**HOW THE EXPERTS
BEAT THE MARKET**
The strategy and tactics
for greatly increasing the odds
in your favor

HOW THE EXPERTS
BEAT THE MARKET

The strategy and tactics
for greatly increasing the odds
in your favor

Thomas C. Noddings

 **DOW JONES-IRWIN** Homewood, Illinois 60430

Some material in this book is adapted from *The Dow Jones-Irwin Guide to Convertible Securities* and from *Listed Call Options: Your Daily Guide to Portfolio Strategy.*

First Printing, August 1976

ISBN 0-87094-126-7
Library of Congress Catalog Card No. 76–13081
Printed in the United States of America

Foreword

You're in serious trouble if you think the stock market is a conservative, sensible place to invest your money. It's not. It's a crapshoot, and the dice are loaded against you.

To begin with, most stock market information you receive is inaccurate, incomplete, or late—whether it comes from your financial newspaper, your advisory service, or your broker. It's censored before release, warped by various middlemen who relay it, and colored by the emotional atmosphere of the marketplace. Complete, accurate, really *profitable* information is just not available to you.

In addition, every time you buy or sell stock—even a single share—you're competing with the full-time professionals of the investment world. Their job is to outperform you, and they do it every time. Simply to compete with them on an equal basis, you'd need a wealth of specialized knowledge, access to a wide variety of research, unlimited time, practical experience in every kind of market, and complete objectivity. That's what you'd need just to compete. And to *beat* them? No way!

Yet even with all their advantages, the so-called experts rarely win the market game either. In this ongoing contest between giants, the majority are defeated. The list of big losers includes the sophisticated elite of Wall Street: mutual funds, pension funds, insurance companies, brokers, financial columnists, bank trust departments, most stock exchange members, and far too many investment counselors. Just look at their performance during the last bear market; it was disastrous.

And if those whom you've been led to believe are experts have such a poor record, what chance does the ordinary investor have? You know very well what chance he has. He loses, too. While the reasons may differ, the final result is the same. Beginner or veteran, odd-lotter or block trader, technician or fundamentalist, speculator or conservative, genius or moron—the stock market treats the majority alike. Most, sooner or later, are brought to their knees. It's an exciting contest, but the chance of winning is rather small.

Nevertheless, the chance is there *if you know where to look for it.*

To beat the odds—to sit at the "house" side of the table for a change—you must first realize the rules of the game are constantly being changed. For example, there are now such new factors to contend with as the impact of large institutions, the option market, increased price volatility, computer monitoring, and changing tax laws, to mention just a few. You can't win if you're still playing by the old conventional rules.

For conventional approaches to investing are obsolete today. In fact, they've become dangerously speculative. Gone is the day when you might set up a portfolio of sound common stocks, with a good bond or two, then sit back and watch your equity grow. No longer can you simply buy shares in a mutual fund and automatically profit from your ownership in American industry. And the banker, broker, or financial columnist, whose advice you might once have thought would be profitable, seems to have lost his golden touch. But don't take my word for it; just ask any investor of recent years. The old stock market that many once considered an automatic "bread" machine unexpectedly ran out of "dough."

Yes, it's a brand new market—and to make money in it you need a new approach. Preferably, it should be one that doesn't require daily price watching, advanced mathematics, or predictions as to which way the market is going to go. It should exploit those areas unavailable to the large institutions. It should not only cope with volatility but actually take advantage of it. And, ideally, it should be profitable in bull markets or bear.

Although not widely known, there *is* such a system; in fact, you're holding it in your hands.

Briefly, it's a panoply of techniques built around convertible securities—techniques that, once mastered, will entitle you to your share of the prize money. Convertible securities offer the ordinary investor his best opportunity to score in the investment game. It's a pity they're so poorly understood, for, compared with their underlying common stocks, carefully selected convertibles have lower risk or higher yield or bigger profit potential—or any combination of the three.

If you're serious about making like a market Midas, you must familiarize yourself with these versatile modern securities. Become knowledgeable about convertibles and, instead of competing with the other players, you'll bypass them. You'll walk safely and confidently in the midst of the fray, protected by your own specialized know-how and guided by Thomas Noddings, whose market classic you're about to begin reading.

The dictionary defines *classic* as "being of the highest rank or excellence"—an apt description of this book. Tom Noddings has generously poured into one overflowing vessel the cream of his encyclopedic knowledge of the entire field of hedging, and has even included the first practical guide to the use of listed put options. Though he's a virtuoso in the use of convertible securities, the author is the first to admit he doesn't know which way the stock markets will go next week—or even tomorrow. Furthermore, he doesn't care. Using the strategies developed herein, convertible hedges can be designed to make money whether the market goes up, down, or even sideways. Best of all, you can learn to do it yourself, as Mr. Noddings explains in detail.

I'm not going to tell you much more about this book. I don't have to. If you've read the author's previous works, you know the wealth of original material he's presented; if you haven't, you're in for an uncommon treat. It's more than a treat—it's a veritable feast. You can "dine out" on it for weeks. And, in addition to a banquet for your mind, it offers nourishment to your purse as well.

Eat hearty! Relish it. *Digest* it.

Then—refreshed and restored—you can return to the game, enjoy it more, and (who knows?) perhaps even make some money.

July 1976   EARL ZAZOVE

Preface

This book was written for the serious investor who is willing to devote time and energy to achieve long-term investment success. It will also be of significant help to stockbrokers in guiding their clients through the constantly expanding field of convertible securities.

Through planned and systematic investment in convertible securities, the safest form of equity investment I know of, the investor may reasonably expect to achieve superior performance over the long term. The concepts and techniques that I propose in this book will help, but they will not provide a panacea for the *institutional* investment community. This specialized investment system simply cannot accept the billions of dollars that flow into Wall Street. However, professional money managers and individual investors will profit from them.

I do not claim that the reader can breeze through this book and then attack the investment world, armed with its sophisticated weaponry. The book must be studied. But, once the techniques are mastered—and they are not really too difficult—the average investor-reader can expect to have a substantial advantage over the rest of the investment community.

The guidelines you are about to learn are valuable. However, they are no substitute for common sense in investing. So, modify them according to your own judgment in every case—your judgment about the general market as well as about the particular company being considered. As you absorb the ideas and concepts presented, weave them into the framework of your own investment knowledge. The more completely you integrate them into your own market expertise, the more useful and profitable they will be.

This book is the result of many years of research and actual investment experience and it includes contributions from several investment professionals—some through direct consultation and others by their writings. I am especially indebted to Earl Zazove and to Stanley Kritzik, two exceptionally sophisticated investors.

Dr. Zazove, my coauthor of *Listed Call Options: Your Daily Guide to Portfolio Strategy,* published in 1975, made invaluable contributions during the countless hours of analysis and development of the concepts and strategies you are about to learn. He also provided much appreciated help in the actual preparation of the manuscript, in addition to writing the stimulating and provocative foreword you have just read.

Stan Kritzik is the inventor of the *Superhedge*—the most dynamic and potentially rewarding investment strategy I have ever had the honor to be associated with. Not only did he originate the idea, but he also reduced it to a practical system that others may employ for achieving investment success.

My thanks also to Carol Sachs, my brokerage partner. Without her enthusiasm and assistance, it would not have been possible for me to make this book the comprehensive work that it is.

July 1976   THOMAS C. NODDINGS

Contents

warrants: *Procedures for evaluating, establishing, and maintaining hedge positions. Specific buy, hold, and sell actions. Anticipated performance in different types of markets.* The six-year study: *Summary of all positions taken during the six-year study.* Performance results from the basic system. Common stock performance. Warrant performance. Warrant/cash performance. Buying on margin. Warrant hedge performance—The basic system. Warrant hedge performance on margin. An additional 2½-year "track record." Alternatives to the basic system: *Continuous review of all warrant opportunities. Over-the-counter warrants. Fine tuning the hedge portfolio. Trading against warrants for profits during sideways markets. Predicting major market swings.* General guides for hedging warrants.

chapter 1

The real world of investing

In the real world of investing, the individual investor has access to a wide variety of strategies and techniques to beat the professionals at their own game: the stock market. These tools will be presented in this book. They range from simple "one-decision" investments to those as sophisticated as you can possibly imagine, but none are really complex—all can be evaluated using simple arithmetic and common sense. Of the various strategies, the best for you will depend on your investment objectives and your ability to analyze, select, and monitor.

It has often been said that if a new strategy were developed to beat the stock market, it would be exploited by professional money managers so quickly that it would soon be rendered worthless. Don't believe it! Most money managers are not receptive to new investment approaches involving nontraditional techniques. The vast majority of them simply can not use the truly sophisticated tools available to the individual investor—i.e., options, warrants, short selling, and margin. Many of the strategies you are about to learn have always been available to Wall Street professionals but have not been used; yet they have given investors, both small and large, a source of extraordinary profits over the years—and the personal satisfaction of knowing they were outperforming the market.

I know of no other endeavor where people make such important decisions without proper training as when investing their money. Because of this lack, even those who should know better, like financial editors and investment advisors, are forced to simplify their advice for ease of understanding. Did you know, for example, that some successful stock market investors seldom buy stocks? It's true! Instead of common stocks, they search out alternative opportunities that offer superior risk/reward characteristics. This book will present more than a dozen basic alternatives to the conventional purchase of common stock—strategies and techniques that might offer lower risk, greater profit potential, higher yield, or any combination of these objectives.

One of my favorite examples in recent times, for illustrating the advantages of alternatives, has been Pan American World Airways—an actively traded stock that advanced from about $2 per share in early 1975 to its recent level of $7. How many stock buyers were even aware of the several Pan American convertible bonds available during this time period? One, for example, the 7½s of 1998, converts into 143 shares of common stock and has always traded at little or no premium over its conversion value. When Pan American stock was at $2, the bond was at 30; when the stock was at $3.50, the bond was at 50; and when the stock reached $7, the bond traded at 100. At all times, the bond offered the same upside potential as the stock while providing a much higher yield than the nondividend-paying common—15 percent, for example, at a price of 50! In addition, the bond provided greater downside safety, being a senior security to the common stock. The common stock buyers simply overlooked an opportunity to increase their probability of return by 15 percent, or higher!

In the real world of investing, the stock market has offered capital appreciation of about 8 to 9 percent over the very long term, and substantially less in recent years. No serious investor or speculator, intent on beating the market, can afford to overlook the many tools available for gaining an edge—like the Pan American convertible bonds. If you ever buy common stock without first examining the available alternatives, you are seriously limiting your opportunity for above-average performance.

What are the alternatives? First, and most conventional, are convertible bonds and convertible preferred stocks—aggressive convertibles like the Pan American bonds or those in blue-chip companies. As shown in the next chapter, convertibles are frequently overlooked in the marketplace, but they should make up the core holdings of your stock market portfolio. Other alternatives to be presented include put and call options, warrants, and a unique method of purchasing stocks at large price discounts.

We will also look at combinations of these various investment vehicles and, in particular, methods to *hedge* them—including a surprising and completely new strategy, the *superhedge*. Properly constructed hedges will permit you not only to reduce risk but also to increase the probability of return on your invested capital. No serious investor in today's stock market can begin to compete successfully without having these modern investment skills.

Real world "track records" will be shown for various investment strategies in cases where I believe performance results have been meaningfully documented. The use of margin to improve investment performance will be recommended and illustrated where it is prudent. The impact of current tax rulings will be evaluated, where appropriate, to help you to manage your portfolio for optimum aftertax performance.

Most of the material will be relatively easy to comprehend but some chapters may require extra study. As most of the strategies are closely interrelated, I suggest that you first read the entire book without paying excessive attention to details, then go back and reread it more carefully.

You will note that I have intentionally avoided the use of complex mathematical formulas; therefore, some people may claim that my approach is too simplistic. If they do, I will consider it a compliment. Having an engineering background, I am comfortable with advanced math and computer printouts; but for making investment decisions, I have found no substitute for good judgment! Also, as you gain experience, most of the better opportunities will be obvious and, since they are usually based on special circumstances or combinations of different strategies, they will seldom be programmed for the computers. Once you have found a potential opportunity, the arithmetic for making a decision is relatively simple.

Let us begin our study of common stock alternatives in the real world of investment with convertible bonds and preferreds— securities that have long offered the sophisticated investor a substantial edge on the market.

chapter 2

Undervalued convertibles

The experienced investor should *never buy* a share of common stock without first checking to see if there is a convertible security available that offers superior risk/reward characteristics. The random walker should *never even consider owning common stock—there are far better alternatives!*

These statements are contrary to the preachings of most Wall Street "professionals"—even many of those who embrace the random walk concept of investing. Nevertheless, they are known to be true by sophisticated investors around the country—investors who laugh at the simplistic advice provided by most brokerage firms, financial columnists, and advisory services.

Undervalued convertibles in well-established companies should constitute the central holdings of your investment portfolio. You may also use them in some of the more advanced investment strategies to be presented later.

For purposes of this discussion, a convertible security is defined as either a convertible bond or a convertible preferred stock. Call options and warrants have related characteristics but are excluded from this narrow definition for ease of reference.

5

Any convertible may be compared with its underlying common stock by simple analytical measurements provided later in this chapter. Its potential upside appreciation and downside risk, relative to its stock, can be estimated with reasonable accuracy. After giving additional consideration to the yields of both securities, the convertible can be judged to be undervalued, normally valued, or overpriced relative to its common stock. The *undervalued* convertible should be purchased in lieu of the common, whereas the *overpriced* convertible should be sold or avoided.

An undervalued convertible may offer the same upside profit opportunity as its common stock at less downside risk. Or, it might offer much of the upside potential at substantially less risk. The convertible will also provide a yield advantage over its stock in terms of both its actual payout and the safety of that payout in most cases. If it is a convertible bond, its guaranteed redemption price provides an additional advantage.

Let us now turn to the real world of investing and evaluate typical convertibles as they are actually traded in the marketplace.

A NORMALLY PRICED CONVERTIBLE— CITICORP BONDS

In July 1975, Citicorp brought its first convertible to the market—a bond yielding 5¾ percent and exchangeable into 24.4 shares of common stock. It was quickly oversubscribed by institutional money managers, and Citicorp was happy to increase the size of its offering to $350 million in response to the enthusiastic reception. It was the largest convertible bond issue on record.

A graphic analysis of the Citicorp bond in July 1975 is presented by Exhibit 2–1. A step-by-step evaluation of its risk/reward characteristics follows.

Conversion value. Each $1,000 bond was immediately convertible into 24.4 shares of common stock at the option of the

EXHIBIT 2–1:   Citicorp 5¾–00 convertible bond, July 1975 (issue size, 350 millon; bond converts into 24.4 shares)

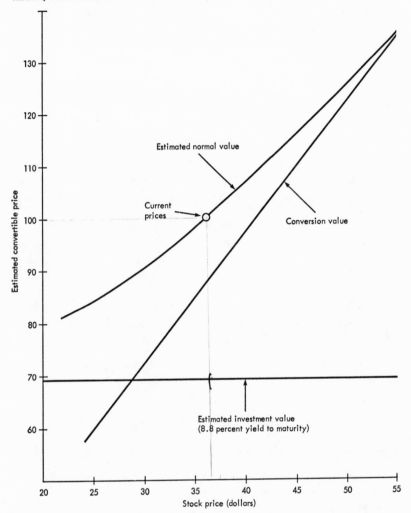

bondholder. Its conversion value, as shown by the sloping solid line on Exhibit 2–1, is simply the market price of the stock multiplied by 24.4 shares. For example, the stock was trading at $36 per share when the bond was issued. The bond's conversion value at that time was:

$$24.4 \text{ shares} \times \$36 \text{ per share} = \$878$$

If the stock were to advance 25 percent to $45, the conversion value would be:

$$24.4 \text{ shares} \times \$45 \text{ per share} = \$1,098$$

If the stock were to decline 25 percent to $27, the conversion value would be:

$$24.4 \text{ shares} \times \$27 \text{ per share} = \$659$$

Since the conversion value is the bond's stock worth if the holder were to exchange it for common stock, any convertible must trade at or above its conversion value. Otherwise, professional arbitragers will profit by purchasing it below conversion value and simultaneously selling the underlying stock. Conversion value, therefore, provides a fixed but sloping "floor" under the market price of a convertible security.

Conversion premium. A convertible's premium over its conversion value is an important tool for measuring worth. At an offering price of $1,000 when the underlying stock was trading at $36, the Citicorp bond's conversion premium was calculated as follows:

$$\text{Conversion premium} = \frac{\$1,000 - 878}{\$878} = 14\%$$

Most new convertibles are issued at conversion premiums ranging from about 10 to 15 percent. Most older convertibles will also trade in this premium range when they are near par.

Investment value. The investment value of a convertible is its worth without its conversion privilege. This value is estimated by bond-rating services in the same way they evaluate conventional nonconvertible bonds. They consider the inherent quality of the bond relative to prevailing interest rates for similar securities. As shown in Exhibit 2–1, the investment value for the high-quality Citicorp bond was estimated at $690 based on an

8.8 percent yield to maturity. This figure is shown as the solid horizontal line on the graph.

Premium over investment value. For analytical purposes, the premium paid for the conversion privilege of the Citicorp bond may be expressed as a percentage over its investment value:

$$\text{Premium over investment value} = \frac{\$1,000 - 690}{\$690} = 45\%$$

The smaller the premium over investment value, the less susceptible is the convertible to a price decline by its underlying stock, since the investment value provides a price floor under the convertible. This floor may move up or down, however, with changing money market rates or the changing fortunes of the company.

Yield advantage. The Citicorp bonds, yielding 5¾ percent when issued in July 1975, provided a yield advantage of 3.3 percent over their low dividend-paying common stock. Practically all new convertibles offer yield advantages. As time passes, however, the advantage may diminish as the common stock's dividend is increased.

Break-even time. Another analytical tool is the number of years it will take for the convertible's yield advantage to make up for its present premium over conversion value. The break-even time for the Citicorp bonds was:

$$\text{Break-even time} = \frac{14 \text{ percent conversion premium}}{3.3 \text{ percent yield advantage}} = 4.2 \text{ years}$$

A small break-even time (under five years) generally means that the convertible offers greater value than its common stock and should be purchased in lieu of the common. However, even convertibles having very long break-even times may be a superior alternative to their common stock if there is a possibility that the dividend may be reduced or eliminated on the stock. For the same reason, some convertibles are better even if their yields are below those of their stocks—Consolidated Edison's convertible preferred in 1974 was a good example. It was yielding about ½ percent less than its common and was trading close to its conversion value prior to the dividend omission on the common. The extra safety of the preferred's payout made it a far better investment than the common stock of Consolidated Edison.

Normal value curve.   The normal value curve for the Citicorp bond, as shown in Exhibit 2–1, is an estimate of the future near-term price of the convertible at any stock price; this is the most important concept presented so far in this book. Taking into consideration all the variables previously discussed, the normal value curve may be calculated from complex mathematical formulas or approximated if you have experience and good judgment in this area.

Upside price estimates for any convertible are controlled by the conversion value, while *downside* price estimates are controlled by the floor provided by the investment value. Since the conversion value is fixed, upside estimates may be made with exceptional accuracy. Downside estimates, however, are subject to uncertainties because the investment value may move up or down with changing money market rates independent of the price action of the underlying common stock—or the market may ignore theoretical investment values during emotional sell-offs.

Risk/reward analysis.   By applying the normal value curve from Exhibit 2–1, we may now make a complete comparison of Citicorp's convertible bond with its underlying common stock in July 1975. Assuming that the common stock would remain unchanged, or advance or decline by either 25 or 50 percent during the following 12 months, a risk/reward analysis of both securities may be made as shown in the accompanying table.

As conclusively demonstrated by the risk/reward analysis, the normally valued Citicorp convertible bond, in July 1975, was a

	Assumed stock price change (next 12 months)				
	−50%	−25%	0%	+25%	+50%
Stock price..............	18	27	36	45	54
Estimated bond price.....	78	87	100	116	133
Stock gain or loss........	−50%	−25%	0%	+25%	+50%
Plus dividends.........	+ 2	+ 2	+ 2	+ 2	+ 2
Net gain or loss........	−48%	−23%	+ 2%	+27%	+52%
Convertible gain or loss..	−22%	−13%	0%	+16%	+33%
Plus interest...........	+ 6	+ 6	+ 6	+ 6	+ 6
Net gain or loss.......	−16%	− 7%	+ 6%	+22%	+39%

superior alternative to its common stock. Its downside risk was only one third that of the common while it provided more than three fourths of the upside potential.

RULE NO. 1:   **Never buy a share of common stock without first checking to see if there is a convertible having superior risk/reward characteristics. Even normally priced convertibles may offer advantages over their underlying common stocks.**

AN UNDERVALUED CONVERTIBLE—
CHASE MANHATTAN BONDS

While the institutional money managers throughout the country were scrambling to get their share of the record-size Citicorp issue, the convertible bonds of Citicorp's sister bank, Chase Manhattan, were not wanted by the investment community. In July 1975, both of these high-quality bank stocks were trading at about $36 and both declined to below $30 during the next few months. The Chase Manhattan bonds were undervalued throughout this period but attracted little buying interest.

Exhibit 2–2 provides a graphic analysis of the Chase Manhattan convertibles in November 1975, similar to the previous analysis for Citicorp. Strange as it seems, the Chase bonds were actually trading within 2 percent of their estimated investment value

**EXHIBIT 2-2: Chase Manhattan 4⅞-93 convertible bond, November 1975
(issue size, 150 million; bond converts into 18.18 shares)**

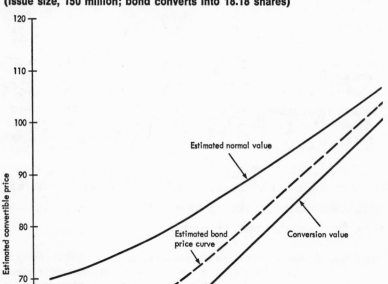

while at only a modest 20 percent premium above conversion
value. They were clearly a far better buy than their underlying
common stock.

Historical experience shows that an undervalued convertible
will tend to remain undervalued for long periods of time. The
estimated bond price curve of Exhibit 2–2 reflects this experience
and assumes that the Chase bonds will be no exception. Despite

this conservative assumption, they offered nearly three-fourths of the upside potential of the common at little or no downside risk. And, if they ever return to their normal value curve, greater relative advantage than presently indicated will be achieved.

Risk/reward analysis. A risk/reward analysis for the Chase Manhattan securities, similar to the previous analysis for Citicorp, is shown in the accompanying table.

	Assumed stock price change (next 12 months)				
	−50%	−25%	0%	+25%	+50%
Stock price..............	14	21	28	35	42
Estimated bond price.....	55	57	61	70	81
Stock gain or loss........	−50%	−25%	0%	+25%	+50%
Plus dividends.........	+ 8	+ 8	+ 8	+ 8	+ 8
Net gain or loss.......	−42%	−17%	+ 8%	+33%	+58%
Convertible gain or loss..	−10%	− 6%	0%	+15%	+33%
Plus interest...........	+ 8	+ 8	+ 8	+ 8	+ 8
Net gain or loss.......	− 2%	+ 2%	+ 8%	+23%	+41%

RULE NO. 2: **Undervalued convertibles offer substantial advantages over their underlying common stocks and should always be purchased in lieu of the common.**

BUYING CONVERTIBLES ON MARGIN

The ability to purchase securities on margin gives the individual investor greater flexibility than most professional money managers have. For example, suppose that both an individual and a pension fund portfolio manager concluded that the common stock of Chase Manhattan was grossly oversold in November 1975 at $28 per share. They were both sure the stock would advance 50 percent within the next 12 months. The pension fund manager, pressured by increasing demand for better performance, might reject the convertible bond because it offered less upside potential than the common stock (41 percent versus 58 percent).

The individual, however, should not even consider the common stock but instead should purchase the convertible bonds on margin. The risk/reward postures for the two investors would be as shown in the table.

	Assumed stock price change		
	−50%	0%	+50%
Common stock purchased for cash............	−42	+8	+58
Bonds purchased on 50 percent margin (assuming margin interest at 8 percent).....	−12	+8	+74

RULE NO. 3:   The purchase of an undervalued convertible on margin may be a prudent alternative to the cash purchase of its underlying common stock.

UNDERVALUED CONVERTIBLES FOR AGGRESSIVE INVESTORS

The most undervalued convertible securities are frequently related to stocks that do not have an institutional following. Investors and speculators alike often buy and sell these stocks without even being aware that a convertible exists; thus price inefficiencies between the related securities occur quite often as the convertibles are overlooked by the marketplace.

Exhibits 2–3 and 2–4 illustrate two grossly undervalued convertible bonds available to aggressive investors during 1975— LTV and Pan American. Risk/reward estimates, assuming a 12-month position, were as shown in the table.

	Assumed stock price changes		
	−50%	0%	+50%
Stock gain or loss..................	−50	0	+50
Gain or loss for convertibles			
LTV............................	−13	+ 7	+50
Pan American..................	−21	+13	+58

EXHIBIT 2–3:   LTV 7½–77 convertible bond, January 1975 (issue size, 36 million; bond converts into 95.24 shares)

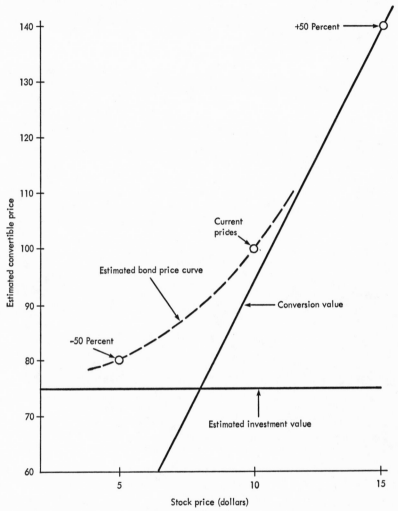

Anyone who purchased the common stock of LTV and Pan American made a serious investment error. The bonds were certain to provide as much upside potential at substantially less downside risk.

RULE NO. 4:   Grossly undervalued convertibles are often found on stocks that do not have an institutional following.

EXHIBIT 2–4:   Pan American 7½–98 convertible bond, October 1975 (issue size, 75 million; bond converts into 142.86 shares)

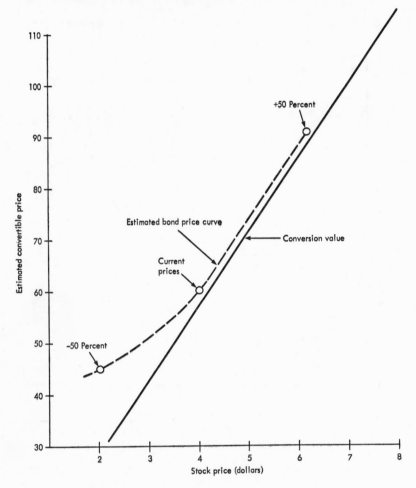

PLACING ORDERS FOR CONVERTIBLE BONDS

The following guidelines should be followed carefully when placing buy or sell orders for convertible bonds.

1. Select bonds that are actively traded whenever possible— they will normally be listed on the New York Stock Exchange and have a large issue outstanding.

2. Monitor both the bond and its underlying stock prices prior to entering orders—a good "feel" for their related prices will save you money whether buying or selling by permitting you to execute orders at favorable prices.

3. Place orders through a brokerage firm that has skills in executing orders in the over-the-counter bond market—many listed bonds are more actively traded in the over-the-counter market than on the floor of the exchange.

4. Work with a stockbroker who has special training in evaluating convertibles and in executing orders—the broker's knowledge and skills are much more critical to your investment success in this area than in conventional buying or selling of common stocks.

RULE NO. 5: **You will gain additional profits by the careful execution of orders and by working with a skilled stockbroker.**

CONVERTIBLE BONDS VERSUS CONVERTIBLE PREFERREDS

Since convertible bonds and convertible preferreds have many similar characteristics, they may both be evaluated on such factors as their conversion values, investment values, and yield advantages. Yet, there are some significant differences which may influence your investment strategy.

Claim on assets. Since bondholder claims to a company's assets are senior to those of preferred stockholders, bonds are inherently safer. This distinction may be of little consequence if the company is financially sound. For a speculative company, however, it may be of major importance.

Continuity of payments. During adverse times, a company will suspend dividends on its preferred stock before discontinuing bond interest payments—the failure of a company to meet bond interest obligations places it in default, the first step toward bankruptcy. Even though the dividends paid on preferred stock are usually cumulative (arrearages must be made up before dividends are paid to common shareholders), the holder of preferred stock may have a long wait before receiving the dividends, once suspended. Eventually, he may even have to accept some sort of exchange offer from the company and may, therefore, never see the dividend arrearages paid.

Tax consequences. Dividends paid on preferred stocks (or common stocks) possess unique tax advantages over interest received on bonds. Bond interest is fully taxable as ordinary income, whereas the first $100 of annual dividends is excluded on individual tax returns ($200 on joint returns). The tax advantage to corporations is even greater because they are permitted to exclude 85 percent of the dividends received on most preferreds (and common stocks). These tax benefits to corporations have historically kept the yields of preferreds close to bonds despite the greater safety of the bond.

Maturity date. Since bonds have a fixed maturity date, they must ultimately be redeemed by the company at par value. An approaching maturity date provides additional protection against broad price swings caused by interest rate changes. It may also protect the convertible bond against a serious price decline by the common stock without limiting its upside potential. Preferred stocks, which seldom have a maturity date, are more sensitive to changing market conditions.

RULE NO. 6. **All other factors being equal, a convertible bond is usually better than a convertible preferred for the individual investor.**

SPECIAL CONVERTIBLES

Our discussion up to now has covered conventional types of convertible bonds and preferreds—those immediately exchangeable into a fixed number of common stock shares. These represent by far the largest part of the convertible securities market. Yet, there are several types of special convertibles that can offer unusual risk/reward opportunities, and all sophisticated investors should be familiar with them.

Plus cash convertible. This is a convertible security that requires an additional cash payment upon conversion. Since the cash payment is constant regardless of the common stock's market price, the conversion value changes faster than the price of the underlying common stock. This type of special convertible may be of interest to the investor seeking greater leverage than that offered by conventional convertibles.

Fabricated convertible. This special convertible is a combination of warrants plus straight bonds that may be used at par value (usually $1,000) in lieu of the cash exercise price when exercising the warrants. To determine the number of warrants to be purchased with each straight bond, simply divide the par value of the bond by the total exercise price of the warrant. The combination results in risk/reward characteristics similar to conventional convertibles but provides greater flexibility as the bonds and warrants are purchased or sold separately.

Unit convertible. This is a convertible issue that, instead of being exchangeable into only common stock, is instead convertible into a "unit"—a package of one or more securities that may not even include the common. The evaluation of a unit convertible requires additional sophistication but can be potentially more rewarding since the marketplace may have extra difficulty in assigning a normal value.

Delayed convertible. The most exciting, and potentially rewarding, special convertibles are the bonds or preferred stocks having delayed conversion features and selling at a discount below the future conversion value. These generally fall into either of two categories:

1. A convertible with fixed conversion terms that specify the number of shares of common stock to be received upon conversion beginning at a specified future date. Price action of the convertible will be related to that of the common stock.

2. A convertible that will convert into common stock beginning on a specified date based upon a formula relating to the future price of the common. Depending on the specific terms, the convertible's price action may or may not be related to that of its common stock's until the date it becomes convertible.

RULE NO. 7: Special convertibles may offer unusually attractive risk/reward opportunities to the sophisticated investor.

UNUSUAL PLUSES AND MINUSES

The complex field of convertible securities offers unusual opportunities to the sophisticated investor—and hidden traps to the unwary.

Short-term convertible bonds. A convertible bond nearing its maturity date may resist decline if its common stock drops while still offering upside potential if the stock advances.

Preferreds in arrears. This situation offers potentially high profits to the aggressive investor if the previously omitted dividends are cumulative and the company is a turnaround candidate.

Tender offers for discounted bonds. In an effort to improve its balance sheet, a company may make a cash tender or exchange offer for its discounted bonds. The value offered is usually well above the current market price of the bond to assure a favorable response.

Changes in terms. Some convertibles have fixed schedules for changing their conversion terms at future specified dates. These changes are usually downward and will therefore reduce the value of the convertible.

Expiration of conversion privileges. The conversion privilege of some convertibles may terminate well before the maturity date. At that point, the convertible's price will immediately drop to its investment value.

Call provisions. Be extra careful of paying a conversion premium if the convertible is subject to call at a price below its current market value. If called, the convertible will immediately drop to its conversion value. In addition, the interest accrued on a bond since its last interest payment date may be lost.

Mergers and tender offers for the common stock. These events may have either positive or negative impact on the market value of a convertible, depending on the specific terms of the package offered to the common stockholders and the convertible's premium over conversion value.

Antidilution provisions. Convertibles are generally protected against stock splits, stock dividends, etc. However, there have been instances where a company has spun off a subsidiary to holders of its common stock without adjusting the conversion terms of its convertibles. You will probably be unable to protect yourself against such deceitful tactics used by some corporate officials.

RULE NO. 8:   The sophisticated investor will profit from a keen awareness of the potential opportunities and hidden traps in the real world of convertible securities.

MODEL CONVERTIBLE PORTFOLIOS

Exhibits 2–5 and 2–6 suggest model portfolios of undervalued convertibles recently available. The convertibles were chosen simply on the basis of their merits relative to their underlying common stocks without evaluating the stocks themselves.

Exhibit 2–5 illustrates conservative convertibles offering upside potential at low downside risk—selected on underlying common

EXHIBIT 2–5: Model portfolio of undervalued convertibles—conservative (January 1976)

Company	Convertible description	Stock volatility*	Estimated convertible gains or loss assuming that stock prices change in 12 months by†		
			−25%	0%	+25%
ARA Services................	4.625–96	85	+3	+ 7	+18
Budd Co....................	5.875–94	90	+9	+10	+20
Chase Manhattan Corp.......	4.875–93	75	+8	+ 8	+17
Consumers Power............	$5.50 preferred	75	−5	+ 9	+39
El Paso Co.................	6.000–93	65	+4	+ 9	+34
Greyhound.................	6.500–90	75	+1	+ 8	+23
International Telephone & Telegraph.................	$4.00 preferred	85	+4	+10	+22
United Merchants & Manufacturers.............	4.000–90	65	+5	+ 8	+20
United Technologies..........	5.375–91	90	+1	+ 8	+33
United Telecommunications...	$1.50 preferred	65	−5	+ 8	+32
Averages.................		77	+2	+ 8	+26

* Volatility figures are courtesy of the *Value Line Convertible Survey*. A volatility of 100 is representative of the average common stock.

† Price projections for the convertibles are also courtesy of the *Value Line Convertible Survey*. Bond interest and preferred stock dividends are included.

EXHIBIT 2–6: Model portfolio of undervalued convertibles—aggressive (January 1976)

Company	Convertible description	Stock volatility*	Estimated convertible gain or loss assuming that stock prices change in 12 months by:†		
			−50%	0%	+50%
Beech Aircraft.............	4.750–93	115	+ 2	+ 8	+38
Colt Industries.............	$4.25 preferred	105	− 4	+ 9	+39
Federal National Mortgage..	4.375–96	105	−16	+ 6	+51
Fibreboard Corp............	6.750–98	105	+11	+11	+36
Grumann Corp.............	4.250–92	130	− 4	+ 9	+39
Kaiser Aluminum and Chemical................	$4.75 preferred	125	− 5	+ 9	+59
McDonnell Douglas........	4.750–91	110	− 3	+ 8	+43
Occidental Petroleum.......	$3.60 preferred	115	−17	+ 8	+58
Republic N.Y..............	5.375–97	130	+ 6	+ 9	+34
Zapata Corp...............	4.750–88	120	− 1	+ 8	+43
Averages.................		116	− 3	+ 8	+44

* Volatility figures are courtesy of the *Value Line Convertible Survey*. A volatility of 100 is representative of the average common stock.

† Price projections for the convertible are also courtesy of the *Value Line Convertible Survey*. Bond interest and preferred stock dividends are included.

stocks having below-average volatility. Stock price changes of plus or minus 25 percent during the next 12 months were assumed for estimating purposes. Exhibit 2–6 shows aggressive convertibles offering greater upside potential at modest downside risk—selected on underlying common stocks having above-average volatility. Stock price changes of plus or minus 50 percent during the next 12 months were assumed based on the higher price volatilities of the underlying stocks.

PORTFOLIO SELECTION

In summary for this chapter, if you are interested in building a portfolio of undervalued convertible securities, you should proceed as follows:

1. Carefully determine your investment objectives.
2. Determine how much diversification you want both in terms of number of different securities and by industry.
3. Establish a plan for selecting convertibles that meet your objectives.
4. Decide whether purchases will be for cash or whether margin will be used.
5. Establish a plan for monitoring your portfolio to assure that it always contains securities having the desired risk/reward characteristics relative to your objectives.

chapter 3

Hedging undervalued convertibles

The previous chapter demonstrated how market inefficiencies allow some convertibles to become grossly undervalued relative to their underlying common stocks. This condition is especially true for speculative securities that do not enjoy an institutional following. The conservative investor, who will not normally consider owning a low-quality convertible, can take advantage of its undervaluation by using hedging techniques.

THE CONVERTIBLE HEDGE

A convertible hedge position involves the short sale of common stock against a convertible security. The hedged investor simply plans to take advantage of the convertible's undervaluation without exposing his investment capital to unnecessary risks. He is not as concerned about the fundamentals of the common stock as he would be if he were considering purchase of the stock or convertible only. He is, however, most concerned about the price volatility of the common and its dividend payout. The following parameters should be carefully applied when selecting hedge candidates:

24

1. The bond, or preferred, should be trading close to its conversion value—it will offer nearly as much upside potential as its common stock.
2. The convertible should not be selling too far above its investment value so as to limit its decline upon a drop in price by the stock.
3. The common stock should pay little or no dividends since the hedger is obligated to pay any dividends on stock he sells short. The hedge position of long convertibles versus short stock will then provide a net cash flow to the hedger.
4. The common stock should have a history of high price volatility to improve the chances for a major price move, but the company should not be a potential bankruptcy candidate.

HEDGING LTV CONVERTIBLE BONDS

Let us look at the LTV 7½s–77 convertible, as of January 1975, for hedging opportunities (Exhibit 2–3 of chapter 2). Since the bond was trading at only a 5 percent conversion premium and its volatile common stock paid no dividend, it was a prime candidate for hedging. A step-by-step evaluation proceeded as follows:

1. *Yield advantage.*   A current yield of 7½ percent was received by the bondholder, whereas the stock paid no dividend.

2. *Upside potential.*   The bond had to advance almost as fast as its common stock since it was selling near conversion value. If LTV common were to double from $10 up to $20, the bond would have to advance 90 percent to its conversion value of 190 (95 shares X $20 = $1,900).

3. *Downside risk.*   The bond would have declined less than the common due to the support provided by its investment floor. As shown by Exhibit 2–3 in the previous chapter, the estimated investment value was 75 and we expected a drop of only 20 per-

cent, from 100 down to 80, if the stock declined by 50 percent to $5.

4. *Mathematical advantage.* Assuming that LTV common either doubled or dropped in half (equal probabilities), the convertible bond's mathematical advantage (or risk/reward ratio) was calculated as follows:

$$MA = \frac{\text{Percent convertible advance}}{\text{100 percent stock advance}}$$
$$\times \frac{\text{50 percent stock decline}}{\text{Percent convertible decline}}$$
$$= \frac{90}{100} \times \frac{50}{20} = 2.2$$

Note that I chose price moves by LTV common stock of -50% and $+100\%$ since these represented equal probabilities for future price action assuming no price bias. If a stock drops in half, it must later double in price to get back to the starting price; or if it first doubles, a 50% decline would also bring it back to the starting price. Other equal probability combinations could also have been considered, i.e., $-20/+25$, $-25/+33$, or $-33/+50$, but price relationships between a convertible and its underlying stock may be predicted more accurately for a major move and such a move is generally needed to close out a hedge position with significant profits after commission expenses. Regardless of the percentages used for estimating purposes, a ratio of 1.0 would be considered neutral and above 1.5 would be a candidate for hedging. The mathematical advantage of 2.2 for the LTV bond was exceptionally high and was even greater if the 7½ percent bond yield was included in the calculation.

5. *Alternate hedge positions.* Depending on your personal investment goals, desired risk posture, and other securities in your portfolio, a convertible hedge in LTV could have been designed to meet a number of different objectives. By definition, the three common types of convertible hedges are:

Bullish hedge—upside profits at low downside risk.

Neutral hedge—modest profits in any kind of market.

Bearish hedge—downside profits at low upside risk.

Bullish and bearish hedges in LTV are shown in Exhibit 3–1, a neutral hedge would fall between these two extremes.

6. *Selecting the best hedge ratio.* How to select the best hedge ratio has been the most frequently raised question during my entire investment career. As illustrated by Exhibit 3–1, a bullish hedge provides greater profit potential during the upside phase of a market cycle than a bearish hedge does during the downside phase. Convertible hedgers who do not exercise market judgment should therefore favor a bullish posture since it will produce optimum profits over a market cycle. On the other hand,

EXHIBIT 3–1: Alternate hedge positions in LTV convertible bonds (investment = 10 bonds × $1,000 = $10,000)

	Stock price move	
	−50%	+100%
Bullish Hedge		
Stock sold short = 400 shares × $10 = $4,000		
Downside risk		
Profit on stock sold short = $ 4,000 × 50%......	$2,000	
Loss on bonds purchased = $10,000 × 20%......	(2,000)	
Upside potential		
Profit on bonds purchased = $10,000 × 90%......		$9,000
Loss on stock sold short = $ 4,000 × 100%.....		(4,000)
Net profit or (loss)...............................	$ 0	$5,000
Return on investment.............................	0%	+50%
Bearish Hedge		
Stock sold short = 900 shares × $10 = $9,000		
Downside potential		
Profit on stock sold short = $ 9,000 × 50%......	$4,500	
Loss on bonds purchased = $10,000 × 20%......	(2,000)	
Upside risk		
Profit on bonds purchased = $10,000 × 90%.....		$9,000
Loss on stock sold short = $ 9,000 × 100%.....		(9,000)
Net profit or (loss)...............................	$2,500	$ 0
Return on investment.............................	+25%	0%

Note: Bond interest and commissions were excluded from the above calculations for simplification.

some investors will employ bearish hedges to protect their un-hedged common stock portfolios against a market crash. Bearish hedges frequently provide cash flows competitive with money market instruments while still offering substantial profits during stock market declines. The choice is yours.

CONVERTIBLE HEDGE WORK SHEETS

Exhibits 3–2 and 3–3 illustrate the use of standard work sheets for evaluating convertible hedges. Using the bullish hedge in LTV

EXHIBIT 3–2

WORK SHEET FOR EVALUATING CONVERTIBLE HEDGES

COMPANY_____LTV_____   DATE _Jan. '75_

DESCRIPTION OF SECURITIES

	Description	Symbol	Target Prices	Current Yield
(a) Common stock.........		LTV	10	0 %
Convertible...........	7½-77		100	7.5

(b) Conversion value =_95.24_ shares x $ _10.00_ = $ _952_
    Conversion premium   = _____5_ %
    Estimated investment value   = $ _750_

	1972	1973	1974
(c) Stock price ranges	9 - 14 3/4	7 ½ - 13 ½	7 7/8 - 12 ½

(d) POSSIBLE HEDGE POSITION: Bullish _✓_, Neutral_____, or Bearish_____

(e)   Convertibles purchased:_10 M_ at $ _1,000_ each = $ _10,000_
(f)   Stock sold short:_400_ shs. at $ _10.00_ each = $ _4,000_
(g)   Investment = $ _10,000_ + $ _150_ commissions = $ _10,150_

(h) PROFIT OR LOSS ESTIMATES – ASSUMING A 12-MONTH POSITION (unleveraged)

	-50%	0%	+50%	+100%
(i) Assumed stock price change	-50%	0%	+50%	+100%
Stock price	5	10	15	20
(j) Estimated convertible price......	80	100	143	190
(k) Profit or (loss) – convertible	(2,000)	0	4,300	9,000
– stock	2,000	0	(2,000)	(4,000)
(l) Commissions....................	(270)	(300)	(320)	(340)
(m) Estimated capital gain or (loss)...	(270)	0	1,980	4,660
(n) Estimated return on investment ...	– 2.7 %	+ 3.0 %	+ 19.5 %	+ 45.9 %
(o) Income received less dividends paid on stock sold short	+ 7.4 %	+ 7.4 %	+ 7.4 %	+ 7.4 %
(p) Net return.....................	+ 4.7 %	+ 4.4 %	+ 26.9 %	+ 53.3 %

EXHIBIT 3–3

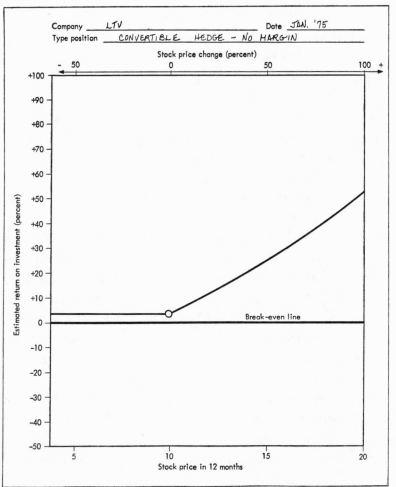

as our example, the following steps are keyed to Exhibit 3–2 for ease of reference.

(*a*) Market prices were 10 and 100 for the stock and bonds, respectively. The bonds provided a current yield of 7½ percent, while the stock paid no dividend.

(*b*) Calculations show that the bonds were trading at only a 5 percent conversion premium and not too far above their estimated investment value of $750.

(*c*) Three-year price ranges for the stock are shown to provide a possible indication of potential price movements in the future.

(*d*) Our investment objective was to establish a bullish hedge position—one that offered upside profits at little or no downside risk.

(*e*) Ten bonds were purchased at $1,000 each.

(*f*) Four hundred shares of stock were sold short at $10 per share.

(*g*) The net investment of $10,150 was the cost of the bonds plus commissions for both sides of the hedge. If full margin were employed, the net investment would have been only 50 percent of the bonds purchased (no margin was required for the short sale since the stock was sold against a convertible security). Accrued bond interest was not considered as it would be recouped at the next bond interest payment date, or upon sale of the bonds.

(*h*) Profit and loss estimates were based on an unleveraged position and on the assumption that it would be held for twelve months.

(*i*) Stock price changes of −50, 0, +50, and +100 percent were selected for estimating potential profit or loss.

(*j*) The convertible bond price was estimated for each of the assumed stock prices—see Exhibit 2–3 for the estimated bond price curve.

(*k*) Profit and loss calculations were based on the assumed stock prices and estimated bond prices.

(*l*) Round-trip commissions were included for conservative estimates, although if the stock price does not change appreciably the position should be held.

(*m*)   The estimated net capital gain or loss was calculated next.

(*n*)   The estimated return on investment was the net capital gain or loss divided by the $10,150 investment. Although we assumed a 12-month position, these returns might be achieved quickly—or never—depending on future price action.

(*o*)   The net income to be received for the next 12 months is the $750 bond interest divided by the $10,150 investment. Since the common stock paid no dividend, no dividend deduction was necessary.

(*p*)   The net return is the sum of the estimated return on investment plus the net income received, assuming a 12-month position.

Exhibit 3–3 graphically illustrates the net return figures from Exhibit 3–2 by plotting the percentage return on investment against stock prices.

MARGINING CONVERTIBLE HEDGES

As in the straight purchase of undervalued convertibles on margin, conservative hedgers will also use margin to leverage their potential profits. Margin calculations could have been included on the standard work sheet but I have found it more meaningful to first evaluate all hedges on a nonleveraged basis. This permits direct comparison of various types of hedge strategies having different margin rules.

Exhibit 3–4 provides convenient tables for adjusting nonleveraged profit and loss estimates for different margin rates and different margin interest charges. You should first study the examples provided by this exhibit. Next, to show the results of a

EXHIBIT 3–4: Factors for adjusting profit and loss estimates when using margin

					Margin rate (percent)						
	30	35	40	45	50	55	60	65	70	75	80
Profit or loss multiplier..	3.33	2.86	2.50	2.22	2.00	1.82	1.67	1.54	1.43	1.33	1.25
Deduction for margin interest (percent)											
6.........	14.0	11.1	9.0	7.3	6.0	4.9	4.0	3.2	2.6	2.0	1.5
7.........	16.3	13.0	10.5	8.6	7.0	5.7	4.7	3.8	3.0	2.3	1.8
8.........	18.7	14.9	12.0	9.8	8.0	6.5	5.3	4.3	3.4	2.7	2.0
9.........	21.0	16.7	13.5	11.0	9.0	7.4	6.0	4.8	3.8	3.0	2.2
10.........	23.3	18.6	15.0	12.2	10.0	8.2	6.7	5.4	4.3	3.3	2.5
11.........	25.7	20.4	16.5	13.5	11.0	9.0	7.3	5.9	4.7	3.7	2.8
12.........	28.0	22.3	18.0	14.7	12.0	9.8	8.0	6.5	5.2	4.0	3.0

Examples: A specific situation is expected to provide an annual return of 15 percent including income and capital gains. It may be margined at 50 percent and current margin interest is
10 percent.

$$\text{Net return} = 2.0\,(15.0) - 10.0 = 30.0 - 10.0 = 20.0\%$$

A diversified portfolio is expected to provide an annual return of 14 percent. The total
portfolio may be margined at 70 percent and current margin interest is 8 percent.

$$\text{Net return} = 1.43\,(14.0) - 3.4 = 20.0 - 3.4 = 16.6\%$$

margined investment, we may adjust the figures for the LTV
hedge from Exhibit 3–2 as follows:

Profit or loss multiplier = 2.00 based on a 50 percent margin
rate.

Deduction for margin interest = 10.0 based on 10 percent interest rates prevailing in January 1975.

	Stock price change			
	−50%	0%	+50%	+100%
Net return from Exhibit 3–2....	+ 4.7%	+ 4.4%	+26.9%	+ 53.3%
Times profit or loss multiplier..	× 2.0	× 2.0	× 2.0	× 2.0
	+ 9.4	+ 8.8%	+53.8%	+106.6%
Less deduction for margin interest.....................	−10.0	−10.0	−10.0	− 10.0
Estimated net return on full margin.....................	− 0.6%	− 1.2%	+43.8%	+ 96.6%

EXHIBIT 3-5

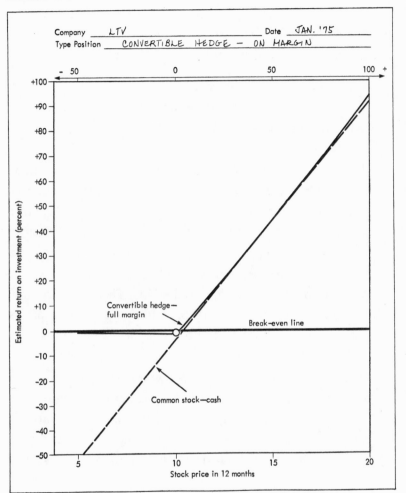

Exhibit 3–5 graphically compares the leveraged hedge position with a cash purchase of LTV common stock, including commissions and interest and assuming a 12-month workout.

MANAGING CONVERTIBLE HEDGE PORTFOLIOS

Once a convertible hedge portfolio is established, the hedger may simply sit back and wait for major price moves before closing positions. Or, he may monitor the portfolio continually for profit opportunities. Aggressive management of a relatively passive hedge portfolio may increase overall investment performance. Management strategies for bullish hedges include:

1. Close out a position for profit if the convertible becomes normally valued, even if the stock has not changed much. There will probably be better opportunities elsewhere for reinvesting the funds.

2. Do not wait for the stock to "double" before taking upside profits. Once the convertible has advanced much above par, the possibility of additional upside profit is offset by the other possibility that paper gains will be given back if the stock retreats.

3. Be prepared to close out positions on the downside even if the close out will result in a modest loss. There will probably be another opportunity available which will produce profits during the next market advance while the old hedge is simply returning to its starting point.

4. The short side of the hedge may be traded against the long side by shorting more stock during market rallies and covering stock on market dips. These adjustments will produce greater profits during sideways market movements at the expense of reduced profits if the stock were to make a sustained price advance.

CLOSING OUT A CONVERTIBLE HEDGE ON THE UPSIDE

The convertible hedger has a choice as to how he can close out his position if his hedge appreciates in value. He could, of course, simply sell the convertibles and purchase stock to cover the short sales. However, if the convertibles were selling at their conversion value, as would be expected after a major advance, he might consider converting a sufficient number of convertibles and covering the short position with the shares received. This maneuver would save much of the expense of close-out brokerage commissions. In this event, the hedger should make sure that the bond interest was just recently paid, since the interest accrued from the previous payment date would be lost upon conversion. This interest loss might exceed commission savings.

Income tax considerations might also favor close-out by sale instead of conversion. Let us evaluate the tax consequences for the LTV hedge from Exhibit 3–2, assuming that the stock doubled after a holding period in excess of six months (commissions are excluded).

1. *Close-out by conversion.* Those bonds converted for covering the 400 shares of stock sold short would be treated as being sold the day the stock was shorted for an approximate break-even, short-term trade. The remaining bonds would provide a long-term capital gain of about $5,000.

2. *Close-out by sale.* A long-term capital gain of $9,000 would be received on the convertible bonds versus a short-term loss of $4,000 on the stock sold short (all short sales are short-term gain or loss regardless of the time held). This result would be even more advantageous if short-term gains on other transactions were taken during the year.

A 2½-YEAR "TRACK RECORD"

Between June 1973 and June 1975, I provided hedge recommendations and follow-up monitoring for an investment advisory service specializing in low-risk investment strategies.[1] Basic recom-

---

[1] Published by S.P.A. Industries, Winnetka, Illinois.

mendations were published eight times annually and were supplemented by occasional special flashes to subscribers to close out or adjust a hedge position. Target prices for establishing or adjusting the hedges were representative of actual market conditions—not closing prices on a specific day, which are frequently impossible to obtain but are used by some services to report results for their recommendations. My objective was to provide responsible and conservative investment advice to clients as opposed to developing a "track record" for expanding subscriptions to the service.

The suggested investments included nonleveraged, convertible hedges and other types of traditional hedging strategies to be presented later in this handbook. Of the 40 total recommendations, 14 were in convertible hedge positions that were designed for upside profits at limited downside risk, similar to the bullish hedge previously shown for LTV in Exhibit 3–2. No attempt was made to predict future price trends for either the overall stock market or individual securities. Those hedges that were still open when I discontinued providing research to the advisory service in June 1975 were assumed to be held until the end of the year and then closed out. All commissions paid, bond interest received, and dividends received or paid were included in the profit or loss calculations for meaningful results.

The actual results of the 2½-year track record for the 14 convertible hedges are presented in Exhibit 3–6. As shown, all hedge positions were profitable despite the worst bear market in over 40 years during the initial 1½-year life of the advisory service. At no time during the 1973–74 stock market crash was this convertible hedge portfolio down more than 5 percent, even though investment values for all convertibles plunged as interest rates rose to historic highs.

The average return on investment for the hedge positions may be calculated in different ways. From Exhibit 3–6, the average profit for all hedges of 14 percent may be adjusted by the average

EXHIBIT 3–6:   Convertible hedges (June 1973 through December 1975)

Convertible Hedge	Date recommended	Date closed	Months	Profit or loss	An-nualized return
Gulf Resources and Chemicals...	6/26/73	2/15/74	7.5	+20%	+ 32%
National General..............	6/26/73	2/15/74	7.5	+ 8	+ 13
Zapata Corp...................	6/26/73	12/03/74	17.0	+ 7	+ 5
LTV.........................	6/26/73	2/12/75	19.5	+21	+ 13
Occidental Petroleum..........	6/26/73	6/16/75	23.5	+15	+ 8
General Host.................	6/26/73	12/31/75	30.0	+39	+ 16
United National..............	6/26/73	12/31/75	30.0	+ 1	+ 0
Pan American.................	2/16/74	12/31/75	22.5	+26	+ 14
Gulf Resources and Chemicals...	5/15/74	3/26/75	10.5	+ 4	+ 5
Brown Co....................	8/12/74	11/11/74	3.0	+ 9	+ 36
Gould Inc...................	8/12/74	12/03/74	17.0	+14	+ 10
Fibreboard..................	10/01/74	3/26/75	6.0	+ 9	+ 18
Republic N.Y................	10/01/74	11/11/74	1.5	+ 8	+ 64
Northwest Industries.........	1/02/75	2/12/75	1.5	+14	+112
Averages (14 positions)......			14	+14%	+ 25%

Note: These hedges were recommended by the author for an investment advisory service. Each hedge was designed for profits during bull markets, at limited downside risk, without attempting to predict future price trends. If a hedge position was proposed more than once (or if a similar hedge position in the same company was suggested) while the initial recommendation was still rated a buy or hold, only the initial recommendation is shown. Profit or loss figures are based on nonleveraged positions and all commission expenses, dividends, and bond interest are included.

14-month time period to arrive at an average annualized return of 12 percent. Or, the return for each individual hedge may be annualized as shown in the last column of Exhibit 3–6 and then averaged for a return of 25 percent. The latter approach, as used by some advisory services, will produce inflated performance results whenever the shorter term positions are highly profitable, as were those in our model portfolio of 14 hedges. Actual performance results would have fallen somewhere between the 12 and 25 percent figures—probably closer to the lower end of the range. But, regardless of the figure used, this experience supports our target objective of 15 percent annual return for a convertible hedge portfolio. Performance results for the other 26 hedge positions recommended during the 2½-year period, to be presented later, will provide additional support.

EXHIBIT 3-7: General guides for hedging convertibles

1. The convertible should be significantly undervalued—a mathematical advantage over its underlying common stock of 1.5 or higher, including yields on both securities.

2. The convertible should be selling close to its conversion value and not too far above its investment value.

3. Select convertibles on common stocks that pay little or no dividends—the short seller must pay these dividends.

4. The common stock should have a history of high price volatility to improve the chances for a major price move.

5. Make sure that the stock is available for short selling and that there is a reasonable probability that it can be held short for as long as desired.

6. Both the convertible and the stock should be actively traded to permit establishing and closing out positions at favorable price relationships.

7. The amount of common stock sold short versus convertibles purchased should be designed to meet your specific investment objectives.

8. The convertibles are held in the brokerage account, even if purchased for cash, to permit the short sale of common stock against them without having to deposit extra collateral for the short side.

9. Employ margin for convertible hedges to obtain the additional leverage.

10. Close out the position if the convertible becomes overpriced or even normally valued—the funds should be employed in another situation having more favorable risk/reward characteristics.

11. Consider closing out the position on the upside by converting the required number of convertibles to save on commission expenses—unless interest lost or tax considerations favor close out by sale of the convertibles and covering the short sales.

12. Avoid companies that are takeover candidates—a cash tender offer for the common stock might reduce the up-

EXHIBIT 3–7:   *(continued)*

side potential for the convertible relative to its common. Also, it might not be possible to hold the short position through the tender offer period.

13. Avoid hedges in companies that are possible bankruptcy candidates unless you plan to establish a full bear hedge.

14. Diversify your convertible hedge portfolio—especially if leverage is to be employed.

chapter 4

Listed call options

Call options have long been an important tool used by sophisticated investors, and with the creation of a listed option market in 1973, their use has been greatly expanded. In fact, many portfolios today employ call option strategies exclusively. Successful option trading is neither mysterious nor difficult. On the contrary, it is a skill you can develop with study and practice. My purpose here is to help you develop this skill by training you in new techniques and by teaching you to protect yourself from some of the dangers you will encounter along the way.

A comprehensive presentation of listed call options is provided in the prospectus issued by the option exchanges. This prospectus, as well as other literature available from member brokerage firms, should be carefully studied before considering the use of call options in your investment program. The option material to be presented in *this* book is not for beginners. It is for the serious investor who has knowledge of the stock market and some experience in the field of options. Basic information is not included, since that is readily available from other, more conventional sources. My primary purpose is to present advanced strategies for employing call options for above-average performance in your investment program.

ADVANTAGES OF LISTED CALL OPTIONS

Most advantages are directly related to the special features of listed options which were unavailable in the conventional over-the-counter (OTC) market. These are:

1. Standardized terms.
2. Secondary trading market.
3. Greater market depth.
4. Lower transaction costs.
5. Tax considerations.

1. Standardized terms

Trading in listed call options is currently available for a broad list of popular stocks. Each call has four fixed expiration months, i.e., January, April, July, and October. Trading in calls of a particular expiration month begins nine months early so that, at any given time, there are options trading with three different expiration months. All options expire on the third Saturday of the month; trading ceases the previous Friday.

Exercise prices are normally fixed at five-point intervals for stocks trading below 100, at ten-point intervals for stocks trading between 100 and 200, and at 20-point intervals for stocks above 200. When trading begins in a new expiration month, the exercise price for the option is fixed at a dollar-per-share figure close to the current market price of the underlying common stock.

If significant price movements take place in an underlying stock between the introduction of new expiration months, additional call options with new exercise prices may be opened for trading. This offers the investor in listed calls a choice of exercise prices and related premiums having widely different risk/reward characteristics. These variations permit the alert investor to take advantage of overpriced or undervalued options resulting from the day-to-day supply/demand imbalances of the marketplace.

Exhibit 4–1 provides pertinent information for those listed calls that were recently trading—their ticker symbols, expirations months, and the exchange(s) where they were listed.

EXHIBIT 4–1: Listed call options

Underlying stock	Stock symbol	Exchange	Expiration months			
Abbott Laboratories............	ABT	PBW	Feb	May	Aug	Nov
Aetna Life & Casualty..........	AET	AMEX	Jan	Apr	Jul	Oct
Alcoa........................	AA	CBOE	Jan	Apr	Jul	Oct
Allied Chemical................	ACD	PBW	Jan	Apr	Jul	Oct
Amerada Hess..................	AHC	PBW	Feb	May	Aug	Nov
American Cyanamid............	ACY	AMEX	Jan	Apr	Jul	Oct
American Electric Power........	AEP	CBOE	Feb	May	Aug	Nov
American Home Products.......	AHP	AMEX	Jan	Apr	Jul	Oct
American Hospital Supply......	AHS	CBOE	Feb	May	Aug	Nov
AMF Inc......................	AMF	AMEX	Feb	May	Aug	Nov
AMP Inc......................	AMP	CBOE	Feb	May	Aug	Nov
ASA Ltd......................	ASA	AMEX	Feb	May	Aug	Nov
Asarco........................	AR	AMEX	Jan	Apr	Jul	Oct
American Telephone & Telegraph...................	T	CBOE	Jan	Apr	Jul	Oct
Atlantic Richfield..............	ARC	CBOE	Jan	Apr	Jul	Oct
Avon Products.................	AVP	CBOE	Jan	Apr	Jul	Oct
Baxter Laboratories............	BAX	CBOE	Feb	May	Aug	Nov
Beatrice Foods................,....	BRY	AMEX	Jan	Apr	Jul	Oct
Bethlehem Steel................	BS	CBOE	Jan	Apr	Jul	Oct
Black & Decker................	BDK	CBOE	Feb	May	Aug	Nov
Boeing........................	BA	CBOE	Feb	May	Aug	Nov
Boise Cascade..................	BCC	PBW	Feb	May	Aug	Nov
Brunswick.....................	BC	CBOE	Jan	Apr	Jul	Oct
Burroughs.....................	BGH	AMEX	Jan	Apr	Jul	Oct
Caterpillar Tractor.............	CAT	AMEX	Feb	May	Aug	Nov
CBS Inc.......................	CBS	CBOE	Feb	May	Aug	Nov
Chase Manhattan Corp..........	CMB	AMEX	Jan	Apr	Jul	Oct
Citicorp......................	FNC	CBOE	Jan	Apr	Jul	Oct

EXHIBIT 4-1 *(continued)*

Underlying stock	Stock symbol	Exchange	Expiration months			
Clorox Co.	CLX	PBW	Jan	Apr	Jul	Oct
Coca-Cola	KO	CBOE	Feb	May	Aug	Nov
Colgate-Palmolive	CL	CBOE	Feb	May	Aug	Nov
Commonwealth Edison	CWE	CBOE	Feb	May	Aug	Nov
Continental Oil	CLL	PBW	Jan	Apr	Jul	Oct
Continental Telephone	CTC	AMEX	Jan	Apr	Jul	Oct
Control Data	CDA	CBOE	Feb	May	Aug	Nov
Deere & Co.	DE	AMEX	Jan	Apr	Jul	Oct
Delta Airlines	DAL	CBOE	Jan	Apr	Jul	Oct
Digital Equipment	DEC	AMEX	Jan	Apr	Jul	Oct
Disney Productions	DIS	AMEX	Jan	Apr	Jul	Oct
Dow Chemical	DOW	CBOE	Jan	Apr	Jul	Oct
Dupont	DD	AMEX	Jan	Apr	Jul	Oct
Eastman Kodak	EK	CBOE	Jan	Apr	Jul	Oct
El Paso Co	ELG	AMEX	Feb	May	Aug	Nov
Engelhard Minerals & Chemicals	ENG	PBW	Jan	Apr	Jul	Oct
Exxon Corp.	XON	CBOE	Jan	Apr	Jul	Oct
Federal National Mortgage	FNM	CBOE	Jan	Apr	Jul	Oct
Firestone Tire & Rubber	FIR	PBW	Feb	May	Aug	Nov
First Charter Financial Corp.	FCF	AMEX	Jan	Apr	Jul	Oct
Ford Motor Co.	F	CBOE	Jan	Apr	Jul	Oct
General Dynamics	GD	CBOE	Feb	May	Aug	Nov
General Electric	GE	CBOE	Jan	Apr	Jul	Oct
General Foods Corp.	GF	CBOE	Feb	May	Aug	Nov
General Motors	GM	CBOE	Jan	Apr	Jul	Oct
General Telephone & Electric	GTE	AMEX	Jan	Apr	Jul	Oct
Gillette	GS	AMEX	Jan	Apr	Jul	Oct
Goodyear Tire & Rubber	GT	AMEX	Jan	Apr	Jul	Oct
Grace, W. R.	GRA	AMEX	Feb	May	Aug	Nov
Great Western Financial Corp.	GWF	CBOE	Jan	Apr	Jul	Oct
Greyhound	G	AMEX	Jan	Apr	Jul	Oct
Gulf Oil	GO	AMEX	Jan	Apr	Jul	Oct
Gulf & Western Industries	GW	CBOE	Jan	Apr	Jul	Oct
Halliburton	HAL	CBOE	Jan	Apr	Jul	Oct
Hercules Inc.	HPC	AMEX	Jan	Apr	Jul	Oct
Hewlett-Packard	HWP	CBOE	Feb	May	Aug	Nov
Holiday Inns Inc.	HIA	CBOE	Feb	May	Aug	Nov

EXHIBIT 4–1 *(continued)*

Underlying stock	Stock symbol	Exchange	Expiration months			
Homestake Mining.............	HM	CBOE	Jan	Apr	Jul	Oct
Honeywell Inc.................	HON	CBOE	Feb	May	Aug	Nov
Household Finance............	HFC	AMEX	Jan	Apr	Jul	Oct
Howard Johnson..............	HJ	PBW	Jan	Apr	Jul	Oct
International Business Machines.	IBM	CBOE	Jan	Apr	Jul	Oct
INA.........................	INA	CBOE	Jan	Apr	Jul	Oct
International Flavors & Fragrances..................	IFF	CBOE	Feb	May	Aug	Nov
International Harvester.........	HR	CBOE	Jan	Apr	Jul	Oct
International Minerals & Chemicals...................	IGL	CBOE	Jan	Apr	Jul	Oct
International Paper............	IP	CBOE	Jan	Apr	Jul	Oct
International Telephone & Telegraph...................	ITT	CBOE	Jan	Apr	Jul	Oct
Jim Walter....................	JWC	CBOE	Feb	May	Aug	Nov
Johns-Manville................	JM	CBOE	Feb	May	Aug	Nov
Johnson & Johnson............	JNJ	CBOE	Jan	Apr	Jul	Oct
Kennecott Copper.............	KN	CBOE	Jan	Apr	Jul	Oct
Kerr-McGee Corp..............	KMG	CBOE	Jan	Apr	Jul	Oct
Kresge, S. S..................	KG	CBOE	Jan	Apr	Jul	Oct
Lilly (Eli) Co.................	LLY	AMEX	Jan	Apr	Jul	Oct
Loews Corp...................	LTR	CBOE	Jan	Apr	Jul	Oct
Louisiana Land & Exploration...	LLX	PBW	Feb	May	Aug	Nov
McDonald's Corp..............	MCD	CBOE	Jan	Apr	Jul	Oct
Merck & Co...................	MRK	CBOE	Jan	Apr	Jul	Oct
Merrill Lynch & Co............	MER	AMEX	Jan	Apr	Jul	Oct
Mesa Petroleum...............	MSA	AMEX	Jan	Apr	Jul	Oct
Minnesota Mining & Manufacturing...............	MMM	CBOE	Jan	Apr	Jul	Oct
Mobil Oil Corp................	MOB	CBOE	Feb	May	Aug	Nov
Monsanto.....................	MTC	CBOE	Jan	Apr	Jul	Oct
Motorola.....................	MOT	AMEX	Jan	Apr	Jul	Oct
National Semiconductor.........	NSM	CBOE	Feb	May	Aug	Nov
Northwest Airlines.............	NWA	CBOE	Jan	Apr	Jul	Oct
Norton Simon Inc..............	NSI	AMEX	Feb	May	Aug	Nov
Occidental Petroleum...........	OXY	CBOE	Feb	May	Aug	Nov
Penney, J. C..................	JCP	AMEX	Feb	May	Aug	Nov
Pennzoil Co...................	PZL	CBOE	Jan	Apr	Jul	Oct
Pfizer Inc.....................	PFE	AMEX	Jan	Apr	Jul	Oct

EXHIBIT 4–1 (continued)

Underlying stock	Stock symbol	Exchange	Expiration months			
Phelps Dodge	PD	AMEX	Jan	Apr	Jul	Oct
Philip Morris	MO	AMEX	Jan	Apr	Jul	Oct
Phillips Petroleum	P	AMEX	Feb	May	Aug	Nov
Pittson Co	PCO	PBW	Feb	May	Aug	Nov
Polaroid Corp	PRD	CBOE	Jan	Apr	Jul	Oct
Procter & Gamble	PG	AMEX	Jan	Apr	Jul	Oct
Raytheon Co	RTN	CBOE	Feb	May	Aug	Nov
RCA Corp	RCA	CBOE	Jan	Apr	Jul	Oct
R. J. Reynolds Industries	RJR	CBOE	Feb	May	Aug	Nov
Rite Aid Corp	RAD	AMEX	Jan	Apr	Jul	Oct
Schlumberger	SLB	CBOE	Feb	May	Aug	Nov
Searle, G. D	SRL	AMEX	Feb	May	Aug	Nov
Sears Roebuck	S	CBOE	Jan	Apr	Jul	Oct
Simplicity Pattern	SYP	AMEX	Feb	May	Aug	Nov
Skyline Corp	SKY	CBOE	Feb	May	Aug	Nov
Southern Co	SO	CBOE	Feb	May	Aug	Nov
Sperry Rand	SY	CBOE	Jan	Apr	Jul	Oct
Standard Oil of California	SD	AMEX	Jan	Apr	Jul	Oct
Standard Oil of Indiana	SN	CBOE	Feb	May	Aug	Nov
Sterling Drugs	STY	AMEX	Feb	May	Aug	Nov
Syntex Corp	SYN	CBOE	Jan	Apr	Jul	Oct
Tandy Corp	TAN	AMEX	Jan	Apr	Jul	Oct
Tenneco Inc	TGT	AMEX	Feb	May	Aug	Nov
Tesoro Petroleum Corp	TSO	CBOE	Jan	Apr	Jul	Oct
Texaco Inc	TX	AMEX	Jan	Apr	Jul	Oct
Texasgulf Inc	TG	CBOE	Feb	May	Aug	Nov
Texas Instruments	TXN	CBOE	Jan	Apr	Jul	Oct
Tiger International Inc	TGR	AMEX	Feb	May	Aug	Nov
TRW	TRW	AMEX	Jan	Apr	Jul	Oct
UAL Inc	UAL	CBOE	Feb	May	Aug	Nov
Union Carbide	UK	AMEX	Jan	Apr	Jul	Oct
United Technologies	UTX	CBOE	Feb	May	Aug	Nov
Upjohn Co	UPJ	CBOE	Jan	Apr	Jul	Oct
U.S. Steel Corp	X	AMEX	Jan	Apr	Jul	Oct
Utah International Inc	UC	CBOE	Feb	May	Aug	Nov
Virginia Electric & Power	VEL	PBW	Jan	Apr	Jul	Oct
Warner-Lambert	WLA	AMEX	Jan	Apr	Jul	Oct
Western Union Corp	WU	PBW	Jan	Apr	Jul	Oct

EXHIBIT 4-1 (concluded)

Underlying stock	Stock symbol	Exchange	Expiration months			
Westinghouse Electric..........	WX	AMEX	Jan	Apr	Jul	Oct
Weyerhaeuser..................	WY	CBOE	Jan	Apr	Jul	Oct
Williams Companies............	WMB	CBOE	Feb	May	Aug	Nov
Woolworth, F. W..............	Z	PBW	Feb	May	Aug	Nov
Xerox Corp....................	XRX	CBOE	Jan	Apr	Jul	Oct
Zenith Radio..................	ZE	AMEX	Feb	May	Aug	Nov

Source: Thomas C. Noddings and Earl Zazove, *Listed Call Options*, Homewood, Ill.: Dow Jones-Irwin, 1975.

Option symbols. Call option symbols consist of the underlying stock's symbol followed by two letters. The first letter represents the expiration month and the second letter represents the exercise price.

Expiration month codes		Exercise price codes			
Code	Month	Code*	Exercise prices		
A.............	Jan	A..........	5	105	205
B.............	Feb	B..........	10	110	210
C.............	Mar	C..........	15	115	215
D.............	Apr	D..........	20	120	220
E.............	May	E..........	25	125	225
F.............	Jun	F..........	30	130	230
G.............	Jul	G..........	35	135	235
H.............	Aug	H..........	40	140	240
I.............	Sep	I..........	45	145	245
J.............	Oct	J..........	50	150	250
K.............	Nov	K..........	55	155	255
L.............	Dec	L..........	60	160	260
		M..........	65	165	265
		N..........	70	170	270
		O..........	75	175	275
		P..........	80	180	280
		Q..........	85	185	285
		R..........	90	190	290
		S..........	95	195	295
		T..........	100	200	300

* The letters U–Z are used for up to six nonstandard exercise prices (uneven splits, spin-offs, synonyms, and other unusual exercise prices).

Source: Thomas C. Noddings and Earl Zazove, *Listed Call Options*, Homewood, Ill.: Dow Jones-Irwin, 1975.

2. Secondary trading market

The most important new feature of listed options is a secondary market in which existing options are freely traded. This innovation clearly sets listed options apart from OTC options, which have virtually no resalability.

In the absence of a secondary trading market, an option holder must exercise the option (or sell it at its salvage value) to profit from any increase in the price of the underlying stock. The holder of such an OTC call has almost no opportunity to realize additional value for the length of time remaining until the option's expiration date. Likewise, the writer of an OTC call option has little or no opportunity to liquidate his position before the expiration date.

On the other hand, the holder of a listed option has a liquid, marketable instrument that resembles a warrant more nearly than the illiquid call option of the OTC market. He can close out his position in the secondary market at any time. And, after buying a listed call, the investor can continuously follow its price as it rises or falls in conjunction with the price movements of the underlying stock. Furthermore, time value remaining in the call will be reflected throughout its life.

Sellers of listed options have similar advantages in being able to redeem their obligations through purchases in the secondary trading market.

3. Market depth

The popularity of listed call options has resulted in a market depth that never existed in the OTC market. This depth permits trading in relatively large volume without significantly disrupting the market. In fact, certain institutional investors have purchased large numbers of calls with the intention of exercising them, as a superior alternative to the outright purchase of their underlying common stocks.

Sellers of listed calls who own the underlying common stocks may be reasonably sure that future calls can be sold on a continuing basis without having to liquidate their stock positions each time and search for other situations that are in demand by buyers.

4. Lower transaction costs

The option exchanges, which have commission structures similar to other security exchanges, offer a significant saving compared to the price spreads experienced in the negotiated OTC options market. Even more important is the ability to sell a profitable call in the secondary market at regular commission rates, without incurring the extraordinarily high commission expense of exercising the call and selling the stock received.

If a call is about to be exercised, the seller may buy it back at nominal expense instead of having to pay the higher commissions on the sale of his common stock (plus the additional cost of repurchasing stock for use in selling future calls).

5. Tax considerations

The present tax treatment of the sale and subsequent repurchase of listed call options has corrected a tax disadvantage applying to writers of OTC options. The OTC call writer incurs ordinary income if the call expires worthless, but he cannot obtain an ordinary loss if the call's value at expiration exceeds the original premium received. The seller of listed calls, however, can simply repurchase the call for an ordinary loss if it rises in value above the price at which it was originally sold. Although I believe the tax ruling that presently applies to listed call options is fair and equitable, some people have claimed that it is a tax loophole that allows an option trader to convert ordinary income into capital gains. This is true for rising markets but the reverse situation exists during bear markets—ordinary income is received versus capital losses. Pending legislation might change the ruling by treating closing transactions on call options sold as short-term capital gain or loss, as in conventional short sales. In my opinion, this loophole closing would be even more advantageous to the seller of listed calls as most options expire worthless over a market cycle. The sophisticated option seller would prefer the short-term capital gain or loss tax treatment to ordinary income or loss.

NORMAL PREMIUMS FOR LISTED CALL OPTIONS

The concept of normal premiums for call options is one of the most important tools provided in this book. By definition, a normal premium is the amount of money an option buyer or seller should receive to compensate him fairly for market risk.

Most option traders with experience in the over-the-counter or listed markets have a good "feel" for normal premiums on typical option contracts—especially those having three or six months to expiration. They recognize that option premiums are primarily related to:

1. The common stock's yield.
2. The price volatility of the common stock.
3. The length of time the option has to run.

1. Yield

Other factors being equal, a listed call option is worth less on a stock paying a high cash dividend than on a low-yielding stock. Unlike the over-the-counter market, where exercise prices are reduced when a dividend is paid, the purchaser of a listed call does not participate in the dividend. So a buyer, evaluating the call as an alternative to the common stock, will expect to pay less for the option if the dividend is high. Likewise, the seller of the call, who normally owns the underlying stock, is willing to accept less since he will receive the dividends. Note that this applies to only ordinary cash dividends. Stock dividends and other distributions require that the options be equitably adjusted to cover the equivalent property value which a holder of the underlying stock would be entitled to receive.

Listed call option premiums should therefore be evaluated to include the underlying stock's yield. The "effective" premium is the sum of both. For example, a six-month call on XYZ Company, having a 4 percent annual yield, should be evaluated by both buyer and seller as follows:

$$
\begin{array}{lcr}
\text{Call's market premium} & = & 10\% \\
\text{Stock's yield for six months} & = & +2\% \\ \hline
\text{Effective premium} & = & 12\%
\end{array}
$$

Exhibit 4–2 provides dividend data for those stocks having listed calls. As can be seen, there are substantial differences in the dividend payout policies of these companies. Later in this chapter we will see that calls on high-yielding stocks—like AT&T and Commonwealth Edison—historically have below-average market premiums. Calls on low-yielding stocks—like McDonald's and Polaroid—have always commanded higher premiums.

2. Price volatility

Assuming that two stocks have the same yield, the one with the greater price volatility will generally command a higher premium for its call options. A volatile stock offers greater opportunity for profits to the call buyer than one whose price action is

EXHIBIT 4–2: Dividend data for stocks having listed call options (January 1976)

Underlying stock	Stock symbol	Stock price	Indicated dividend rate*	Yield	Earnings and division ranking†
Abbott Laboratories...........	ABT	$ 41	$0.80	2.0%	A
Aetna Life & Casualty.........	AET	24	1.08	4.5	—
Alcoa.......................	AA	39	1.34	3.4	B+
Allied Chemical..............	ACD	33	1.80	5.4	B+
Amerada Hess.................	AHC	17	0.30	1.8	B+
American Cyanamid...........	ACY	25	1.50	6.0	A
American Electric Power.......	AEP	21	2.00	9.5	A—
American Home Products......	AHP	33	0.92	2.8	A+
American Hospital Supply......	AHS	30	0.34	1.1	A+
AMF Inc.....................	AMF	19	1.24	6.5	A—
AMP Inc.....................	AMP	26	0.37	1.4	A
ASA Ltd.....................	ASA	30	0.80	2.7	—
Asarco......................	AR	13	0.60	4.6	B+
American Telephone & Telegraph...................	T	51	3.40	6.7	A+
Atlantic Richfield.............	ARC	90	2.50	2.8	A
Avon Products................	AVP	35	1.60	4.6	A
Baxter Laboratories...........	BAX	40	0.21	0.5	A+
Beatrice Foods................	BRY	24	0.76	3.2	A+
Bethlehem Steel..............	BS	33	2.00	6.1	B+
Black & Decker..............	BDK	23	0.40	1.7	A+
Boeing......................	BA	24	0.95	4.0	B
Boise Cascade................	BCC	24	0.65	2.7	B
Brunswick...................	BC	11	0.40	3.6	B+
Burroughs...................	BGH	84	0.60	0.7	A+
Caterpillar Tractor...........	CAT	70	2.00	2.9	A—
CBS Inc.....................	CBS	47	1.66	3.5	A
Chase Manhattan Corp.........	CMB	28	2.20	7.9	—
Citicorp.....................	FNC	30	0.88	2.9	—
Clorox Co...................	CLX	12	0.52	4.3	B+
Coca-Cola...................	KO	82	2.30	2.8	A+
Colgate-Palmolive............	CL	29	0.76	2.6	A+
Commonwealth Edison........	CWE	30	2.30	7.7	A
Continental Oil..............	CLL	61	2.00	3.3	A
Continental Telephone.........	CTC	12	1.00	8.3	B+
Control Data.................	CDA	18	nil	nil	B
Deere & Co..................	DE	52	1.90	3.6	B+
Delta Airlines................	DAL	38	0.60	1.6	A—

EXHIBIT 4–2 (*continued*)

Underlying stock	Stock symbol	Stock price	Indicated dividend rate*	Yield	Earnings and division ranking†
Digital Equipment............	DEC	$137	$ nil	nil%	B+
Disney Productions............	DIS	50	0.12	0.02	A
Dow Chemical................	DOW	92	1.60	1.7	A
Dupont.......................	DD	126	4.25	3.3	A–
Eastman Kodak...............	EK	106	2.06	1.9	A+
El Paso Co....................	ELG	12	1.10	9.2	B
Engelhard Minerals & Chemicals..................	ENG	23	1.00	4.4	A–
Exxon Corp...................	XON	89	5.00	5.6	A+
Federal National Mortgage.....	FNM	15	0.80	5.3	—
Firestone Tire & Rubber.......	FIR	22	1.10	5.0	A–
First Charter Financial Corp....	FCF	12	nil	nil	—
Ford Motor Co................	F	44	2.40	5.4	A–
General Dynamics.............	GD	38	nil	nil	B–
General Electric...............	GE	46	1.60	3.5	A+
General Foods Corp............	GF	28	1.40	5.0	A
General Motors...............	GM	58	2.40	4.1	A–
General Telephone & Electric...	GTE	25	1.80	7.2	A
Gillette......................	GS	33	1.50	4.6	A–
Goodyear Tire & Rubber.......	GT	22	1.10	5.0	A
Grace, W. R..................	GRA	24	1.70	7.1	B+
Great Western Financial Corp...	GWF	14	0.44	3.1	—
Greyhound...................	G	13	1.04	8.0	B+
Gulf Oil......................	GO	21	1.70	8.1	A
Gulf & Western Industries......	GW	22	0.78	3.6	B+
Halliburton...................	HAL	146	1.32	0.9	A
Hercules Inc..................	HPC	28	0.80	2.9	A–
Hewlett-Packard..............	HWP	95	0.30	0.3	A
Holiday Inns Inc..............	HIA	14	0.35	2.5	B+
Homestake Mining............	HM	36	1.25	3.5	B+
Honeywell Inc.................	HON	33	1.40	4.2	A–
Household Finance............	HFC	16	1.10	6.9	A–
Howard Johnson..............	HJ	15	0.24	1.6	B+
International Business Machines..................	IBM	224	7.00	3.1	A+
INA.........................	INA	35	2.10	6.0	—
International Flavors & Fragrances..................	IFF	24	0.32	1.3	A

EXHIBIT 4–2 (continued)

Underlying stock	Stock symbol	Stock price	Indicated dividend rate*	Yield	Earnings and division ranking†
International Harvester.........	HR	$ 22	$1.70	7.7%	B+
International Minerals & Chemicals..................	IGL	38	2.00	5.3	B+
International Paper...........	IP	58	2.00	3.4	A—
International Telephone & Telegraph..................	ITT	23	1.60	7.0	A—
Jim Walter...................	JWC	37	1.00	2.7	A—
Johns-Manville...............	JM	23	1.20	5.2	A—
Johnson & Johnson............	JNJ	90	0.85	0.9	A+
Kennecott Copper.............	KN	31	1.00	3.2	B+
Kerr-McGee Corp..............	KMG	70	1.00	1.4	A
Kresge, S. S..................	KG	34	0.24	0.7	A+
Lilly (Eli) Co.................	LLY	52	1.10	2.1	A+
Loews Corp...................	LTR	21	1.20	5.7	B+
Louisiana Land & Exploration..	LLX	22	1.12	5.1	A
McDonald's Corp..............	MCD	58	nil	nil	B+
Merck & Co...................	MRK	69	1.40	2.0	A+
Merrill Lynch & Co............	MER	15	0.60	4.0	—
Mesa Petroleum...............	MSA	19	0.05	0.3	B+
Minnesota Mining & Manufacturing.....................	MMM	56	1.35	2.4	A+
Mobil Oil Corp................	MOB	47	3.40	7.2	A+
Monsanto....................	MTC	76	2.60	3.4	A
Motorola.....................	MOT	41	0.70	1.7	A
National Semiconductor........	NSM	41	nil	nil	B
Northwest Airlines............	NWA	23	0.45	2.0	B+
Norton Simon Inc..............	NSI	22	0.50	2.3	B+
Occidental Petroleum..........	OXY	14	1.00	7.1	B
Penney, J. C..................	JCP	50	1.16	2.3	A
Pennzoil Co...................	PZL	19	1.20	6.3	B+
Pfizer Inc....................	PFE	28	0.81	2.9	A+
Phelps Dodge.................	PD	36	2.20	6.1	B+
Philip Morris.................	MO	53	1.00	1.9	A+
Phillips Petroleum.............	P	54	1.60	3.0	A
Pittston Co...................	PCO	32	1.02	3.2	A
Polaroid Corp.................	PRD	31	0.32	1.0	B+
Procter & Gamble.............	PG	89	2.00	2.2	A+
Raytheon Co..................	RTN	46	1.00	2.2	A
RCA Corp....................	RCA	19	1.00	5.3	B+

EXHIBIT 4–2 *(concluded)*

Underlying stock	*Stock symbol*	*Stock price*	*Indicated dividend rate**	*Yield*	*Earnings and division ranking†*
R. J. Reynolds Industries.......	RJR	$ 62	$ 3.08	5.0%	A+
Rite Aid Corp.................	RAD	15	0.16	1.1	B+
Schlumberger.................	SLB	76	0.80	1.0	A+
Searle, G. D..................	SRL	15	0.52	3.5	A+
Sears Roebuck................	S	65	1.85	2.8	A+
Simplicity Pattern............	SYP	16	0.40	2.5	A
Skyline Corp.................	SKY	17	0.24	1.4	B
Southern Co..................	SO	15	1.40	9.3	A−
Sperry Rand.................	SY	39	0.76	2.0	B+
Standard Oil of California......	SD	29	2.00	6.9	A+
Standard Oil of Indiana........	SN	43	2.00	4.6	A+
Sterling Drugs...............	STY	19	0.70	3.7	A+
Syntex Corp..................	SYN	30	0.40	1.3	A−
Tandy Corp..................	TAN	26	nil	nil	B+
Tenneco Inc..................	TGT	27	1.76	6.5	B+
Tesoro Petroleum Corp.........	TSO	14	1.00	7.1	B+
Texaco Inc...................	TX	23	2.00	8.7	A+
Texasgulf Inc.................	TG	28	1.20	4.3	B+
Texas Instruments............	TXN	95	1.00	1.0	A−
Tiger International Inc.........	TGR	14	0.40	2.9	B
TRW.......................	TRW	27	1.20	4.4	A−
UAL Inc.....................	UAL	28	0.60	2.1	B
Union Carbide................	UK	61	2.40	3.9	A
United Technologies...........	UTX	46	2.00	4.4	B+
Upjohn Co....................	UPJ	42	0.96	2.3	A
U.S. STeel Corp...............	X	65	2.80	4.3	B+
Utah International Inc.........	UC	47	1.05	2.2	A
Virginia Electric & Power......	VEL	14	1.18	8.4	A−
Warner-Lambert..............	WLA	36	0.92	2.6	A+
Western Union Corp...........	WU	16	1.40	8.8	B
Westinghouse Electric.........	WX	13	0.97	7.5	B+
Weyerhaeuser.................	WY	37	0.80	2.2	A−
Williams Companies...........	WMB	26	0.60	2.3	B+
Woolworth, F. W.............	Z	22	1.20	5.4	A−
Xerox Corp..................	XRX	51	1.00	2.0	A+
Zenith Radio.................	ZE	24	1.00	4.2	B+

* Standard & Poor's projection of dividend payments for next 12 months was used to compute percent yield (stock dividends and possible extra dividends excluded).
† Standard & Poor's rankings based on scientific weighting of earnings and dividends.
Source: Thomas Noddings and Earl Zazove, *Listed Call Options*, Homewood, Ill.: Dow Jones-Irwin, 1975.

relatively stable. Likewise, an option seller would expect to receive a higher premium on a volatile security to compensate for the additional risk of holding the underlying stock in a declining market or for the loss of opportunity for large profits during a market upsurge.

Exhibit 4–3 provides volatility calculations for the past three years on all stocks having listed calls. As indicated, volatility was determined by dividing the stock's price range $(H - L)$ by its average price for that year $\frac{1}{2}(H + L)$. Although historical price actions may not predict the future exactly, they do have an important bearing on market premiums paid for calls. Of course, if the market expects a stock to exhibit greater or less price volatility in the future than it did in the past, it will make corresponding adjustments to premiums.

Calls on stocks with high price volatility—like Disney and Holiday Inns—have historically commanded high premiums. Calls on stable stocks—like AT&T and Exxon—can be expected to sell for low premiums.

3. Normal premiums for six-month listed calls

Exhibit 4–4 combines yield and price volatility from Exhibits 4–2 and 4–3 and places each call option in a normal premium range—assuming that it has six months to run and that the stock is selling at the call's exercise price. These premium ranges are not definite or fixed, but are intended to be flexible guides for evaluation purposes.

It cannot be overemphasized that the indicated premium ranges are approximations. The future will bring major changes to many of these companies and their option premiums will change accordingly. The phase of the market cycle will also affect premiums, which are a measure of investor optimism. Finally, supply/demand price pressures and additional experience with listed options will

EXHIBIT 4–3:   Stock volatility calculations

$$V = \frac{H - L}{\frac{1}{2}(H + L)}$$

Where
V = Volatility
L = Stock's low for the year
H = Stock's high for the year

	1973			1974			1975		
Underlying stock	*Low*	*– High*	*V*	*Low*	*– High*	*V*	*Low*	*– High*	*V*
Abbott Laboratories.........	23.75–	40.44	0.52	15.25–	30.62	0.67	23.25–	42.75	0.59
Aetna Life & Casualty.......	28.75–	41.00	0.35	15.12–	39.25	0.89	17.25–	29.38	0.52
Alcoa......................	31.88–	53.75	0.51	25.88–	52.62	0.68	27.12–	50.25	0.60
Allied Chemical............	28.12–	49.00	0.54	23.00–	54.25	0.81	27.00–	42.00	0.43
Amerada Hess..............	26.25–	47.00	0.57	12.50–	38.12	1.01	14.50–	23.38	0.47
American Cyanamid.........	17.75–	32.12	0.58	17.12–	25.00	0.37	20.62–	30.88	0.40
American Electric Power.....	21.25–	30.75	0.37	13.50–	27.12	0.67	14.75–	21.62	0.38
American Home Products....	36.38–	48.75	0.29	26.12–	44.88	0.56	27.75–	43.25	0.44
American Hospital Supply...	36.38–	52.75	0.37	18.75–	41.38	0.75	25.88–	38.50	0.39
AMF Inc...................	17.25–	57.12	1.07	9.00–	24.00	0.91	9.62–	22.00	0.78
AMP Inc...................	35.75–	52.88	0.39	20.38–	45.25	0.76	23.12–	40.88	0.56
ASA Ltd...................	11.31–	34.88	1.02	26.06–	52.25	0.67	26.00–	47.75	0.59
Asarco.....................	17.25–	26.12	0.41	13.00–	27.38	0.71	12.00–	19.75	0.49
American Telephone & Telegraph................	45.38–	55.00	0.19	39.62–	53.00	0.29	44.75–	52.00	0.15
Atlantic Richfield...........	66.50–	113.25	0.52	73.00–	113.75	0.44	75.50–	110.00	0.37
Avon Products..............	57.25–	140.00	0.84	18.62–	65.00	1.11	27.88–	51.25	0.59
Baxter Laboratories.........	41.25–	61.62	0.40	24.12–	48.62	0.67	31.50–	51.38	0.48
Beatrice Foods..............	16.62–	30.25	0.58	12.12–	23.38	0.63	14.12–	24.88	0.55
Bethlehem Steel.............	24.62–	35.62	0.37	23.50–	36.12	0.42	24.75–	40.25	0.48
Black & Decker.............	31.00–	42.38	0.31	20.00–	41.50	0.70	20.12–	36.75	0.58
Boeing.....................	11.75–	26.88	0.78	11.62–	20.50	0.55	15.12–	31.88	0.71
Boise Cascade..............	8.25–	18.38	0.76	9.88–	19.00	0.63	10.50–	27.25	0.89
Brunswick..................	11.88–	37.88	1.04	7.12–	18.62	0.89	9.00–	15.75	0.55
Burroughs..................	92.00–	126.38	0.31	61.38–	113.00	0.59	61.12–	110.75	0.58
Caterpillar Tractor..........	53.62–	77.62	0.37	39.38–	69.75	0.56	48.00–	75.88	0.45
CBS Inc....................	24.38–	52.00	0.72	25.00–	40.38	0.47	28.88–	54.00	0.61
Chase Manhattan Corp......	41.50–	60.25	0.37	24.62–	56.50	0.79	24.75–	38.75	0.44
Citicorp....................	33.62–	51.50	0.42	20.88–	46.25	0.76	24.75–	39.00	0.45
Clorox Co..................	11.50–	53.00	1.29	5.50–	14.75	0.91	6.12–	13.50	0.75
Coca-Cola..................	115.50–	150.00	0.26	44.62–	127.75	0.96	53.25–	93.50	0.55
Colgate-Palmolive..........	21.00–	35.12	0.50	15.75–	30.25	0.63	22.00–	34.88	0.45
Commonwealth Edison......	27.38–	36.62	0.29	19.25–	30.38	0.45	22.62–	31.88	0.34
Continental Oil.............	26.75–	55.38	0.70	29.00–	58.50	0.67	40.62–	75.00	0.59
Continental Telephone.......	17.12–	25.88	0.41	9.25–	19.00	0.69	10.00–	14.38	0.36
Control Data...............	30.38–	62.00	0.68	9.50–	39.12	1.22	10.62–	23.50	0.75

EXHIBIT 4–3 *(continued)*

	1973			1974			1975		
Underlying stock	*Low*	*– High*	*V*	*Low*	*– High*	*V*	*Low*	*– High*	*V*
Deere & Co................	35.62–	65.50	0.59	27.75–	53.88	0.64	34.50–	52.00	0.40
Delta Airlines..............	35.25–	68.38	0.64	27.88–	56.12	0.61	25.38–	41.38	0.48
Digital Equipment.........	73.25–	119.25	0.48	49.00–	122.75	0.86	45.38–	141.00	1.03
Disney Productions.........	37.75–	115.62	1.02	16.12–	51.88	1.05	20.62–	54.12	0.90
Dow Chemical.............	46.50–	68.00	0.38	49.88–	70.00	0.34	53.75–	95.50	0.56
Dupont...................	145.25–	203.50	0.33	84.50–	179.00	0.72	87.12–	133.88	0.42
Eastman Kodak.............	103.50–	151.75	0.38	57.62–	117.50	0.68	63.00–	110.00	0.54
El Paso Co................	12.75–	21.00	0.49	9.12–	16.62	0.58	10.25–	13.75	0.29
Englehard Minerals & Chemicals...............	12.62–	27.25	0.73	12.38–	21.25	0.53	14.88–	24.00	0.47
Exxon Corp................	83.88–	103.25	0.21	54.88–	99.75	0.58	65.00–	94.00	0.36
Federal National Mortgage..	13.50–	23.50	0.54	11.12–	20.75	0.60	12.00–	19.88	0.49
Firestone Tire & Rubber.....	13.00–	27.75	0.72	12.25–	20.00	0.48	13.62–	23.75	0.54
First Charter Financial Corp....................	9.88–	27.12	0.93	4.50–	15.25	1.08	9.00–	15.88	0.55
Ford Motor Co.............	38.62–	82.38	0.72	28.75–	54.38	0.62	32.38–	45.25	0.33
General Dynamics...........	15.62–	28.62	0.59	13.50–	28.75	0.72	19.00–	56.25	0.99
General Electric...........	55.00–	75.88	0.32	30.00–	65.00	0.74	32.38–	52.88	0.48
General Foods Corp........	21.75–	30.50	0.33	16.00–	28.62	0.57	18.38–	29.38	0.46
General Motors.............	44.88–	84.62	0.61	28.88–	55.50	0.63	31.25–	59.12	0.62
General Telephone & Electric..................	22.88–	31.62	0.32	16.12–	26.62	0.49	16.88–	26.00	0.43
Gillette...................	31.75–	66.12	0.70	20.75–	40.50	0.64	21.25–	35.38	0.50
Goodyear Tire & Rubber....	12.50–	31.88	0.87	11.75–	18.38	0.44	12.75–	23.12	0.58
Grace, W. R...............	19.88–	30.38	0.42	18.00–	28.38	0.45	22.12–	29.62	0.29
Great Western Financial Corp....................	14.62–	34.75	0.82	6.38–	23.00	1.13	10.75–	19.00	0.55
Greyhound.................	13.25–	18.88	0.35	9.75–	18.62	0.63	10.50–	15.25	0.37
Gulf Oil..................	20.00–	28.88	0.36	16.00–	25.25	0.45	17.62–	23.50	0.29
Gulf & Western Industries...	10.69–	17.88	0.50	9.00–	14.56	0.47	11.75–	22.38	0.62
Halliburton...............	125.25–	194.50	0.43	104.00–	194.00	0.60	115.00–	189.00	0.49
Hercules Inc..............	28.50–	40.25	0.34	21.00–	44.00	0.71	21.50–	34.75	0.47
Hewlett-Packard...........	71.00–	100.62	0.35	52.00–	92.25	0.56	56.38–	120.50	0.73
Holiday Inns. Inc..........	10.75–	42.88	1.20	4.25–	18.38	1.25	5.12–	16.50	1.05
Homestake Mining.........	11.50–	35.44	1.02	29.25–	69.62	0.82	31.50–	55.50	0.55
Honeywell Inc..............	67.50–	140.38	0.70	17.50–	86.25	1.33	20.88–	40.50	0.64
Household Finance.........	15.75–	35.62	0.77	9.75–	22.00	0.77	11.88–	18.50	0.44
Howard Johnson...........	10.00–	34.88	1.11	4.00–	13.12	1.07	4.50–	16.00	1.12
International Business Machines...............	235.12–	365.25	0.43	150.50–	254.00	0.51	157.25–	227.38	0.36

EXHIBIT 4–3 (continued)

	1973			1974			1975		
Underlying stock	*Low*	*– High*	*V*	*Low*	*– High*	*V*	*Low*	*– High*	*V*
INA......................	30.62–	49.62	0.47	19.25–	38.38	0.66	28.00–	40.38	0.36
International Flavors & Fragrances................	33.25–	49.38	0.39	19.88–	42.38	0.72	22.50–	35.12	0.44
International Harvester......	22.12–	39.00	0.55	16.75–	29.25	0.54	19.75–	30.50	0.43
International Minerals & Chemicals................	15.25–	30.25	0.66	21.50–	40.75	0.62	30.88–	48.50	0.44
International Paper..........	33.00–	57.00	0.53	31.62–	56.00	0.56	34.62–	61.50	0.56
International Telephone & Telegraph................	25.00–	60.38	0.83	12.00–	29.50	0.84	14.62–	25.12	0.53
Jim Walter.................	13.38–	33.00	0.85	13.38–	24.00	0.57	22.75–	44.00	0.64
Johns-Manville.............	14.50–	33.00	0.78	14.38–	22.50	0.44	19.00–	26.75	0.34
Johnson & Johnson..........	101.25–	132.25	0.27	73.12–	119.38	0.48	72.25–	99.75	0.32
Kennecott Copper...........	23.00–	44.38	0.63	25.38–	49.50	0.64	27.12–	41.00	0.41
Kerr-McGee Corp...........	52.88–	95.88	0.58	47.12–	92.50	0.65	60.00–	95.12	0.45
Kresge, S.S.................	28.75–	51.12	0.56	18.25–	38.88	0.72	20.38–	35.38	0.54
Lilly (Eli) Co...............	69.75–	92.50	0.28	55.75–	82.75	0.39	49.50–	79.75	0.47
Loews Corp.................	16.25–	48.00	0.99	10.88–	23.25	0.73	14.50–	26.50	0.59
Louisiana Land & Exploration..............	32.00–	53.00	0.49	16.75–	54.88	1.06	19.38–	32.88	0.52
McDonald's Corp...........	44.12–	76.88	0.54	21.25–	63.25	0.99	26.75–	60.50	0.77
Merce & Co................	76.25–	101.50	0.28	46.62–	86.00	0.59	57.50–	85.75	0.39
Merrill Lynch & Co.........	12.38–	32.75	0.90	6.25–	15.12	0.83	10.12–	20.62	0.68
Mesa Petroleum............	28.75–	42.75	0.39	10.88–	43.88	1.21	17.88–	29.00	0.47
Minnesota Mining & Manufacturing.....	70.00–	91.62	0.27	44.62–	80.50	0.57	43.00–	68.00	0.45
Mobil Oil Corp.............	42.25–	75.50	0.56	30.62–	56.50	0.59	34.12–	48.88	0.36
Monsanto..................	43.12–	75.75	0.55	39.38–	69.50	0.55	41.00–	80.88	0.65
Motorola..................	41.25–	69.00	0.50	31.62–	61.88	0.65	33.75–	57.88	0.53
National Semiconductor.....	7.75–	36.25	1.30	6.25–	25.12	1.20	9.25–	48.38	1.36
Northwest Airlines.........	17.12–	36.62	0.73	10.62–	27.25	0.88	11.62–	23.25	0.67
Norton Simon Inc...........	15.00–	39.00	0.89	7.75–	16.12	0.70	10.62–	23.50	0.76
Occidental Petroleum........	7.75–	13.50	0.54	7.38–	14.62	0.66	12.62–	22.62	0.57
Penney, J. C...............	58.50–	101.00	0.53	35.00–	79.25	0.77	36.50–	63.25	0.54
Pennzoil Co................	17.50–	32.00	0.59	12.75–	30.50	0.82	17.00–	23.50	0.32
Pfizer Inc..................	38.50–	52.38	0.31	21.38–	45.00	0.71	23.75–	36.88	0.43
Phelps Dodge...............	38.75–	50.25	0.26	25.50–	49.88	0.65	29.00–	40.25	0.32
Philip Morris...............	48.75–	68.38	0.34	34.12–	61.38	0.57	40.88–	59.25	0.37
Phillips Petroleum..........	40.50–	70.50	0.54	31.62–	71.38	0.77	37.00–	60.38	0.48
Pittson Co.................	9.38–	16.50	0.55	11.00–	18.88	0.53	18.25–	40.62	0.76
Polaroid Corp..............	65.12–	143.50	0.75	14.12–	88.50	1.45	15.00–	43.50	0.97
Procter & Gamble..........	89.00–	120.00	0.30	67.00–	105.88	0.45	78.50–	100.75	0.25

EXHIBIT 4–3 *(concluded)*

Underlying stock	1973 Low – High	V	1974 Low – High	V	1975 Low – High	V
Raytheon Co...............	21.38– 34.75	0.48	20.00– 39.88	0.66	25.25– 59.75	0.81
RCA Corp.................	16.50– 39.12	0.81	9.25– 21.50	0.80	10.38– 21.38	0.69
R. J. Reynolds Industries....	36.50– 55.75	0.42	37.25– 53.38	0.36	49.50– 61.50	0.22
Rite Aid Corp.............	12.00– 56.75	1.30	2.50– 18.75	1.53	4.12– 16.38	1.20
Schlumberger Ltd...........	55.00– 92.62	0.51	48.75– 89.12	0.59	60.75– 90.50	0.39
Searle, G. D...............	22.75– 40.75	0.57	11.38– 28.25	0.85	13.50– 25.75	0.62
Sears Roebuck.............	78.25–123.25	0.45	41.50– 90.38	0.74	48.38– 74.38	0.42
Simplicity Pattern..........	32.75– 58.88	0.57	6.12– 38.00	1.45	8.00– 18.88	0.81
Skyline Corp..............	9.12– 33.12	1.14	10.25– 21.62	0.71	12.75– 26.00	0.68
Southern Co...............	14.75– 20.88	0.34	7.88– 17.25	0.75	8.75– 15.12	0.53
Sperry Rand...............	35.12– 56.00	0.46	23.12– 44.62	0.63	25.38– 48.62	0.63
Standard Oil of California...	27.00– 45.00	0.50	20.12– 36.62	0.58	22.12– 33.00	0.39
Standard Oil of Indiana......	38.25– 51.88	0.30	34.88– 55.00	0.45	36.00– 53.25	0.39
Sterling Drugs.............	24.25– 37.25	0.42	16.00– 31.25	0.65	15.25– 25.50	0.50
Syntex Corp...............	23.12– 64.25	0.94	27.75– 63.00	0.78	28.50– 44.62	0.44
Tandy Corp................	7.81– 23.44	1.00	4.88– 13.00	0.91	5.81– 26.88	1.29
Tenneco Inc...............	19.75– 30.38	0.42	16.75– 24.75	0.39	19.75– 27.38	0.32
Tesoro Petroleum Corp.......	12.00– 24.75	0.69	11.25– 28.94	0.88	12.75– 20.62	0.47
Texaco Inc.................	25.00– 43.12	0.53	20.00– 32.88	0.49	21.12– 28.38	0.29
Texasgulf Inc..............	17.12– 33.12	0.64	20.12– 36.62	0.58	23.88– 36.38	0.41
Texas Instruments..........	74.38–138.88	0.60	58.75–115.75	0.65	61.00–119.38	0.65
Tiger International Inc.......	14.00– 39.75	0.96	6.25– 22.88	1.14	7.25– 16.88	0.80
TRW.....................	17.50– 34.88	0.66	10.12– 20.50	0.68	14.25– 28.38	0.66
UAL Inc..................	15.38– 34.50	0.77	13.00– 29.88	0.79	13.62– 28.50	0.71
Union Carbide.............	29.25– 51.75	0.56	31.75– 46.00	0.37	40.12– 66.50	0.49
United Technologies........	20.75– 46.25	0.76	22.50– 32.75	0.37	31.25– 62.12	0.66
Upjohn Co.................	58.50–104.75	0.57	41.62– 88.25	0.72	30.00– 53.00	0.55
U.S. Steel Corp.............	26.75– 38.25	0.35	35.38– 48.50	0.31	38.25– 71.38	0.60
Utah International Inc.......	39.81– 57.00	0.36	32.62– 52.88	0.47	39.50– 74.88	0.62
Virginia Electric & Power...	13.00– 23.38	0.57	6.88– 15.75	0.78	8.25– 13.88	0.51
Warner-Lambert............	33.62– 58.00	0.53	18.12– 39.88	0.75	25.00– 38.50	0.43
Western Union Corp.........	10.00– 49.50	1.33	8.50– 15.88	0.61	9.12– 17.38	0.62
Westinghouse Electric.......	24.25– 47.38	0.65	8.00– 26.00	1.06	9.75– 20.00	0.69
Weyerhaeuser.......	22.12– 41.12	0.60	23.88– 46.00	0.63	27.62– 43.25	0.44
Williams Companies.........	19.50– 37.00	0.62	22.69– 38.50	0.52	22.50– 37.38	0.50
Woolworth, F. W...........	15.75– 31.88	0.68	8.00– 19.38	0.83	9.38– 22.75	0.83
Xerox Corp................	114.75–170.00	0.39	49.00–127.12	0.89	46.38– 87.62	0.62
Zenith Radio..............	23.00– 56.00	0.84	9.38– 31.38	1.08	10.00– 28.62	0.96

Source: Thomas C. Noddings and Earl Zazove, *Listed Call Options*, Homewood, Ill.: Dow Jones-Irwin, 1975.

EXHIBIT 4–4:   Approximate premiums for six-month listed call options

Underlying stock	Low 5–7 1/2 percent	Below average 7 1/2–10 percent	Average 10–12 1/2 percent	Above average 12 1/2–15 percent	High 15–20 percent
Abbott Laboratories			X		
Aetna Life & Casualty			X		
Alcoa			X		
Allied Chemical		X			
Amerada Hess			X		
American Cyanamid		X			
American Electric Power	X				
American Home Products		X			
American Hospital Supply			X		
AMF Inc.			X		
AMP Inc.			X		
ASA Ltd.				X	
Asarco		X			
American Telephone & Telegraph	X				
Atlantic Richfield		X			
Avon Products			X		
Baxter Laboratories			X		
Beatrice Foods		X			
Bethlehem Steel	X				
Black & Decker			X		
Boeing			X		
Boise Cascade				X	
Brunswick				X	
Burroughs			X		
Caterpillar Tractor		X			
CBS Inc.			X		
Chase Manhattan Corp.		X			
Citicorp			X		
Clorox Co.				X	
Coca-Cola		X			
Colgate-Palmolive			X		
Commonwealth Edison	X				
Continental Oil			X		
Continental Telephone		X			
Control Data					X
Deere & Co.			X		
Delta Airlines			X		

EXHIBIT 4–4 *(continued)*

Underlying stock	Low 5–7½ percent	Below average 7½–10 percent	Average 10–12½ percent	Above average 12½–15 percent	High 15–20 percent
Digital Equipment				X	
Disney Productions				X	
Dow Chemical		X			
Dupont		X			
Eastman Kodak		X			
El Paso Co.	X				
Engelhard Minerals & Chemicals			X		
Exxon Corp.	X				
Federal National Mortgage			X		
Firestone Tire & Rubber		X			
First Charter Financial Corp.					X
Ford Motor Co.		X			
General Dynamics					X
General Electric		X			
General Foods Corp.		X			
General Motors		X			
General Telephone & Electric	X				
Gillette		X			
Goodyear Tire		X			
Grace, W. R.	X				
Great Western Financial Corp.				X	
Greyhound	X				
Gulf Oil	X				
Gulf & Western Industries			X		
Halliburton			X		
Hercules Inc.			X		
Hewlett-Packard			X		
Holiday Inns Inc.					X
Homestake Mining				X	
Honeywell Inc.			X		
Household Finance			X		
Howard Johnson					X
International Business Machines		X			
INA		X			
International Flavors & Fragrances			X		

EXHIBIT 4–4 (continued)

Underlying stock	Low 5–7½ percent	Below average 7½–10 percent	Average 10–12½ percent	Above average 12½–15 percent	High 15–20 percent
International Harvester		X			
International Minerals & Chemicals			X		
International Paper		X			
International Telephone & Telegraph		X			
Jim Walter			X		
Johns-Manville		X			
Johnson & Johnson		X			
Kennecott Copper			X		
Kerr-McGee Corp.			X		
Kresge, S. S.			X		
Lilly (Eli) Co.		X			
Loews Corp.			X		
Louisiana Land & Exploration			X		
McDonalds Corp.				X	
Merck & Co.		X			
Merrill Lynch & Co.				X	
Mesa Petroleum				X	
Minnesota Mining & Manufacturing		X			
Mobil Oil Corp.	X				
Monsanto		X			
Motorola			X		
National Semiconductor					X
Northwest Airlines				X	
Norton Simon Inc.				X	
Occidental Petroleum			X		
Penney, J. C.			X		
Pennzoil Co.			X		
Pfizer Inc.			X		
Phelps Dodge	X				
Philip Morris		X			
Phillips Petroleum			X		
Pittson Co.			X		
Polaroid Corp.					X
Procter & Gamble		X			
Raytheon Co.			X		

EXHIBIT 4–4 *(concluded)*

Underlying stock	Low 5–7½ percent	Below average 7½–10 percent	Average 10–12½ percent	Above average 12½–15 percent	High 15–20 percent
RCA Corp.			X		
R. J. Reynolds Industries	X				
Rite Aid Corp.					X
Schlumberger			X		
Searle, G. D.			X		
Sears Roebuck		X			
Simplicity Pattern				X	
Skyline Corp.					X
Southern Co.	X				
Sperry Rand			X		
Standard Oil of California		X			
Standard Oil of Indiana	X				
Sterling Drugs			X		
Syntex Corp.				X	
Tandy Corp.					X
Tenneco Inc.	X				
Tesoro Petroleum Corp.			X		
Texaco Inc.	X				
Texasgulf Inc.			X		
Texas Instruments			X		
Tiger International Inc.				X	
TRW			X		
UAL Inc.				X	
Union Carbide		X			
United Technologies			X		
Upjohn Co.			X		
U.S. Steel Corp.		X			
Utah International Inc.			X		
Virginia Electric & Power		X			
Warner-Lambert			X		
Western Union Corp.			X		
Westinghouse Electric			X		
Weyerhaeuser			X		
Williams Companies			X		
Woolworth, F. W.			X		
Xerox Corp.			X		
Zenith Radio				X	

Source: Thomas C. Noddings and Earl Zazove, *Listed Call Options*, Homewood, Ill.: Dow Jones-Irwin, 1975.

result in further modifications to the basic premium guidelines presented here.

Each investor must use his judgment, when assessing a premium, as to where in its range the option should be at the time or whether it should be placed in a higher or lower range. Successful investors in call options will establish a normal premium, as in Exhibit 4–4, before making an investment decision.

In the exhibit, the majority of listed calls currently trading have been placed in average or below-average premium ranges. This reflects the high overall quality of the companies selected for trading. Future additions to the trading list will likely include more secondary or speculative companies.

4. Other option lengths

Our discussion to this point has been based on the popular six-month call. Options currently trading on exchanges, however, have a life of zero to nine months, and 12-month calls are often available in the over-the-counter market.

A good rule of thumb for premiums is that the value of the call increases 50 percent as the time is doubled. For example, a six-month call is worth 50 percent more than a three-month call, and a 12-month call is worth 50 percent more than a six-month call. Using this time-tested formula, Exhibit 4–5 provides relative premiums for options ranging from one to 12 months. The investor should first establish a reasonable premium range for a *six-month option* from Exhibit 4–4, then use Exhibit 4–5 to determine expected premium ranges for other lengths of time.

For example, six-month calls on IBM should trade in the 7½–10 percent premium range, per Exhibit 4–4. We would therefore expect new nine-month calls to sell in the 9.5–12.7 percent range, from Exhibit 4–5. If existing calls had only three months to run, their premium range should be 5.0–6.7 percent.

EXHIBIT 4–5:   Relative premiums for one- to 12-month options

Months to ex- piration	Low	Below average	Average	Above average	High
1	1.8	2.6	3.5	4.4	5.2	7.0
2	2.6	3.9	5.2	6.6	7.8	10.5
3	3.3	5.0	6.7	8.3	10.0	13.3
4	3.9	5.9	7.9	9.8	11.8	15.7
5	4.5	6.8	9.0	11.2	13.5	18.0
6	5.0 to	7.5 to	10.0 to	12.5 to	15.0 to	20.0
7	5.5	8.2	10.9	13.7	16.4	21.9
8	5.9	8.9	11.8	14.8	17.7	23.6
9	6.4	9.5	12.7	15.9	19.0	25.4
10	6.8	10.1	13.5	16.9	20.2	27.0
11	7.2	10.7	14.3	17.9	21.4	28.6
12	7.5	11.2	15.0	18.8	22.5	30.0

Note: The figures in the above table were rounded to the nearest $\frac{1}{10}$ of 1 percent for convenience. This is not intended to imply that the actual ranges are that precise. You must use your own judgment in evaluating option premiums, with this table as a guide.

Source: Thomas C. Noddings, and Earl Zazove, *Listed Call Options*, Homewood, Ill.: Dow Jones-Irwin, 1975.

If IBM's call options actually traded below these indicated ranges, they would be considered undervalued; if above these ranges, they would be overpriced.

NORMAL VALUE CURVES FOR LISTED CALL OPTIONS

So far, this chapter has provided procedures for determining normal premiums for call options when the underlying common stock was trading at the call's exercise price. Factors considered were the cash dividend paid on the common, the stock's price volatility, and the length of time the call had to run. These variables were illustrated in tables for your convenience and future reference. However, since the underlying common stock of a listed call option seldom trades at exactly the call's exercise price, analysis of listed calls is considerably more difficult than conventional OTC call options. Fortunately, this difficulty creates unusual opportunities for the alert and sophisticated investor.

Let us consider, for example, a six-month call on XYZ Company having a $50 exercise price when the common stock is trading at $50. Considering the average price volatility of the common and its 4 percent cash dividend, a 10 percent premium would be reasonable for the call—for a market price of $5. But what would be a fair market value for the call if the common were trading at $45, or $55, or even farther than five points from the exercise price?

Exhibit 4–6 shows a normal value curve based on historical

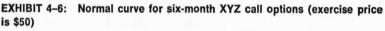

EXHIBIT 4–6: Normal curve for six-month XYZ call options (exercise price is $50)

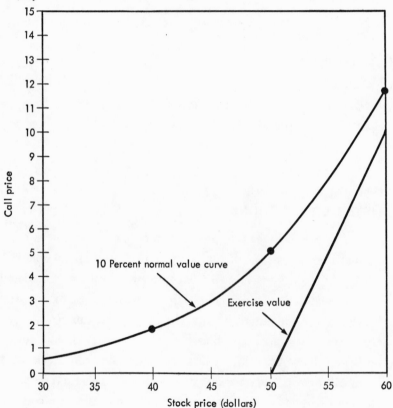

trading experience for the typical 10 percent premium for a six-month call on XYZ stock. This curve reflects the time value remaining in the call, as actually evaluated in the secondary market. When the common stock declines well below the call's exercise price, the market value of the call approaches zero. At a stock price of $40, for example, the call would be expected to trade at a small premium of about $1.75. On the upside, the call price approaches its exercise (intrinsic) value. At a price of $60 for the common, we would expect the call to trade at a modest $1.75 premium over its $10 intrinsic value for a market price of about $11.75.

A FAMILY OF NORMAL VALUE CURVES
FOR XYZ CALL OPTIONS

Exhibit 4–7 includes 5 and 15 percent premium curves for XYZ calls. These reflect typical values for shorter- or longer-term XYZ call options than the 10 percent curve for the six-month option. From this family of normal value curves, an investor interested in buying or selling XYZ calls could easily and quickly determine if they were overpriced or undervalued. He would first determine the remaining call option life, then assign a reasonable premium from Exhibit 4–4, assuming that the stock was trading at the exercise price, and finally compare actual stock and call market prices with the appropriate normal value curve in Exhibit 4–7.

For example, if XYZ common were trading at $40 and a call having a $50 exercise price had eight months time remaining, a reasonable market price for the call would be estimated as follows:

1. Based on stock yield and volatility, the normal premium for a *six-month* call would be 10 percent, assuming that the stock were trading at the $50 exercise price.

EXHIBIT 4-7: Normal value curves for XYZ call options (exercise price is $50)

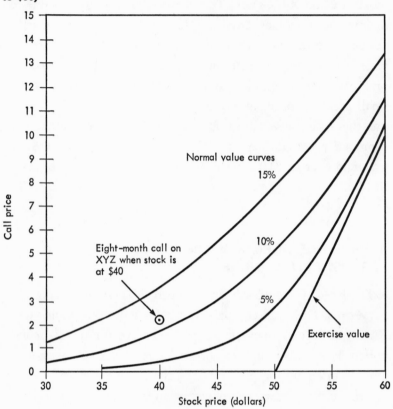

10 percent curve is for a six-month option.
15 percent curve is for a longer period.
 5 percent curve is for a shorter period.

2. From Exhibit 4–4, the expected premium for an *eight-month* call is about 12 percent (11.8 percent from the exhibit).

3. From Exhibit 4–7, the fair market price for the call is determined to be about $2.25 as indicated—the 12 percent factor is located between the 10 and 15 percent normal value curves at a stock price of $40.

If the call being evaluated were trading at less than $2.25, it would be considered undervalued. If trading at a higher price, it would be overvalued.

A FAMILY OF NORMAL VALUE CURVES FOR ALL LISTED CALL OPTIONS

A family of normal value curves could be prepared for each listed call option. However, the time and effort required would

EXHIBIT 4-8:   Normal value curves for call options

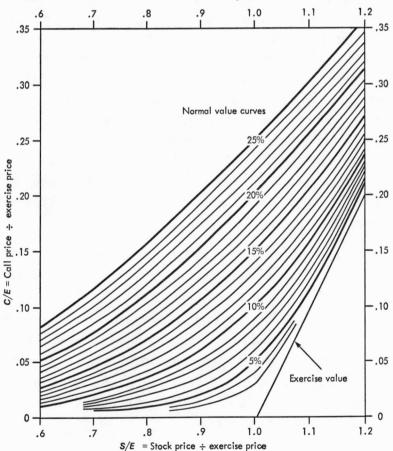

S/E = Stock price ÷ exercise price

be unrealistic. Fortunately, it is not necessary to prepare individualized curves for every call. Since the stock's dividend rate, its volatility, and the time to expiration have already been taken into consideration by Exhibits 4–4 and 4–5, the only remaining variable at the time the curves would be used is the price of the common stock in relation to the call's exercise price.

We can construct a family of normal curves that can be used for *all* call options. This is accomplished by dividing both the call and stock prices by the exercise price. Standardized curves may then be plotted using C/E (call price divided by exercise price) and S/E (stock price divided by exercise price). This family of curves will allow you to conveniently evaluate prices by a single chart for all calls, for comparison with the theoretical norm.

This family of normal value curves is the most important call option tool provided so far in this book. It is presented as Exhibit 4–8 and covers a range of call option premiums from 5 to 25 percent (at call's exercise price) and a range of S/E factors from 0.6 to 1.2. Most opportunities will fall within these ranges.

To illustrate the use of Exhibit 4–8, let us assume that IBM's stock is trading at $220 and we want to evaluate a four-month call option having an exercise price of $200. We would proceed as follows:

1. From Exhibit 4–4, the normal premium range for a *six-month* call is seen to be 7½ to 10 percent, assuming that the stock were trading at the $200 exercise price.

2. From Exhibit 4–5, the expected premium range for a *four-month* call is adjusted to 5.9 to 7.9 percent (we will round this off to 6.0 to 8.0 percent for convenience).

3. From Exhibit 4–8, at $S/E = 1.1$ ($220 market price divided by the $200 exercise price), C/E factors should range from about 0.125 (the 6 percent curve) to 0.14 (the 8 percent curve).

4. Our estimated fair market price for the call would therefore fall in the range of $25 (0.125 × $200) to $28 (0.14 × $200).

In summary, the normal value curves of Exhibit 4–8 are applied after these variables are taken into consideration: the stock's yield, its volatility, and the call option's remaining life. You must first refer to the other exhibits to determine a fair market value for the call option, while assuming that the common stock is trading at the call's exercise price. Once having made this fair value determination, you then use Exhibit 4–8 to evaluate premiums when the stock is trading away from the exercise price. These curves, in conjunction with the procedures for evaluating the variables, provided earlier in this chapter, will permit you to scan all listed call options to determine which ones should be studied in greater detail. Buy or sell decisions should be made only after additional evaluation, as will be shown in the following chapters.

ACTUAL MARKET EXPERIENCE WITH EXHIBIT 4–8

This family of normal value curves was prepared based on empirical data and practical market experience. When initially introduced in 1974, it closely reflected actual trading on the option exchanges—more so than computerized formulas provided by others. As time passed, out-of-the-money calls (those trading below their exercise prices) tended to drop below these normal valu~ curves, while in-the-money calls stayed close to or drifted moderately above the curves. This could indicate that some adjustments to these curves should be considered, or it might indicate market inefficiencies caused by these general conditions:

1. Aggressive speculators favor selling out-of-the-money calls naked without giving proper consideration to their inherent

risk/reward characteristics. This would depress prices in the absence of sufficient demand on the buy side to offset this selling pressure.

2. Stockbrokers tend to recommend that in-the-money calls be purchased, since they find them easier to explain to their unsophisticated clients. This would provide greater demand on the buy side when calls are above their exercise prices.

I believe it is too early to change the curves, but current supply/ demand pressures of the marketplace should always be considered when you evaluate call options—there is no substitute for good judgment.

CAUTION: Sellers of listed call options should not accept less than normal premiums. If they do, they are giving away their fair rate of return in the long run. Conversely, buyers should not pay more than normal premiums.

chapter 5

Buying listed calls

This chapter on buying call options is relatively short because the purchase of listed calls affords few opportunities for using sophisticated strategies to outperform the market. Call options do, however, offer straightforward alternatives to the conventional purchase of common stocks for conservative investors, aggressive speculators, and any type of investor or speculator between these extremes. The key to success for the buyer is to search out those calls that are undervalued relative to their underlying common stocks using the procedures developed in chapter 4.

WHEN SHOULD THE CONSERVATIVE INVESTOR BUY CALLS?

Suppose a conservative investor (or institutional money manager) has evaluated the merits of XYZ Company's common stock, trading at 50 per share and paying a $0.50 quarterly dividend, and he has decided to buy 100 shares. Total cost, including commissions, is $5,075. Before making the purchase, he checks the listed option markets and finds that a call on XYZ common, having an exercise price of $40 and with three months time remaining, is tradiing at its $10 intrinsic value. Does the purchase of the call option, as an alternative investment to the common stock, offer the investor any advantages? The answer is a very positive yes, as will be shown by the following analysis.

Obvious advantage

Let us simply assume that the call will be held until its expiration date and then exercised for 100 shares of XYZ common at $40 per share. We will also assume that the funds saved on the initial investment by buying the low-priced call instead of the common will be placed in short-term money market instruments paying 8 percent interest. Calculations to determine if there is an advantage in buying the call option may be made as follows:

Premium paid for call, less its exercise value
$= \$1,000 - \$1,000$ .... $= (\$\ 0)$
Commission expense for purchase of the call .... $= (\ 28)$
Dividends not received on XYZ common stock .... $= (\ 50)$
Interest on funds saved $= (\$5,075 - \$1,028)$
$\times\ 8\%\ \times\ 3$ months .... $=\quad 81$
Commission savings for purchase of common stock
at $40 instead of at $50 $= \$75 - \$64$ .... $=\quad \underline{11}$
Net advantage .... $= \$14$

Although a saving of $14 may appear to be only a modest amount, it results in an annualized saving of over 1 percent, or more than the annual fee charged by many money managers. In addition, this strategy provides other advantages which are even more significant.

Upside advantage

On the upside, a sharp advance by XYZ common stock during the three-month time period to the investor's target sell price of, say, $70 would permit the sale of the call, instead of exercising it and then selling the common. This strategy would result in an additional saving by reducing brokerage commissions. Assuming that the call option is sold for its $30 exercise value when the common reaches $70, the additional saving would be $98 ($152 round-trip commissions plus tax for the common, less $54 commissions for selling the call). If the investor preferred to exercise the call and hold the common stock, he would still have the original $14 saving.

Downside advantage

The *major* advantage offered by the call option is its limited risk in declining markets. The call option would provide much greater downside safety if the price of XYZ common were to drop substantially during the three-month period that the option is held. For example, if the stock were to decline to $30, a $2,000 loss would be experienced by the holder of the common stock. The purchase of the call, however, limits the investor's downside risk exposure to the premium paid—saving $1,000. If the investor still wanted to own XYZ stock, he could purchase it for $30 upon expiration of the call.

In this example, the decision to purchase the call option is clearly a superior alternative to the conventional purchase of the common stock. Investors should *always* check the listed option markets before purchasing related stocks. Many call options, both in the money and out of the money, offer substantial advantages when all risk/reward aspects are properly evaluated. Large investors may also find that substantial stock positions may be taken via the call option route at more favorable prices than if they made sizable purchases of the common stock. In fact, I wonder if it is *prudent* for institutional money managers *not* to consider calls as alternatives to their stock purchases.

AN ALTERNATIVE TO BUYING LOW-YIELDING GROWTH STOCKS

When short-term interest rates are high, the conservative investor may gain significant advantages by combining call options with cash as an alternative to buying low-yielding growth stocks like IBM and Eastman Kodak—even if the options are not undervalued. Let us assume that nine-month listed calls, trading at a 10 percent premium, are combined with short-term money market instruments yielding 10 percent. We will assume also that 90 percent of the available funds is placed in the money market instruments and 10 percent is used to purchase call options. A risk/reward analysis may be made as shown in the accompanying table.

Gain or (loss) as a percent of the total funds invested	Stock price change in nine months				
	−50%	−25%	0%	+25%	+50%
Call options.....................	−10%	−10%	−10%	+15%	+40%
Money market instruments.......	+ 7	+ 7	+ 7	+ 7	+ 7
Net gain or loss...............	− 3%	− 3%	− 3%	+22%	+47%

As shown, the combination of call options and cash offered nearly the same upside potential as the stock but at substantially less downside risk. How many professional buyers of growth stocks, who claim to be investing in accordance with the prudent man rule, would even consider the above strategy? I believe the answer is obvious.

SELLING STOCK SHORT AGAINST CALL OPTIONS

The short sale of common stock against calls is a strategy similar to hedging warrants, a subject to be covered in a later chapter of this book. Due to the shorter time to expiration, however, it is more of a trading strategy than the longer-term investment merits of warrant hedging. Another major difference is the present requirement that the short sale of common against call options must be fully margined as in a conventional short sale. This would be of no consequence to portfolios not employing leverage—the collateral value of nonmargined securities held long in the account would satisfy the margin required for the short sale. If the portfolio is fully margined, however, this strategy would tie up too much capital in a nonproductive manner (although the rules may be improved in the near future).

Subject to the above limitation, option traders should consider selling stock short against profitable calls as an alternative to taking profits in the calls. Should the stock drop back, it would permit the trader to cover the profitable short sale and continue to hold the call for a potential rally and additional trades. If, instead, the stock continued to rise, the call could simply be exercised to obtain stock for covering the short sale, or the short sale could be covered for short-term losses and the call sold for long-term profits if it has been held longer than six months.

It is certainly hoped that the Federal Reserve Board will revise their margin regulations for shorting stock against calls to reflect the low risks of this trading strategy. Lower margins would also increase the demand for buying calls and provide greater trading liquidity.

GENERAL GUIDES FOR BUYING LISTED CALL OPTIONS—CONSERVATIVE INVESTORS

1. Call options should be evaluated only as an alternative investment to their underlying common stocks. Be sure you have studied and like the stock before considering purchase of the call.
2. The call option length is not of major importance since the investor generally expects to exercise the option.

3.   Before purchasing the call, calculate S/E and C/E factors and compare them with the normal value curves provided in this book. The call should generally be undervalued to be of interest to the investor.

4.   Compare applicable expense and income items for the purchase of the call option versus the common stock to determine relative costs. Also evaluate risk/reward aspects of both positions based on the common stock advancing or declining prior to the call's expiration date.

5.   Sell the call option if it becomes overpriced in relation to the common as determined by the procedures provided in this book. The funds should be switched into the common stock or into another undervalued call option.

6.   When short-term interest rates are high, all investors should consider a combination of cash and call options as a low-risk alternative to a common stock portfolio. Even normally priced calls may offer advantages to the conservative investor during periods of high short-term interest rates.

GENERAL GUIDES FOR BUYING LISTED CALL OPTIONS—AGGRESSIVE TRADERS

1.   Call options should be evaluated only as an alternative investment to their underlying common stocks. Be sure you have studied and like the stock before considering purchase of the call.

2.   The common stock should have an upside potential that will permit the market price of the call option to at least double by its expiration date. If the common is trading below the call's exercise price, the appreciation potential should be even greater to compensate for the higher probability that the call will expire worthless.

3. Before purchasing the call, calculate S/E and C/E factors and compare them with the normal value curves provided in this book. The call should not be overpriced to be of interest to the trader, otherwise he will not receive sufficient potential return to compensate for the risk of owning the call.

4. Stagger your option purchases to smooth out the effect of market cycles.

5. Sell the call if it becomes significantly overpriced in relation to the common. The funds should be switched into another call having more favorable risk/reward characteristics.

6. Continually monitor other calls on the same stock since there may be possibilities for advantageous switches or spread positions.

7. Consider shorting stock against a profitable call having some time to run, in lieu of selling the call.

chapter 6

Selling calls against common stocks

Since the publication of *Listed Call Options* in early 1975,[1] I have had the opportunity to discuss call option selling with dozens of investors throughout the country. Except for those using the sophisticated tools available, option sellers have generally been disappointed with their performance. They have not received the 20, 30, or 40 percent returns on their portfolios promised by brokers and advisory services. Most, in fact, have struggled to just break even! But why should they have expected to do much better than break even? Are option buyers so naive as to permit unreasonably large returns to the sellers? I doubt it! A simple example will serve to illustrate my point.

Let us assume that a covered writer sells a three-month call at 10 percent premium against 100 shares of a relatively volatile, nondividend-paying stock trading at $50. As each call expires, a new three-month call at 10 percent premium will be sold. We will also assume that the stock trades in a price range of between $40

---

[1] Thomas Noddings and Earl Zazove, *Listed Call Options: Your Daily Guide to Portfolio Strategy* (Homewood, Ill.: Dow Jones-Irwin, 1975).

and $60 over a one-year market cycle. Now, I have heard brokers and investors alike claim that this strategy will return 40 percent on one's investment—doesn't 10 percent per quarter times four quarters per year equal a 40 percent return? In the real world of investing, the potential results from a continual covered call-selling program for the typical market conditions described above may be estimated as shown in the table below.

Three-month cycle	Security	Beginning price	Ending price	Profit or (loss) Stock	Call
Stock goes from 50 to 40.........	Stock	$50	$40	($1,000)	—
	Call	5	0	—	$500
Stock goes from 40 to 50.........	Stock	40	50	1,000	—
	Call	4	10	—	(600)
Stock goes from 50 to 60.........	Stock	50	60	1,000	—
	Call	5	10	—	(500)
Stock goes from 60 to 50.........	Stock	60	50	(1,000)	—
	Call	6	0	—	600
Net profit or loss for one year (excluding commissions)...............				0	0

If you are an option seller or are considering the sale of call options as one of your investment tools, please take a few minutes to study the analysis—it may save you thousands of dollars, and much disappointment, if its impact is fully appreciated.

Promised returns of 20 percent and higher from a typical call-selling program are financial fantasy! In the real world, above-average investment performance from an option-selling program can be achieved *only* by employing the most sophisticated tools available. These tools *are* available to the serious investor if he is willing to study and to discard all the time-consuming trivia that is continually pushed at him by those wanting his commission or subscription dollars. These tools will be fully disclosed in this and following chapters.

The first, and simplest, way to improve your chances when selling calls is to take advantage of supply/demand price imbalances that result from a less-than-perfect marketplace. These distortions usually favor the selling side of a call option portfolio, although there are circumstances when purchases are in order, as was shown in chapter 5.

SELECTING OVERPRICED CALLS

The normal value curves of Exhibit 4–8 were derived from market experience. These curves favor the seller to a small degree, reflecting the fact that option sellers are generally more percentage-minded than are buyers. However, this small advantage is insufficient in itself to produce the above-average investment performance you should be seeking. Therefore, you should not be satisfied to accept normal premiums. Instead, search for situations that offer premiums higher than usual.

Compare, for example, two different six-month calls on XYZ Company common stock selling at $50—one with a normal 10 percent premium and another with an overpriced 15 percent premium (caused by temporary overenthusiasm on the part of buyers of XYZ calls). Assume that the exercise price of each is $50 and that in each case two calls are sold against ownership of 200 shares[1] of stock (the ratio of calls to stock = 1:1). A risk/reward analysis may be made as shown in the table to follow. Commissions and dividends are excluded to simplify the calculations.

The 15 percent premium offers an advantage over the 10 percent premium ranging from 3.9 to 6.5 percent for the six-month

---

[1] Using 200 shares of stock in our examples will permit us to conveniently study calls to stock ratios of greater than 1:1. For example, the sale of three calls would provide a ratio of 3:2 or 1.5:1 and the sale of four calls a ratio of 4:2 or 2:1. Incidentally, two or more calls should generally be bought or sold at one time anyway to avoid minimum commission charges.

	10 percent premium		15 percent premium	
Investment				
Cost of stock......................	$10,000		$10,000	
Less premiums received...............	−1,000		−1,500	
Net investment.....................	$ 9,000		$ 8,500	

	Dollars	Percent	Dollars	Percent
Profit or (loss) in six months				
Stock price = $30...............	(3,000)	−33.3	(2,500)	−29.4
40...............	(1,000)	−11.1	(500)	− 5.9
50...............	1,000	+11.1	1,500	+17.6
60...............	1,000	+11.1	1,500	+17.6
70...............	1,000	+11.1	1,500	+17.6

position, or more than 10 percent on an annualized basis—the difference between mediocre and superior investment performance.

The above call option hedge positions are graphically illustrated in Exhibit 6–1. Included, for comparison purposes, is the common stock with no calls sold against it (unhedged). An analysis of this chart shows that the sale of call options at 15 percent premium is significantly superior to ownership of the common stock alone in most cases. It reduces downside risk while offering substantially greater return if the stock were to end up in the area of $50 six months hence. The unhedged stock outperforms the call hedge position only at prices above $59 (an 18 percent advance). The construction of a simple probability table,[2] assuming a maximum stock gain or loss of 40 percent, also supports this conclusion.

Similar calculations for the 10 percent premium call indicate an advantage (expected profit) over the unhedged stock of only 2.2

---

[2] A true probability table (or model) lists all possible results that can occur and their expected frequencies. Although there is no certainty in the investment world, a probability table is useful in making decisions and permits comparison of alternate choices.

EXHIBIT 6–1:   XYZ Company

Stock purchased at $50 (*S/E* = 1.0)
Ratio = 1:1 (two call options sold versus 200 shares of stock)

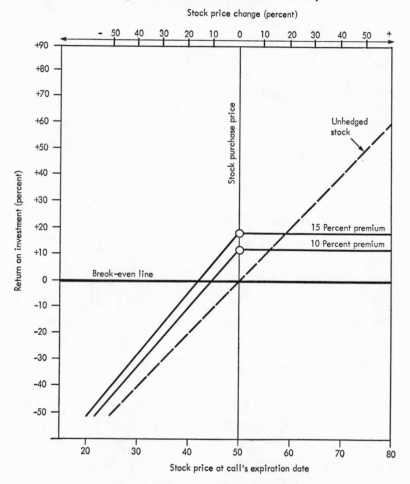

percent. This small advantage reflects the bias of the normal value curves, which favor the sellers to a small degree. It is also partially offset by the possibility that the common stock might advance above the $70 upper limit used in the probability table, in which case there would be a large profit differential favoring the stock over the call option hedge.

Stock price			Profit or loss (percent)			
$30	0.1	×	−29.4	=	−2.9	
40	0.2	×	− 5.9	=	−1.2	
50	0.4	×	+17.6	=	+7.0	
60	0.2	×	+17.6	=	+3.5	
70	0.1	×	+17.6	=	+1.8	

+8.2% expected profit*

* The expected profit is the average six-month return on investment if the decision were made a great number of times. Note that the expected profit for an unhedged investment in the common stock would be zero since possible gains or losses are equally weighed.

SELECTING THE BEST RATIO OF CALLS TO STOCK

The previous example for XYZ Company was based on two calls sold against 200 shares of common stock owned. This 1:1 covered hedge ratio is the conventional approach but not necessarily the most profitable from a probability standpoint. Let us examine other possible hedge ratios for calls sold at a 15 percent premium against 200 shares of stock purchased at their $50 exercise price. *Variable* ratios of 1.5:1 and 2:1 are analyzed as shown in the accompanying table.

	Three calls sold Ratio = 1.5:1		Four calls sold Ratio = 2:1	
Investment				
Cost of stock	$10,000		$10,000	
Premiums received	−2,250		−3,000	
Net investment	$ 7,750*		$ 7,000*	

	Dollars	Percent	Dollars	Percent
Profit or (loss) in six months				
Stock price = $30	(1,750)	−22.6	(1,000)	−14.3
40	250	+ 3.2	1,000	+14.3
50	2,250	+29.0	3,000	+42.9
60	1,250	+16.1	1,000	+14.3
70	250	+ 3.2	(1,000)	−14.3

* Calls sold in excess of a 1:1 ratio are "naked," or uncovered, and must therefore be margined in accordance with applicable regulations. In these examples, the collateral value of the common stock held long in the account is sufficient to carry the uncovered calls.

Probability estimates for these variable hedge positions are presented in the following table. The 1:1 position is also repeated for comparison purposes.

Stock price change	Probability	Two calls sold Ratio = 1:1 (percent)	Three calls sold Ratio = 1.5:1 (percent)	Four calls sold Ratio = 2:1 (percent)
−40	0.1 ×	−29.4 = −2.9	−22.6 = − 2.3	−14.3 = − 1.4
−20	0.2 ×	− 5.9 = −1.2	+ 3.2 = + 0.6	+14.3 = + 2.9
0	0.4 ×	+17.6 = +7.0	+29.0 = +11.6	+42.9 = +17.2
+20	0.2 ×	+17.6 = +3.5	+16.1 = + 3.2	+14.3 = + 2.9
+40	0.1 ×	+17.6 = +1.8	+ 3.2 = + 0.3	−14.3 = − 1.4
		+8.2	+13.4	+20.2

As shown by the table and by the graphic analysis presented in Exhibit 6–2, the probable return on investment increases as additional call options are sold. The higher ratio of 2:1 provided the greatest return, if the stock were to end up close to the call's exercise price, while offering more downside protection because of the extra premiums received—the downside break-even point is a full 30 percent decline by the common stock to $35. On the upside, the unhedged common stock outperforms the call hedge positions only at prices above $59. The 2:1 ratio will not lose money unless the common advances 30 percent to $65. This ratio, therefore, offers profits over a broad stock price range of $35 to $65 for the six-month period, with a possible return of up to about 42 percent (84 percent annualized). If either the $35 or $65 break-even limits were approached by the common while the call option still had some time remaining, the total position could likely be closed out with minimal loss. The 2:1 ratio may also be called a neutral hedge since downside and upside break-even points are equally distant from the stock price.

Given this opportunity in an overpriced call option, the best ratio of calls sold versus shares of stock held long would depend on numerous factors relating to the individual portfolio and its investment objectives. For example, if the portfolio contained other securities that are not hedged, the 2:1 ratio would be recom-

EXHIBIT 6–2:   XYZ Company

Stock purchased at $50 (S/E = 1.0)
Calls sold at 15 percent premium

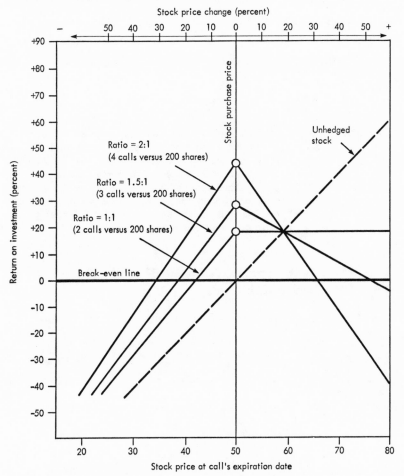

mended to help balance the risk/reward characteristics of the total portfolio.

If the XYZ position is only one of numerous call hedges, and the portfolio contains no unhedged securities, it may be desirable to use lower ratios despite their reduced probability of return. This would be especially true if the portfolio performance will be measured by others against popular market averages during a bull market. Even a conventional ratio of 1 : 1 should still outperform unhedged portfolios of common stocks over the long term, while also providing adequate performance during a bull market.

The above comments pertain to pretax performance of a call option hedge portfolio. Tax considerations, to be presented in the next chapter, may alter any recommendation made here, depending on the individual's personal tax situation.

CAUTION: The conventional ratio of 1:1 doth not insulate a portfolio's equity from downside risk. For example, between April 30 and July 31, 1974, the average CBOE stock declined 19 percent. Typical option premiums received during this three-month period would only have reduced the loss to about 12 percent. Despite those who claim that covered hedges are the most prudent, variable hedges are safer and offer a higher probability of return over the long term.

SELLING CALLS WHEN STOCK IS BELOW THE EXERCISE PRICE

Let us assume that XYZ stock is at $40—20 percent below the call's $50 exercise price—and that the calls are trading on the 15 percent premium curve at $3.50 (Exhibit 4–8). Alternate positions may be evaluated as shown in the table below. Again, 200

	Two calls sold Ratio = 1:1	Four calls sold Ratio = 2:1	Six calls sold Ratio = 3:1
Investment			
Cost of stock.................	$8,000	$8,000	$8,000
Premiums received............	−700	−1,400	−2,100
Net investment...............	$7,300	$6,600	$5,900

	Dollars	Percent	Dollars	Percent	Dollars	Percent
Profit or (loss) in six months						
Stock price = $20.......	(3,300)	−45.2	(2,600)	−39.4	(1,900)	−32.2
30.......	(1,300)	−17.8	(600)	− 9.1	100	+ 1.7
40.......	700	+ 9.6	1,400	+21.2	2,100	+35.6
50.......	2,700	+37.0	3,400	+51.5	4,100	+69.5
60.......	2,700	+37.0	1,400	+21.2	100	+ 1.7
70.......	2,700	+37.0	(600)	− 9.1	(4,100)	−69.5

shares of XYZ stock are purchased for each call hedge position.

Exhibit 6–3 presents a graphic analysis of these alternate hedge positions compared to unhedged ownership of the common stock. As you can see, all three hedges will outperform the common at any price below $55 (a 37 percent advance). The maximum return for each call hedge position is at the $50 exercise price since profits would be made on both sides of the positions. These maxi-

EXHIBIT 6–3:   XYZ Company

Stock purchased at $40 (S/E = 0.80)
Calls sold on 15 percent normal premium curve (C/E = 0.07)

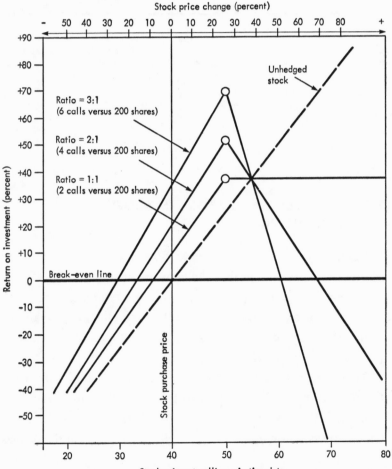

Stock price change (percent)

Return on investment (percent)

Ratio = 3:1
(6 calls versus 200 shares)

Ratio = 2:1
(4 calls versus 200 shares)

Ratio = 1:1
(2 calls versus 200 shares)

Unhedged stock

Break-even line

Stock purchase price

Stock price at call's expiration date

mums range from 37 percent for the 1:1 ratio to about 70 percent for the 3:1 position (140 percent annualized).

Exhibit 6–3 indicates that a 3:1 ratio offers the highest probability of return. Its break-even range is from about $30 to $60, or a 25 percent stock decline versus a 50 percent advance. If either of these limits were approached while the calls had remaining life, the total position could probably be closed out without serious loss. Assuming a maximum gain or loss of 40 percent by the common, as in the previous example, probability estimates are presented in the table below.

Stock price change (percent)	Probability	Two calls sold Ratio = 1:1 (percent)	Four calls sold Ratio = 2:1 (percent)	Six calls sold Ratio = 3:1 (percent)
−40	0.1 ×	−34.3 = −3.4	−27.3 = − 2.7	−18.6 = − 1.9
−20	0.2 ×	−12.3 = −2.5	− 3.0 = − 0.6	+ 8.5 = + 1.7
0	0.4 ×	+ 9.6 = +3.8	+21.2 = + 8.5	+35.6 = +14.2
+20	0.2 ×	+31.5 = +6.3	+45.5 = + 9.1	+62.7 = +12.5
+40	0.1 ×	+37.0 = +3.7	+33.3 = + 3.3	+28.8 = + 2.9
		+7.9	+17.6	+29.4

SELLING CALLS WHEN STOCK IS ABOVE THE EXERCISE PRICE

Assuming that XYZ stock is at $60—20 percent above the $50 exercise price—and that the calls are trading on the 15 percent premium curve at $13.50 (Exhibit 4–8), alternate positions may be evaluated as shown in the following table. It is again assumed that 200 shares of XYZ stock are purchased for each of the call hedge positions.

These alternate call hedge positions are shown in Exhibit 6–4. Contrary to previous examples, the maximum return would be achieved if the common were to *decline* to the call's exercise price. On the upside, the common stock begins to outperform the hedges

	Two calls sold Ratio = 1:1		Three calls sold Ratio = 1.5:1		Four calls sold Ratio = 2:1	
Investment						
Cost of stock................	$12,000		$12,000		$12,000	
Premiums received..........	−2,700		−4,050		−5,400	
Net investment..............	$ 9,300		$ 7,950		$ 6,600	

	Dollars	Percent	Dollars	Percent	Dollars	Percent
Profit or (loss) in six months						
Stock price = $30.......	(3,300)	−35.5	(1,950)	−24.5	(600)	− 9.1
40.......	(1,300)	−14.0	50	+ 0.6	1,400	+21.2
50.......	700	+ 7.5	2,050	+25.8	3,400	+51.5
60.......	700	+ 7.5	1,050	+13.2	1,400	+21.2
70.......	700	+ 7.5	50	+ 0.6	(600)	− 9.1
80.	700	+ 7.5	(950)	−11.9	(2,600)	−39.4

on an advance of only 7 percent to $64. Up to that point, each of the call hedges offers a higher probability of return than unhedged ownership of the stock.

The following probability table shows a lower advantage than in previous situations where the common was trading at or below the exercise price, but it is still greater than unhedged stock.

Stock price change (percent)	Probability	Two calls sold Ratio = 1:1 (percent)	Three calls sold Ratio = 1.5:1 (percent)	Four calls sold Ratio = 2:1 (percent)
−40.................	0.1 ×	−22.6 = −2.3	− 9.4 = −0.9	+ 9.1 = + 0.9
−20.................	0.2 ×	+ 3.2 = +0.6	+20.8 = +4.2	+45.5 = + 9.1
0.................	0.4 ×	+ 7.5 = +3.0	+13.2 = +5.3	+21.2 = + 8.5
+20.................	0.2 ×	+ 7.5 = +1.5	− 1.9 = −0.4	−15.2 = − 3.0
+40.................	0.1 ×	+ 7.5 = +0.8	−17.0 = −1.7	−51.5 = − 5.2
		+3.6	+7.3	+10.3

CAUTION: Although high ratios offer the greatest probability of return and less downside risk, a substantial price advance could result in large losses. You should plan to monitor all high-ratio hedge positions continually to permit prompt action to reduce upside risk if the stock approaches a dangerous price level.

EXHIBIT 6–4:   XYZ Company

Stock purchased at $60 (S/E = 1.20)
Calls sold on 15 percent normal premium curve (C/E = 0.27)

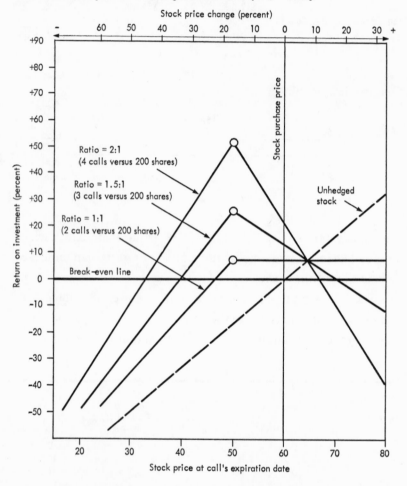

ANALYZING AN ACTUAL CALL OPTION HEDGE POSITION

This chapter has provided procedures for studying the sale of call options against the typical common stock of XYZ Company. Alternate ratios of calls sold versus shares of common were pre-

EXHIBIT 6-5

WORK SHEET FOR EVALUATING CALL OPTIONS SOLD AGAINST COMMON STOCK

COMPANY__FEDERAL NATIONAL MORTGAGE__ DATE _JULY___

DESCRIPTION OF SECURITIES

	Exercise Price	Expir. Date	Symbol	Target Prices	Annual Div.
(a) Common stock			FNH	15	$ .80
(b) Call option	$ 15	JAN.	AC	2	

(c) POSSIBLE HEDGE POSITION   Bullish __✓__, Neutral_____, Bearish_____

(d) Common stock: 1,000 at $ 15 = $5,000 + 270 comm. = $ 15,270
(e) Calls sold: 10 at $ 200 = $2,000 - 110 comm. = $ 1,890
(f) Net investment - unleveraged (15,270 - 1,890) = $ 13,380

(g) PROFIT OR LOSS AT CALL'S EXPIRATION DATE (unleveraged)

	Downside	Exercise Price	Upside
(h) Stock price..................	10	15	20
(i) Call price....................	0	0	5
(j) Profit or (loss) - call options...	2,000	2,000	(3,000)
- stock.........	(5,000)	0	5,000
(k) Commissions*................	(110)	(110)	(250)
(l) Net profit or (loss)............	(3,110)	1,890	1,750
(m) Return on investment (ROI)	- 23.2 %	+ 14.1 %	+ 13.1 %
(n) Annualized ROI (0.50 years)..	- 46.4 %	+ 28.2 %	+ 26.2 %
(o) Plus annual income...........	+ 6.0 %	+ 6.0 %	+ 6.0 %
(p) Total annualized ROI	- 40.4 %	+ 34.6 %	+ 32.2 %

*Commissions for the stock shares held long are not included in the calculations
as it is assumed they will be held for selling future call options. If the stock is trading
above the call's exercise price at the expiration date, it is assumed the calls will be
bought in instead of allowing them to be exercised.

sented at various stock prices relative to the call's exercise price.
Let us now apply these same techniques to calls on Federal National Mortgage (FNM), which were available on the Chicago Board Options Exchange.

Exhibits 6-5 through 6-10 present original work sheets for analyzing possible call option hedge positions. Ratios of 1:1, 1.5:1, and 2:1 are evaluated. Using the 1:1 ratio shown in Exhibit 6-5 for study purposes, a step-by-step approach for estimating potential profit or loss is as follows:

EXHIBIT 6–6

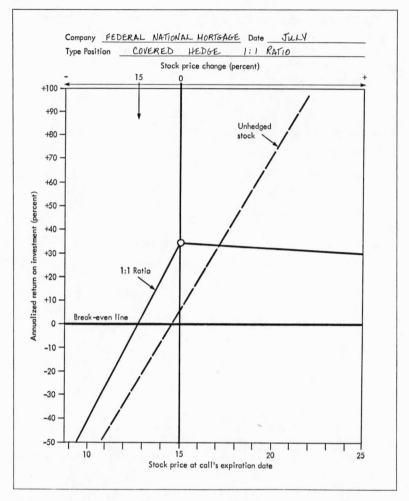

a. The common stock was trading at $15 and paid a $0.80 annual dividend (5.3 percent).

b. The call option, expiring six months later, had an exercise price of $15 and was trading at $2.

c. Our investment objective was to establish a bullish hedge position—one that offered upside profits at modest downside risk.

EXHIBIT 6-7

WORK SHEET FOR EVALUATING CALL OPTIONS SOLD AGAINST COMMON STOCK

COMPANY FEDERAL NATIONAL MORTGAGE   DATE JULY

DESCRIPTION OF SECURITIES

	Exercise Price	Expir. Date	Symbol	Target Prices	Annual Div.
Common stock			FNM	15	$ .80
Call option	$ 15	JAN.	AC	2	

POSSIBLE HEDGE POSITION   Bullish_____, Neutral___✓___, Bearish_____

Common stock: 1,000 at $ 15 = $15,000 + 270 comm. = $ 15,270
Calls sold: 15 at $ 200 = $ 3,000 - 140 comm. = $ 2,860
Net investment - unleveraged (15,270 - 2,860) = $ 12,410

PROFIT OR LOSS AT CALL'S EXPIRATION DATE (unleveraged)

	Downside	Exercise Price	Upside
Stock price...................	10	15	20
Call price.....................	0	0	5
Profit or (loss) - call options...	3,000	3,000	(4,500)
- stock.........	(5,000)	0	5,000
Commissions*..................	(140)	(140)	(340)
Net profit or (loss)............	(2,140)	2,860	160
Return on investment (ROI)	- 17.2 %	+ 23.0 %	+ 1.3 %
Annualized ROI (0.50 years)..	- 34.4 %	+ 46.0 %	+ 2.6 %
Plus annual income...........	+ 6.4 %	+ 6.4 %	+ 6.4 %
Total annualized ROI	- 28.0 %	+ 52.4 %	+ 9.0 %

*Commissions for the stock shares held long are not included in the calculations as it is assumed they will be held for selling future call options. If the stock is trading above the call's exercise price at the expiration date, it is assumed the calls will be bought in instead of allowing them to be exercised.

d. One thousand shares of common stock were purchased at $15 per share.

e. Ten calls were sold at $200 each—a fully covered 1:1 hedge.

f. The net investment (unleveraged) was the cost of the stock plus commissions less the net proceeds received from sale of the call options, or $13,380.

g. Profit and loss estimates were based on holding the position until the call's expiration date in six months.

EXHIBIT 6-8

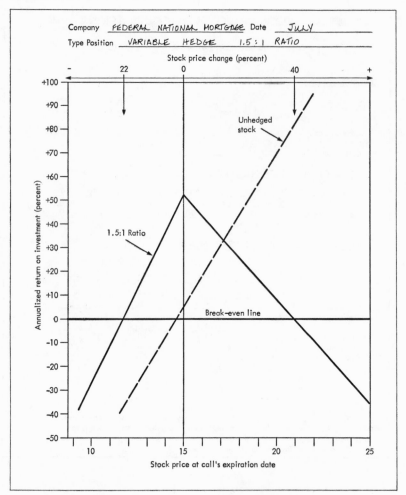

b. Since the major variable (and resulting risk) is the price of
.FNM stock on the call's expiration date, three different
prices were assumed for calculation purposes. These included
the call's exercise price (this always provides the maximum
return on investment) plus representative downside and upside prices for the common stock.

EXHIBIT 6–9

WORK SHEET FOR EVALUATING CALL OPTIONS SOLD AGAINST COMMON STOCK

COMPANY___FEDERAL NATIONAL MORTGAGE___   DATE JULY_____

DESCRIPTION OF SECURITIES

	Exercise Price	Expir. Date	Symbol	Target Prices	Annual Div.
Common stock			FNM	15	$ .80
Call option	$ 15	JAN.	AC	2	

POSSIBLE HEDGE POSITION   Bullish_____, Neutral___✓___, Bearish_____

Common stock: 1,000 at $ 15 = $ 15,000 + 270 comm. = $ 15,270
Calls sold: _____ 20 at $ 200 = $ 4,000 − 170 comm. = $ 3,830
Net investment – unleveraged   (15,270 − 3,830   ) = $ 11,440

PROFIT OR LOSS AT CALL'S EXPIRATION DATE (unleveraged)

	Downside	Exercise Price	Upside
Stock price.................	10	15	20
Call price....................	0	0	5
Profit or (loss) – call options...	4,000	4,000	(6,000)
– stock.........	(5,000)	0	5,000
Commissions*	(170)	(170)	(420)
Net profit or (loss).............	(1,170)	3,830	1,420
Return on investment (ROI)	− 10.2%	+ 33.5%	− 12.4%
Annualized ROI (0.50 years)..	− 20.4%	+ 67.0%	− 24.8%
Plus annual income..........	+ 7.0%	+ 7.0%	+ 7.0%
Total annualized ROI	− 13.4%	+ 74.0%	− 17.8%

*Commissions for the stock shares held long are not included in the calculations as it is assumed they will be held for selling future call options. If the stock is trading above the call's exercise price at the expiration date, it is assumed the calls will be bought in instead of allowing them to be exercised.

i. Call prices shown are exercise values at the various assumed stock prices.

j. Profit and loss calculations are based on the indicated stock and call prices at expiration.

k. Round-trip commissions for the call options are included for realistic estimates. Note that commissions for the stock held long are not included as it is assumed that the shares will be held for selling future call options.

EXHIBIT 6–10

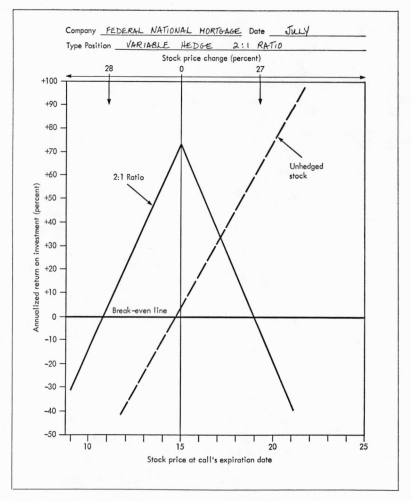

l. The estimated net profit or loss for the stock and calls is determined next.

m. The return on investment is determined by dividing the net profit or loss by the $13,380 investment.

n. Annualized return on investment is determined. Since the time is six months, annualized return will be twice the actual return.

o. Percent annual income is calculated by dividing the $800 annual dividends paid on the 1,000 shares of common stock by the $13,380 investment.

p. The total annualized return on investment is the sum of the annualized return plus the annual income.

Exhibit 6–11 graphically presents the total annualized return on investment calculations for each of the hedge positions. The unhedged purchase of Federal National Mortgage common stock

EXHIBIT 6–11

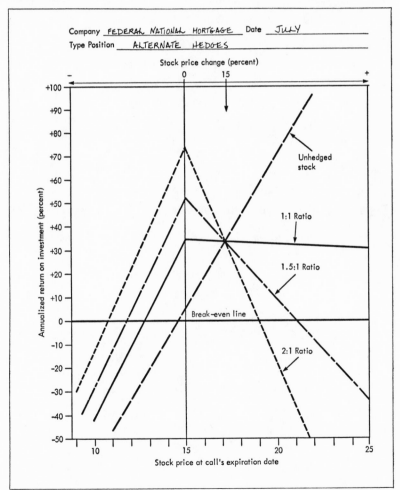

is also shown for comparison purposes (dividends included). All hedges provided greater downside safety than the common as well as more profit at all prices up to $17.25—a 15 percent stock advance. At the optimum price of $15, the annualized returns ranged from 34 percent for the 1:1 ratio up to 74 percent for the 2:1 ratio.

SHORTCUTS FOR CALCULATING BREAK-EVEN POINTS

The following simple formulas may be used for quickly calculating downside and upside break-even points for variable hedges (dividends and commissions are excluded).

$$R = \text{Ratio}$$
$$C = \text{Call price}$$
$$S = \text{Stock price}$$
$$E = \text{Exercise price}$$

$$\textit{Downside break-even} = S - (R \times C)$$

$$\textit{Upside break-even} = \frac{R(C + E) - S}{R - 1}$$

Example: Two calls, having a $50 exercise price, are sold at 7½ points each against 100 shares of stock purchased at $50.

$$
\begin{aligned}
\textit{Downside break-even} &= S - (R \times C) \\
&= 50 - (2 \times 7\tfrac{1}{2}) \\
&= 50 - 15 \\
&= 35
\end{aligned}
$$

$$
\begin{aligned}
\textit{Upside break-even} &= \frac{R(C + E) - S}{R - 1} \\
&= \frac{2(7\tfrac{1}{2} + 50) - 50}{2 - 1} \\
&= \frac{2(57\tfrac{1}{2}) - 50}{1} \\
&= 115 - 50 \\
&= 65
\end{aligned}
$$

PROBABILITY TABLES

Many of those who recommend covered or variable call option hedges, advisory services and brokerage firms alike, indulge in the practice of emphasizing the potential results only if optimal conditions are met; for example, they will show the return for a covered hedge if the stock ends at or above the call's exercise price but hardly ever comment on the downside risk. Their computer printouts might also list the available positions in descending order of maximum potential return, thus encouraging investors to sell calls against the more volatile stocks—the greater premiums received naturally offer the highest potential returns. Where annualized returns are stressed (but not annualized risks), their recommendations may also encourage sale of the higher-risk, shortest-term calls.

The way to avoid these deceptions is to make your own analysis of all risk/reward aspects before taking a position. The probability table used for the examples presented earlier in this section was intended to encourage you to think in terms of risk as well as potential gain. This probability table, however, was simplified for ease of evaluating the arithmetic for the different examples shown. Recent statistical studies of stock price movements have been provided by *Systems and Forecasts,* an investment advisory service specializing in sophisticated investment strategies. Although they caution that each stock has its own volatility pattern, that stock volatility groupings are rough, and that volatility changes over time, this research is an important contribution to the investment art and is presented in Exhibit 6–12. Also shown are shortcut probability distributions that establish broader groups by averaging the results of the columns·to their left. Their experience has shown little difference by using the fewer probable outcomes.

EXHIBIT 6–12:   Probability tables for common stock price movement

Six months				*Three months*			
Percent of change in stock price	*Probability*	*Shortcut method*		*Percent of change in stock price*	*Probability*	*Shortcut method*	
		Low to average stock volatility					
± 2.0%	20%			± 1.5%	20%		
6.0	18			4.0	18		
9.5	16			6.5	16		
13.0	14			9.0	14		
17.0	10	± 4.0%	38%	11.5	10	± 2.5%	38%
20.5	8	11.0	30	14.0	8	7.5	30
24.5	6	19.0	18	16.5	6	12.5	18
28.0	4	26.0	10	19.0	4	17.5	10
34.0+	4	34.0+	4	22.5+	4	22.5+	4
	100%		100%		100%		100%
		Average to above average stock volatility					
± 2.5%	20%			± 1.5%	20%		
7.5	18			5.0	18		
12.5	16			8.5	16		
17.5	14			11.5	14		
22.5	10	± 5.0%	38%	15.0	10	± 3.5%	38%
27.5	8	15.0	30	18.5	8	10.0	30
32.5	6	25.0	18	22.0	6	17.0	18
37.5	4	35.0	10	25.0	4	22.5	10
45.0+	4	45.0+	4	30.0+	4	30.0+	4
	100%		100%		100%		100%
		High stock volatility					
± 4.0%	20%			± 2.5%	20%		
11.5	18			7.5	18		
19.0	16			12.5	16		
26.0	14			17.5	14		
34.0	10	± 7.5%	38%	22.5	10	± 5.0%	38%
41.0	8	22.5	30	27.5	8	15.0	30
49.0	6	37.5	18	32.5	6	25.0	18
56.0	4	52.5	10	37.5	4	35.0	10
67.5+	4	67.5+	4	45.0+	4	45.0+	4
	100%		100%		100%		100%

Note: The above material is the courtesy of *Systems and Forecasts*, published by Signalert Corporation, P.O. Box 1227, Old Village Station, Great Neck, N.Y. 11023.

CONCLUSIONS

1. Overpriced call options offer the seller a significant advantage over unhedged ownership of the common stock. This advantage will contribute to the above-average investment performance you should be seeking.

2. The optimum ratio of calls sold versus shares of stock held long increases as the common declines farther below the call's exercise price. Suggested guidelines for preliminary selection are:

Stock price	Ratio
Above the exercise price.....................	1:1
10 percent below the exercise price...........	2:1
20 percent below the exercise price...........	3:1
30 percent below the exercise price...........	4:1

3. Best positions will generally be found when the stock is below the exercise price.

4. Be sure to evaluate potential risks before taking a position. Recognizing and dealing with risk is the most important aspect of successful money management.

5. Monitor your hedge positions continually.

CAUTION: Numerous recommendations for hedged option positions emphasize the potential profits but ignore the risks. They are generally based on computer selection of those calls offering the highest return, assuming favorable price action by the stock. These narrow parameters always favor selling calls against the higher risk stocks and can only lead to poor investment performance. These one-sided projections have been distorted further by basing them on full margin when, in fact, the probability of return was well below the cost of margin interest—or even negative.

chapter **7**

Tax strategies when selling calls

It is not my intention to provide tax advice since this complex topic is best left to the professionals in the field. Also, the tax rulings applying to call options are subject to change because this new investment tool is under continual review by the Internal Revenue Service and others. It *is* my intention, however, to alert you to dangers and opportunities with listed call options and to encourage you to plan your investment strategies for optimum *aftertax* return on your investment. Aftertax strategies are particularly important when *selling* listed call options as opposed to straightforward purchases.

Before proceeding with the primary subject of this section, let us briefly review the tax aspects of call option purchases or sales as they currently apply to individual investors.

PURCHASES

1. The purchase and subsequent sale of a call option will result in a short-term or long-term capital gain or loss depending on

the time period the option is held. If the call is allowed to expire worthless, it is treated as having been sold on the expiration date.

2. If the call option is exercised instead of sold, the call's purchase cost is added to the exercise price to determine the cost basis of the stock acquired. The holding period for the common stock starts on the date the call is exercised, not on the date the call was acquired.

3. Call options and their underlying common stocks are not substantially identical properties. Therefore, a gain on the sale of a call held for more than six months is long term, even if a short sale of the related stock was made during the period the call was held.

SALES

1. If the call option is not exercised, the total proceeds received from the sale (premium) are considered to be income to the seller on the call's expiration date.

2. If the call is allowed to be exercised, the premium received by the seller is treated as an increase in the proceeds realized from the sale of the underlying stock in the exercise transaction. The gain or loss on the sale constitutes a capital gain or loss, long term or short term, depending upon how long the stock was held.

3. If the seller buys back the call, the difference between the premium received in the original sale transaction and the amount paid in the closing transaction is ordinary income or loss (expense) realized on the day of the closing transaction.

As indicated in chapter 4, this ruling might be changed to short-term capital gain or loss.

ALTERNATE STRATEGIES FOR
CALL OPTION HEDGES

Let us assume that we purchase 200 shares of XYZ Company common stock for $50 per share and sell calls having a $50 exercise price for 7½ points each ($750), as in the examples used in chapter 6. We will also assume that the calls have six months and a few days to run to permit us to evaluate both short-term and long-term capital gain or loss aspects. Looking first at the 1:1 ratio (two calls sold against 200 shares), let us examine both pretax and aftertax consequences for different market conditions —*under the present tax rulings.* Commissions and dividends will be excluded to simplify the calculations.

Declining market

If the stock were to decline to $40 per share by the call's expiration date, we would experience a $2,000 *capital loss* on the 200 shares of stock purchased versus $1,500 *income* from the call options sold. Our net pretax position would be a minus $500, but it would be worse *after taxes* since we must pay taxes at our full tax rate on the $1,500 income received. The capital loss on the stock, if it were sold, would only partially reduce our tax bill, depending on our total capital gain or loss situation for the year.

Note that as the call approaches its expiration date, it may be desirable to sell the stock just prior to its six-month holding period to receive a short-term capital loss instead of a long-term loss. Use of this strategy would also depend on our total situation for the year.

Sideways market

If the stock were to end up at $50 or slightly below, our only choice would be to permit the calls to expire worthless as in the above example. We would receive $1,500 pretax income versus an approximate break-even position on the stock. The stock would be held for selling additional call options.

However, if the stock were to end up above $50, at say $51, we have *two* choices. We could buy back the calls for about one point each for a net pretax income of $1,300 (two calls × 6½ point profit = $1,300) and hold the stock with its $200 paper profit for selling future call options. Or we could permit the calls to be exercised against us and purchase new stock for selling additional calls. Even after the additional commission expense, this latter strategy *might* be advantageous in terms of taxes by giving us a *long-term capital gain* of $1,200 as shown below.

Proceeds received = 200 shares × $50 plus
    $1,500 in premiums   = $11,500
    Less cost of stock purchased   =   −10,000
    Less round-trip commissions on 200 shares =   −   300
    Net long-term capital gain   = $ 1,200

The strategy of permitting the calls to be exercised is most appropriate for the investor in a high tax bracket who can take maximum advantage of the favorable treatment on long-term capital gains. This strategy would be considered for any stock price up to 57½ (the exercise price plus premium received) if commissions were not a factor. Including round-trip commissions on the stock, however, the strategy is appropriate for a stock price up to about $53 to $55, depending on your tax bracket and total tax situation for the year.

Advancing market

If the stock were to rise to $60 per share, we again have the same two choices as in the above example at $51. But in this event, we would gain additional tax advantages by repurchasing the calls at their $10 intrinsic value for an *ordinary loss* of $500 (two calls × 2½ point loss = $500). The stock could be held with its $2,000 paper profit for selling future calls or sold at $60 for a long-term capital gain of about $1,700 after commissions. If the stock were to have advanced higher than $60, the tax advantages would be even greater. At a stock price of $70, for example, we would receive a $2,500 ordinary loss by repurchasing the calls at their $20 intrinsic value versus a $4,000 long-term gain on the stock.

Summary of aftertax performance

Assuming that the taxpayer is in the 50 percent tax bracket and that capital gains or losses are at 25 percent, the aftertax consequences for different market conditions are shown in the table below. Commissions and dividends are again excluded as is the unique exercise strategy at a stock price just above $50.

	Stock price at call's expiration date				
	30	40	50	60	70
Capital gain or (loss)...................	(4,000)	(2,000)	0	2,000	4,000
Taxes (paid) or saved at 25 percent......	1,000	500	0	(500)	(1,000)
Income or (expense)....................	1,500	1,500	1,500	(500)	(2,500)
Taxes (paid) or saved at 50 percent......	(750)	(750)	(750)	250	1,250
Net aftertax profit or (loss)........	(2,250)	(750)	750	1,250	1,750

Exhibit 7–1 graphically compares the aftertax impact with pretax profits or losses for the 50 percent tax bracket investor. As shown, the conventional covered hedge ratio of 1 : 1 provides increasing aftertax profits as the stock rises above the exercise price compared to constant pretax profits. On the other hand, the downside aftertax loss would be greater than the pretax loss unless the stock were to decline to below $35.

CAUTION: Contrary to a popular Wall Street myth (a sales gimmick for merchandising a complex product to unsophisticated investors), call options are not sold to increase one's income. The ideal environment for selling covered calls is a bull market where the ordinary loss on the calls sold provides a tax-deductible expense. Call options should therefore be sold to increase one's total aftertax return on investment.

EXHIBIT 7-1

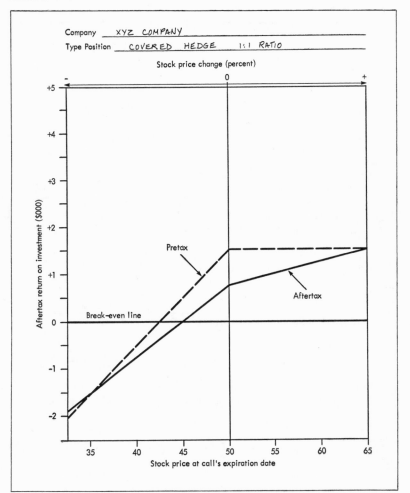

Company ___XYZ COMPANY___

Type Position ___COVERED HEDGE   1:1 RATIO___

Stock price change (percent)

AFTERTAX PERFORMANCE FOR VARIABLE HEDGES

Again assuming that the investor is in the 50 percent tax bracket and that capital gains or losses are at 25 percent, Exhibit 7-2 presents aftertax performance calculations for the 1:1 covered hedge plus variable hedge ratios of 1.5:1 and 3:1. The performance results for the variable hedges are graphically illustrated by Exhibit 7-3. As shown, the 1.5:1 variable hedge

EXHIBIT 7–2: Aftertax performance for alternate hedge ratios—no tax loss carry-over (200 shares of stock at 50 versus calls at 7½)

	Stock price at call's expiration date				
	30	40	50	60	70
1:1 Ratio—two calls sold					
Capital gain or (loss)................	(4,000)	(2,000)	0	2,000	4,000
Taxes (paid) or saved at 25 percent....	1,000	500	0	(500)	(1,000)
Income or (expense)..................	1,500	1,500	1,500	(500)	(2,500)
Taxes (paid) or saved at 50 percent....	(750)	(750)	(750)	250	1,250
Net aftertax profit or (loss)........	(2,250)	(750)	750	1,250	1,750
1.5:1 Ratio—three calls sold					
Capital gain or (loss)................	(4,000)	(2,000)	0	2,000	4,000
Taxes (paid) or saved at 25 percent....	1,000	500	0	(500)	(1,000)
Income or (expense)..................	2,250	2,250	2,250	(750)	(3,750)
Taxes (paid) or saved at 50 percent....	(1,125)	(1,125)	(1,125)	375	1,875
Net aftertax profit or (loss)........	(1,875)	(375)	1,125	1,125	1,125
3:1 Ratio—six calls sold					
Capital gain or (loss)................	(4,000)	(2,000)	0	2,000	4,000
Taxes (paid) or saved at 25 percent....	1,000	500	0	(500)	(1,000)
Income or (expense)..................	4,500	4,500	4,500	(1,500)	(7,500)
Taxes (paid) or saved at 50 percent....	(2,250)	(2,250)	(2,250)	750	3,750
Net aftertax profit or (loss)........	(750)	750	2,250	750	(750)

provides constant aftertax profits as the stock rises above the call's exercise price, similar to a 1:1 ratio on a pretax basis. The 3:1 variable hedge provides a neutral aftertax posture similar to a 2:1 ratio on a pretax basis.

The following simple formulas will permit you to quickly select ratios based on your particular tax bracket.

$$R = \text{Ratio}$$
$$T = \text{Tax rate on income}$$
$$(\text{expressed as a decimal})$$

Bullish hedge (constant aftertax profits on the upside)

$$R = \frac{1 - 0.5T}{1 - T}$$

Neutral hedge (break-even points equally distant from stock price)

$$R = \frac{2(1 - 0.5T)}{1 - T}$$

EXHIBIT 7–3

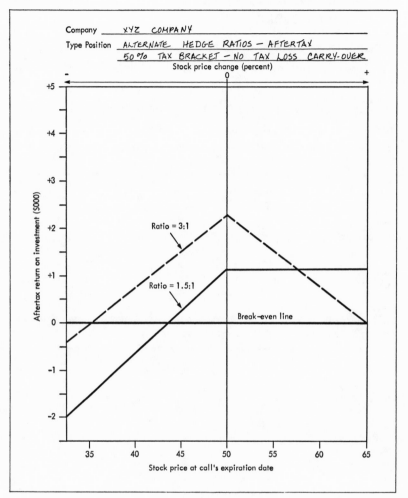

Company ___XYZ COMPANY___

Type Position ___ALTERNATE HEDGE RATIOS — AFTERTAX___
___50% TAX BRACKET — NO TAX LOSS CARRY-OVER___

Example: the investor is in the 40 percent tax bracket. Alternate hedge ratios are:

$$Bullish\ R = \frac{1 - 0.5T}{1 - T} = \frac{1 - 0.2}{1 - 0.4} = \frac{0.8}{0.6} = 1.33$$

$$Neutral\ R = \frac{2(1 - 0.5T)}{1 - T} = \frac{2(1 - 0.2)}{1 - 0.4} = \frac{2(0.8)}{0.6} = 2.67$$

INVESTORS WITH LARGE TAX
LOSS CARRY-OVERS

Suppose the investor is again in the 50 percent tax bracket but he has a large tax loss carry-over with little hope of recouping the losses for years to come. In this case, capital gains or losses on the common stock are just as important to him but are of little or no *tax consequence* to him. He might, therefore, evaluate the 1 : 1 covered hedge ratio, illustrated earlier, as follows.

	Stock price at call's expiration date				
	30	40	50	60	70
Capital gain or (loss)...................	(4,000)	(2,000)	0	2,000	4,000
Taxes (paid) or saved at 0 percent.......	0	0	0	0	0
Income or (expense)....................	1,500	1,500	1,500	(500)	(2,500)
Taxes (paid) or saved at 50 percent......	(750)	(750)	(750)	250	1,250
Net aftertax profit or (loss)........	(3,250)	(1,250)	750	1,750	2,750

EXHIBIT 7–4: Aftertax performance for alternate hedge ratios—with tax loss carry-over (200 shares of stock at 50 versus calls at 7½)

	Stock price at call's expiration date				
	30	40	50	60	70
1:1 Ratio—two calls sold					
Capital gain or (loss)...............	(4,000)	(2,000)	0	2,000	4,000
Taxes (paid) or saved at 0 percent....	0	0	0	0	0
Income or (expense)................	1,500	1,500	1,500	(500)	(2,500)
Taxes (paid) or saved at 50 percent...	(750)	(750)	(750)	250	1,250
Net aftertax profit or (loss).......	(3,250)	(1,250)	750	1,750	2,750
2:1 Ratio—four calls sold					
Capital gain or (loss)...............	(4,000)	(2,000)	0	2,000	4,000
Taxes (paid) or saved at 0 percent....	0	0	0	0	0
Income or (expense)................	3,000	3,000	3,000	(1,000)	(5,000)
Taxes (paid) or saved at 50 percent...	(1,500)	(1,500)	(1,500)	500	2,500
Net aftertax profit or (loss).......	(2,500)	(500)	1,500	1,500	1,500
4:1 Ratio—eight calls sold					
Capital gain or (loss)...............	(4,000)	(2,000)	0	2,000	4,000
Taxes (paid) or saved at 0 percent....	0	0	0	0	0
Income or (expense)................	6,000	6,000	6,000	(2,000)	(10,000)
Taxes (paid) or saved at 50 percent...	(3,000)	(3,000)	(3,000)	1,000	5,000
Net aftertax profit or (loss).......	(1,000)	1,000	3,000	1,000	(1,000)

Like the previous investor with no tax loss carry-over, the investor with a large carry-over will also increase his ratio of calls sold for optimum aftertax performance, but even higher ratios will be used to achieve comparable bullish or neutral postures. These are illustrated by the calculations and graphs of Exhibits 7–4 and 7–5. For the investor in the 50 percent tax bracket, a 2:1 ratio provides a bullish aftertax hedge and a 4:1 ratio gives a neutral

EXHIBIT 7–5

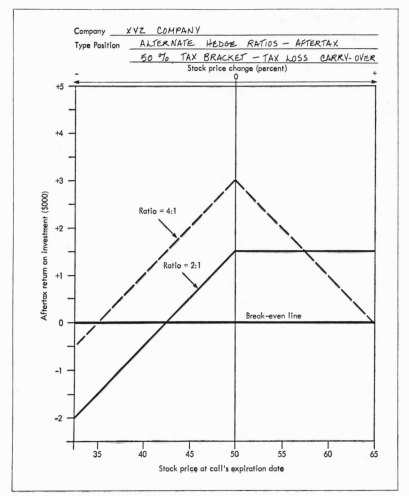

hedge, as shown. These ratios may also be determined by the following formulas.

$$Bullish\ R = \frac{1}{1-T} = \frac{1}{1-0.5} = \frac{1}{0.5} = 2.0$$

$$Neutral\ R = \frac{2}{1-T} = \frac{2}{1-0.5} = \frac{2}{0.5} = 4.0$$

SHORTCUTS FOR CALCULATING AFTERTAX BREAK-EVEN POINTS

The formulas for calculating pretax break-even points for variable hedges from chapter 6 may be adjusted for tax consequences.

R = Ratio
C = Call price
S = Stock price
E = Exercise price
T = Tax rate on income (expressed as a decimal)
t = Tax rate on capital gains (expressed as a decimal)

Downside
  break-even $= S - \dfrac{(1-T)(R \times C)}{(1-t)}$

Upside
  break-even $= \dfrac{R(C+E) - RT(C+E) - S(1-t)}{R(1-T) - (1-t)}$

Example: Two calls, having a $50 exercise price, are sold at 7½ points each against 100 shares of stock purchased at $50. Tax rates are 50 percent on income or expense and 25 percent on capital gains or losses.

Downside
break-even $= S - \dfrac{(1 - T)(R \times C)}{(1 - t)}$

$\qquad = 50 - \dfrac{(1 - 0.5)(2 \times 7\frac{1}{2})}{(1 - 0.25)}$

$\qquad = 50 - \dfrac{(0.5)(15)}{0.75}$

$\qquad = 50 - \dfrac{7.5}{0.75}$

$\qquad = 50 - 10$

$\qquad = 40$

Upside
break-even $= \dfrac{R(C + E) - RT(C + E) - S(1 - t)}{R(1 - T) - (1 - t)}$

$\qquad = \dfrac{2(7\frac{1}{2} + 50) - 2(0.5)(7\frac{1}{2} + 50) - 50(1 - 0.25)}{2(1 - 0.5) - (1 - 0.25)}$

$\qquad = \dfrac{2(57\frac{1}{2}) - (1)(57\frac{1}{2}) - 50(0.75)}{2(0.5) - 0.75}$

$\qquad = \dfrac{115 - 57.5 - 37.5}{1 - 0.75}$

$\qquad = \dfrac{20}{0.25}$

$\qquad = 80$

Note: Investors with large tax loss carry-overs would assign no value to t—the tax rate for capital gains.

CONCLUSIONS

1. The unique tax treatment presently given to profits or losses on call options sold requires that investors think in terms of aftertax risk/reward when designing call option hedges—the higher one's tax bracket, the higher the ratio.

2. Investors with a large tax loss carry-over from prior years should use even higher ratios.

3. The following table summarizes these conclusions for tax-payers in the 50 percent bracket. Others should make adjustments as shown previously.

		Optimum ratio	
Market outlook	Pretax	No tax loss carry-over	Large tax loss carry-over
Bullish................	1:1	1.5:1	2:1
Neutral................	2:1	3:1	4:1

4. The above recommendations apply to call option hedges when the stock is selling close to the call's exercise price. Additional adjustments should be made when considering in-the-money or out-of-the-money calls similar to the procedures of chapter 6.

5. If the tax ruling is changed from ordinary income or loss to short-term capital gain or loss, the ratio adjustments and exercise strategies provided in this chapter will no longer apply. Life will be much simpler since we will be able to evaluate most call option hedges without having to introduce aftertax complications, and the sophisticated hedger of options will probably be able to achieve even greater aftertax profits.

chapter 8

Selling call options against convertibles

Just as they prefer undervalued convertibles as a superior alternative to common stocks in a conventional investment program, experienced hedgers will seldom, if ever, use stocks as the underlying securities when selling call options. The large number of listed calls presently trading provides numerous opportunities for selecting undervalued convertibles for the long side of the hedge. A diversified portfolio of five to ten positions can normally be achieved within a reasonable period of time.

Common stocks are usually used in call option hedges by the sophisticated investor when the calls are *overpriced*. However, when the overpriced call expires, the probabilities are that new calls will be only normally valued. The hedger is then faced with two choices. He may sell a normally valued call which amounts to little more than "trading dollars" on his investment funds; or he may close out his position and search for a better opportunity. The latter approach will probably cost too many commission dollars relative to invested capital and thus reduce overall investment performance.

The sale of *normally valued* calls against *undervalued con-*

vertibles generally offers superior risk/reward opportunities compared to the sale of overpriced calls against common stocks. As
long as the convertibles remain undervalued, future calls that are
just normally priced may be continually sold against them. In
addition to the risk/reward advantages, the lower commission
costs over the long term for this less aggressive (almost passive)
strategy will also enhance investment performance. Of course, if
the convertible becomes overpriced relative to its underlying common stock, the unexpected profits should be taken by closing out
the entire hedge position.

To assist you in evaluating the use of convertibles in your
option-selling program, Exhibit 8–1 presents a recent list of those
having listed calls. Pertinent statistical information is provided but
you should always check with your broker or advisory service for
current data before buying any convertible.

CONVERTIBLES TRADING NEAR THEIR
CONVERSION VALUE

The sale of call options against convertibles trading near their
conversion value may be evaluated in the same manner as the
common stock hedges of chapters 6 and 7. For example, Exhibit
8–2 presents a convertible hedge in Federal National Mortgage
similar to the covered call option/stock hedge in Exhibit 6–5. The
bond was convertible into about 51 shares of common. At a stock
price of $15 per share, its conversion value was $765 as shown.
At a market price of 78 ($780), the bond was trading at only a
2 percent conversion premium. It offered upside potential comparable to the common in addition to its modest yield advantage.
But, more important, the bond provided greater safety. On the
downside, it was expected to decline at only about half the rate of
its underlying common stock, as estimated by a major advisory
service specializing in convertible securities.

EXHIBIT 8–1: Information on convertibles having listed call options (January 1976)

Description	Symbols B.R.	Symbols Ult.	Number of shares	Price	Investment value*	Current yield	Conversion premium	Notes
Aetna Life & Casualty... $2.00 preferred	AET+	AETPr	1.500	37	22	5.4%	3%	
Alcoa... 5.25–91	AA.M	APrA	17.857	84	61	6.2	21	
Amerada Hess... $3.50 preferred	AHC+	AHCPr	2.200	46	33	7.6	23	
American Home Products... $2.00 preferred	AHP+	AHPPr	4.500	144	21	1.4	0	
American Hospital Supply... 5.75–99	AHSK	AHSR	33.898	115	64	5.0	13	
AMF Inc... 4.25–81	AMFL	APrMF	17.510	77	73	5.5	131	
American Telephone & Telegraph... $4.00 preferred	T+	TPr	1.053	55	40	7.3	2	
Atlantic Richfield... $3.00 preferred	ARCA	ARCA	1.700	150	28	2.0	0	
2.80 preferred	ARCC	ARCC	0.600	60	26	4.7	11	
4.375–86	L.N	SPrLO	12.500	141	62	3.1	0	1
Baxter Laboratories... 4.375–91	BAXJ	BWsAX	26.316	116	58	3.8	10	
Brunswick... 4.50–81	BC.L	BPrC	19.739	80	75	5.6	269	
Caterpillar Tractor... 5.50–00	CATU	CAT-RG	13.201	107	65	5.1	16	
CBS Inc... $1.00 preferred	CBS+	CBSPr	0.689	31	10	3.2	0	
Chase Manhattan Corp... 4.875–93	CMBK	CPrMB	18.182	61	60	8.0	20	
6.50–96	CMBJ	CWiMB	17.391	70	72	9.3	44	
Citicorp... 5.75–00	FNCD	FNC-RB	24.390	88	70	6.5	20	
Commonwealth Edison... $1.425 preferred	CWEA	CWEA	0.670	20	14	7.1	0	
Continental Oil... $2.00 preferred	CLL+	CLLPr	1.350	80	21	2.5	0	
Continental Telephone... 5.25–86	CTCL	CTCA	40.920	65	64	8.1	32	
Delta Airlines... 6.50–86	NEAK	NEAA	4.00	72	71	9.0	374	2

EXHIBIT 8-1 (continued)

Description		Symbols		Number of shares	Price	Investment value*	Current yield	Conversion premium	Notes
		B.R.	Ult.						
El Paso Co..........	6.00–93A	ELG.	EWsLG	59.030	68	61	8.8	0	3
	8.50–95A	ELGE	ERtLG	75.130	88	79	9.7	0	4
	4.25–90A	BEMK	BWiEM	48.780	56	46	7.6	0	5
Engelhard Minerals & Chemicals.	$4.25 preferred	ENG+	ENGPr	6.300	139	40	3.1	0	
	5.25–97	ENGK	EPrNG	34.000	88	56	6.0	12	
Federal National Mortgage......	4.375–96	FNMK	FPrNM	50.995	78	53	5.6	2	
Ford Motor...........	4.50–96	FMCD	FMCR	12.800	65	51	6.9	15	6
	4.875–98	FMCC	FMCS	14.430	72	53	6.8	13	7
General Telephone & Electric.....	$2.50 preferred	GTE+	GTEPr	0.950	31	22	8.1%	30%	8
	4.0–90	GTEL	GPrTE	21.231	58	49	6.9	9	
	5.0–92	GTEH	GWiTE	21.697	65	53	7.7	20	
	6.25–96	GTEF	GZTE	29.740	83	60	7.5	12	
Grace, W. R..........	4.25–90	GRAK	GPrRA	17.446	62	51	6.8	48	
	6.50–96	GRAG	GWsRA	33.755	89	62	7.3	10	
Greyhound..........	6.50–90	G.K	GPrC	54.422	81	67	8.0	14	
Gulf & Western Industries.........	$3.88 preferred C	GW+C	GWPrC	3.508	76	28	5.1	0	
	$2.50 preferred D	GW+D	GWPrD	1.488	36	18	6.9	10	9
	5.50–93	GW.O	GPrW	35.499	82	46	6.7	5	
Hercules Inc..........	6.50–99	HPCK	HPrPC	28.571	98	67	6.6	22	
Holiday Inns Inc........	Series A	HIAA	HIAA	1.500	24	12	—	14	10
Household Finance........	$2.375 preferred	HFCB	HFCB	2.250	36	22	6.6	0	
	$2.50 preferred	HFCC	HFCC	1.500	30	23	8.3	25	
International Minerals & Chemicals........	4.00–91	IGLK	IPrGL	26.330	98	44	4.1	0	

Company											11	12			13
International Telephone & Telegraph	$4.00 preferred H	ITTH	ITTH	1.818	43	35	9.3	5							
	$4.50 preferred I	ITT+	ITTI	1.639	45	39	10.0	22							
	$4.00 preferred J	ITTJ	ITTJ	1.626	42	35	9.5	15							
	$4.00 preferred K	ITTK	ITTK	1.563	41	35	9.8	17							
	$2.25 preferred N	ITTN	ITTN	1.200	28	20	8.0	4							
	$5.00 preferred O	ITTO	ITTO	1.408	47	43	10.6	48							
	8.625–00	ITTX	ITT–RG	39.409	101	79	8.5	14							
Jim Walter	$1.60 preferred D	JWCD	JWCD	1.080	40	13	4.0	0							
	5.75–91	JWCK	JPrWC	23.810	99	56	5.8	12							
Kresge, S. S.	6.0–99	KG.K	KPrG	28.169	114	67	5.3	19							
Loews Corp.	6.875–93	—	—	26.667	76	55	9.1	36							
Mesa Petroleum	$1.60 preferred B	MSAB	MSAB	0.985	24	14	6.7	28							
Minnesota Mining & Manufacturing	4.25–97	D..	DPrA	10.750	82	52	5.2	36							
Monsanto	$2.75 preferred	MTC+	MTCPr	1.120	85	28	3.2	0							
Norton Simon Inc.	$1.60 preferred	NSIA	NSIA	2.154	49	14	3.2	3							
Occidental Petroleum	$2.16 preferred	OXYC	OXYC	1.600	26	17	8.3	16							
	$3.60 preferred	OXYB	OXYB	3.237	47	29	7.7	4							
	$4.00 preferred	OXYA	OXYA	3.155	49	32	8.2	11							
	7.50–96	OXYK	OPrXY	50.000	87	64	8.6	24							
Pennzoil Co.	$1.33	PZL+	PZLPr	1.296	24	12	5.5%	0%							
	5.25–96	PZLZ	PPrZL	26.144	66	53	8.0	33							
Pfizer Inc.	4.0–97	PFEK	PPrFE	21.053	75	54	5.3	27							
RCA Corp.	$4.00 preferred	RCAB	RCAB	2.120	51	37	7.8	27							
	4.5–92	RCAK	RPrCA	16.949	61	54	7.4	89							
R. J. Reynolds Industries	$2.25 preferred	RJRB	RJRB	1.500	70	21	3.2	0							

EXHIBIT 8–1 (concluded)

Description	Symbols B.R.	Ult.	Number of shares	Price	Investment value*	Current yield	Conversion premium	Notes
Searle, G. D.								
5.25–89	WR.K	WPrR	22.748	72	67	7.3	111	14
4.50–92	WR..	WWiR	21.818	61	58	7.4	87	15
Sperry Rand								
6.00–00			23.952	106	66	5.7	14	
Tenneco Inc.								
6.25–92	TGTK	TPrGT	35.100	95	63	6.6	0	
$5.50 preferred	TGT+	TGTPr	3.730	100	48	5.5	0	
Tesoro Petroleum Corp								
5.25–89	TSOJ	TPrSO	59.172	83	55	6.3	0	
$2.16 preferred	TSO+	TSOPr	1.724	26	17	8.3	8	
UAL Inc.								
$0.40 preferred	UAL+	UALPr	1.000	28	3	1.4	0	
5.00–91	UALK	UPrAL	24.403	70	50	7.1	54	16
4.25–92	UALL	UWiAL	16.197	55	44	7.7	79	17
United Technologies								
$8.00 preferred	UTXA	UTXA	2.222	114	75	7.0	11	
5.375–91	UTX.	UWiTX	15.500	72	62	7.5	0	18
4.50–92	UTXE	UWsTX	13.500	67	54	6.7	8	19
5.375–96	EXCJ	EPrXC	8.399	97	58	5.5	0	20
Virginia Electric & Power								
3.625–86	VELN	VPrEL	37.037	63	58	5.8	22	
Western Union Corp								
$4.60 preferred	WU+A	WUPrA	2.035	44	30	10.5	35	
$4.90 preferred	WU+C	WUPrC	2.349	46	32	10.6	22	
5.25–97	WU.K	WPrU	15.152	44	38	11.9	82	
Weyerhaeuser								
$2.80 preferred	WY+	WYPr	1.212	53	29	5.3	18	
Williams Companies								
$0.80 preferred	WMB+	WMBPr	1.800	45	7	1.8	0	
Woolworth, F. W.								
$2.20 preferred	Z+A	ZPrA	1.420	33	21	6.7	6	
Xerox Corp.								
6.0–95	XRXK	XPrRX	10.870	89	72	6.7	61	

* Estimated investment values are courtesy of the *Value Line Convertible Survey.*

Notes:

1. The bond trades as Sinclair Oil Corp. 4.375–86; unit consists of 0.6 share of Atlantic Richfield common (ARC) and 1.0 share of Atlantic Richfield $2.80 convertible preferred (ARCC); convertible into 11.76 units after 12/1/76 and 11.11 units after 12/1/81.

2. Bond trades as Northeast Airlines 6.50–86.

3. Bond was issued by and is still an obligation of El Paso Natural Gas, a subsidiary of El Paso Co.—trades as El Paso Natural Gas 6s–93A—conversion ratio decreases from 59.03 to 50.98 after 2/1/85.

4. Bond was issued by and is still an obligation of El Paso Natural Gas, a subsidiary of El Paso Co.—trades as El Paso Natural Gas 8.5s–95A—conversion ratio decreases from 75.13 to 67.08 after 2/1/85.

5. Bond was issued by and is still an obligation of Beanuit Corp., a subsidiary of El Paso Natural Gas—trades as Beanuit 4.25s–90A.

6. Bond trades as Ford Motor Credit 4.50–96.

7. Bond trades as Ford Motor Credit 4.875–98.

8. Number of shares decreases to 0.81 after 6/30/77.

9. Conversion ratio decreases to 1.455 after 12/31/80; to 1.391 after 12/21/83.

10. Series A stock pays noncumulative dividend of $1.70 payable in market value of common stock quarterly.

11. This is a fabricated convertible bond consisting of a nonconvertible 6.875–93 bond plus 26.667 Loews warrants, each to buy 1.0 share of Loews common for $37.50; exercise price increases to $40 after 11/29/76. Warrants expire 11/29/80. For discussion of fabricated convertibles, refer to *The Dow-Jones Irwin Guide to Convertible Securities* (Homewood, Ill.: Dow Jones-Irwin, 1973) pp. 135–38.

12. The bond was issued by and is an obligation of Dart Industries; it trades as Dart Industries 4.25–97.

13. Payment of $22 cash required on conversion.

14. Bond trades as Will Ross 5.25–89.

15. Bond trades as Will Ross 4.50–92.

16. Payment of $350 cash required on conversion; trades as United Air Lines.

17. Payment of $260 cash required on conversion; trades as United Air Lines.

18. Conversion terms expire 10/1/76.

19. Conversion terms expire 10/1/77.

20. Trades as Essex 5.375–96; convertible into 8.399 shares of United Technologies $8.00 convertible preferred (UTXA).

EXHIBIT 8-2

WORK SHEET FOR EVALUATING CALL OPTIONS SOLD AGAINST CONVERTIBLES

COMPANY _FEDERAL NATIONAL MORTGAGE_ DATE _JULY_

DESCRIPTION OF SECURITIES

Convertible: _4 3/8 – 96_

	Exercise Price	Expir. Date	Symbol	Target Prices	Annual Div.	
Common stock			FNM	15	5.3 %	
Convertible			FPr NM	78	5.6 = 6.2 YTM	
Call option	$ 15	JAN.	AC	2		

Conversion value = _50.955_ shares x $ _15_ per share = $ _765_
Conversion premium = _2_ %
Estimated investment value = $ _530_

POSSIBLE HEDGE POSITION   Partial _____, Covered _✓_, Variable _____

Convertibles: _20 M_ at $ _780_ = $ 15,600 + _200_ comm. = $ 15,800
Calls sold: _10_ at $ _200_ = $ 2,000 – _110_ comm. = $ 1,890
Net investment – unleveraged (_15,800 – 1,890_) = $ 13,910

PROFIT OR LOSS AT CALL'S EXPIRATION DATE (unleveraged)

	Downside	Exercise Price	Upside
Stock price..................	10	15	20
Estimated convertible price	65	78	103
Call price....................	0	0	5
Profit or (loss) – call options...	2,000	2,000	(3,000)
– convertibles...	(2,600)	0	5,000
Commissions*	(110)	(110)	(250)
Net profit or (loss)............	(710)	1,890	1,750
Return on investment (ROI)	5.1 %	+ 13.6 %	+ 12.6 %
Annualized ROI (0.50 years) ..	– 10.2 %	+ 27.2 %	+ 25.2 %
Plus annual income	+ 6.3 %	+ 6.3 %	+ 6.3 %
Total annualized ROI	– 3.9 %	+ 33.5 %	+ 31.5 %

*Commissions for the convertibles held long are not included in the calculations as it is assumed that they will be held for selling future call options. If the stock is trading above the call's exercise price at the expiration date, it is assumed the calls will be bought in instead of allowing them to be exercised.

The purchase of 20 bonds is approximately equivalent to the 1,000 share stock position used in previous examples for Federal National Mortgage. The sale of ten call options against the bonds results in a *covered* hedge position. *Pretax* profit and loss calculations are shown in Exhibit 8–2 similar to those previously made for the common stock hedge from Exhibit 6–5.

Exhibit 8–3 graphically presents the estimated annualized re-

EXHIBIT 8–3

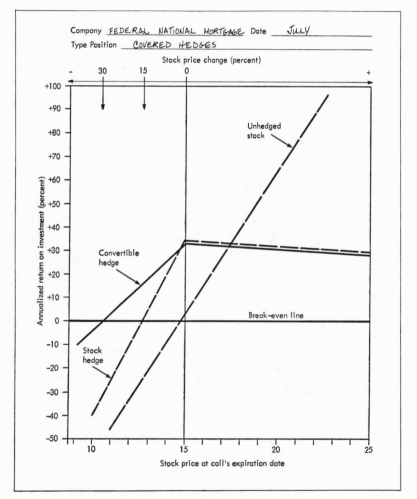

turn on investment for the six-month position. Also shown is the hedge against common stock from Exhibit 6–6. A comparison of the convertible hedge with the common stock hedge indicates about the same upside potential for both positions but significantly greater downside safety for the convertible bond hedge. At the $12.75 downside break-even price for the common stock hedge, for example, the convertible bond hedge is expected to return an annualized profit of 17 percent. The downside break-even protection was doubled from 15 percent to 30 percent.

The downside advantage provided by the convertible bond is *substantial.* If you are an active call option seller, or if you are seriously considering this investment strategy, you should restudy this example for Federal National Mortgage. It is representative of opportunities available to you in the real world of investing and will go a long way toward helping you to achieve the superior investment performance you should be seeking.

HEDGING CONVERTIBLES ON MARGIN

Like the conventional purchase of undervalued convertibles on margin, the use of leverage in a convertible hedge program may be a *prudent alternative* to nonmargined hedges against common stocks. The net investment on margin and the resulting debit balance for the convertible hedge in Federal National Mortgage from Exhibit 8–2 are calculated as follows:

50 percent × $15,800 total cost of bonds purchased	=	$7,900
Minus net call premiums received	=	−1,890
Net investment on full margin	=	$6,010
Debit balance = $15,800 − $1,890 − $6,010	=	$7,900

Profit and loss estimates are shown in the table below.

This convertible hedge on margin is graphically compared with the unleveraged common stock hedge in Exhibit 8–4. As shown,

	Stock price at call's expiration date		
	10	15	20
Profit or (loss) on bonds and calls from			
Exhibit 8–2..........................	($710)	$1,890	$1,750
Plus six-month bond interest			
(20 × $43.75 × 6/12)................	435	435	435
Minus six-month margin interest at 8 percent			
($7,900 × 8% × 6/12)...............	(315)	(315)	(315)
Net profit or (loss) on full margin.........	($590)	$2,010	$1,870
Annualized return on investment...........	−20%	+67%	−62%

the downside safety of the bonds permits the leveraging of potential profits without seriously adding to downside risk.

CONVERTIBLES TRADING AT A PREMIUM OVER CONVERSION VALUE

When a convertible is trading at a premium over its conversion value, the selection of the desired number of call options to be sold against it requires careful analysis. If the full number of calls are sold, as in a conventional covered hedge, the investor may be disappointed in a rising market. Since the bond or preferred will lose its conversion premium on the upside, it will not provide as much profit as would its underlying common stock. The risk/reward characteristics for a covered hedge, when the convertible is at a premium above its conversion value, are similar to a conventional variable hedge.

Exhibits 8–5 and 8–6 illustrate this characteristic for the previously discussed Chase Manhattan convertible bonds. Fifty bonds are the approximate equivalent to 900 shares of common stock. A covered hedge involving nine call options results in declining profits as the stock rises above the call's $30 exercise price.

If the investor is seeking risk/reward characteristics comparable to a conventional covered hedge when considering the Chase bonds, he must reduce the number of call options sold. The num-

EXHIBIT 8–4

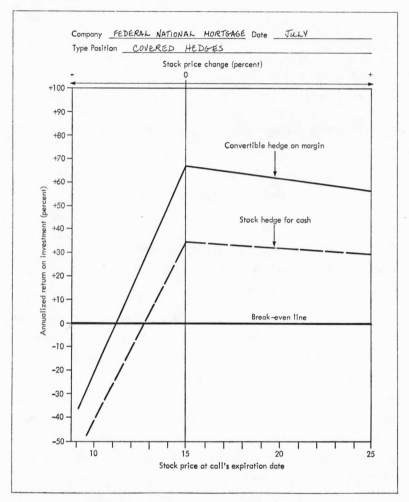

Company _FEDERAL NATIONAL MORTGAGE_ Date _JULY_

Type Position _COVERED HEDGES_

ber can quickly be approximated and the resulting *partial hedge* for Chase Manhattan is shown by Exhibits 8–7 and 8–8. The sale of only seven call options against the 50 bonds provides a reasonably constant return as the stock advances above the $30 exercise price.

EXHIBIT 8–5

WORK SHEET FOR EVALUATING CALL OPTIONS SOLD AGAINST CONVERTIBLES

COMPANY___CHASE MANHATTAN_____   DATE _OCTOBER____

DESCRIPTION OF SECURITIES

Convertible:___4 7/8 – 93_____

	Exercise Price	Expir. Date	Symbol	Target Prices	Annual Div.
Common stock			CMB	28	7.9 %
Convertible			CPr MB	61	8.0 = 9.6 YTM
Call option	$ 30	APR.	ZF	2	

Conversion value = ___18.18_____ shares x $__28____ per share = $ _510__
Conversion premium   = ___20 %__
Estimated investment value   = $ _600__

POSSIBLE HEDGE POSITION   Partial_____, Covered___✓___, Variable_____

Convertibles: _50 M_ at $ _610_ = $ 30,500 + _500_ comm. = $ _31,000_
Calls sold: ___9___ at $ _200_ = $ _1,800_ - _100_ comm. = $ _1,700_
Net investment – unleveraged   (___31,000 – 1,700___) = $ _29,300_

PROFIT OR LOSS AT CALL'S EXPIRATION DATE (unleveraged)

	Downside	Exercise Price	Upside
Stock price..................	20	30	40
Estimated convertible price	56	63	78
Call price....................	0	0	10
Profit or (loss) – call options ...	1,800	1,800	(7,200)
– convertibles...	(2,500)	1,000	8,500
Commissions*	(100)	(100)	(280)
Net profit or (loss)............	(800)	2,700	1,020
Return on investment (ROI)	– 2.7 %	+ 9.2 %	+ 3.5 %
Annualized ROI (0.50 years)..	– 5.4 %	+ 18.4 %	+ 7.0 %
Plus annual income	+ 8.3 %	+ 8.3 %	+ 8.3 %
Total annualized ROI	+ 2.9 %	+ 26.7 %	+ 15.3 %

*Commissions for the convertibles held long are not included in the calculations
as it is assumed that they will be held for selling future call options. If the stock
is trading above the call's exercise price at the expiration date, it is assumed the
calls will be bought in instead of allowing them to be exercised.

EXHIBIT 8-6

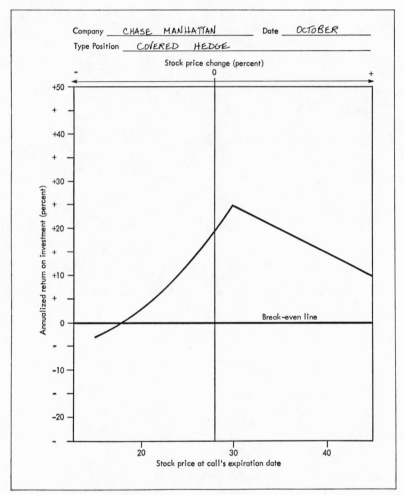

EXHIBIT 8–7

WORK SHEET FOR EVALUATING CALL OPTIONS SOLD AGAINST CONVERTIBLES

COMPANY ___CHASE MANHATTAN_____   DATE _OCTOBER___

DESCRIPTION OF SECURITIES

Convertible: __4⅞ – 93___

	Exercise Price	Expir. Date	Symbol	Target Prices	Annual Div.	
Common stock			CMB	28	7.9 %	
Convertible			CBr-HB	61	8.0	= 9.6 YTM
Call option	$ 30	APR.	ZF	2		

Conversion value = _____18.18_____ shares x $ _28_ per share = $ _510_
Conversion premium   = _20_ %
Estimated investment value   = $ _600_

POSSIBLE HEDGE POSITION   Partial __✓__, Covered_____, Variable_____

Convertibles: _50 M_ at $ _610_ = $30,500 + _500_ comm. = $ _31,000_
Calls sold: ___7___ at $ _200_ = $ 1,400 - _80_ comm. = $ _1,320_
Net investment – unleveraged   (__31,000 – 1,320__) = $ _29,680_

PROFIT OR LOSS AT CALL'S EXPIRATION DATE (unleveraged)

	Downside	Exercise Price	Upside
Stock price..................	20	30	40
Estimated convertible price....	56	63	78
Call price....................	0	0	10
Profit or (loss) – call options...	1,400	1,400	(5,600)
– convertibles...	(2,500)	1,000	8,500
Commissions*.................	(80)	(80)	(230)
Net profit or (loss)...........	(1,180)	2,320	2,670
Return on investment (ROI)	– 4.0 %	+ 7.8 %	+ 9.0 %
Annualized ROI (0.50 years)..	– 8.0 %	+ 15.6 %	+ 18.0 %
Plus annual income...........	+ 8.2 %	+ 8.2 %	+ 8.2 %
Total annualized ROI.........	+ 0.2 %	+ 23.8 %	+ 26.2 %

*Commissions for the convertibles held long are not included in the calculations
as it is assumed that they will be held for selling future call options. If the stock
is trading above the call's exercise price at the expiration date, it is assumed the
calls will be bought in instead of allowing them to be exercised.

EXHIBIT 8-8

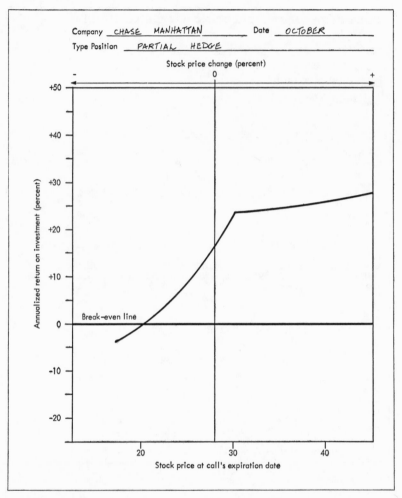

CONCLUSIONS

1. The use of *undervalued* convertibles in a call option-selling program is far superior to hedging against common stocks—substantial risk/reward advantages plus fewer commission dollars expended over the long term.

2. The use of margin in a convertible hedge program may be a *prudent alternative* to nonleveraged hedges against common stocks.

3. When a convertible is trading at a premium over its conversion value, a *partial hedge* should be considered to compensate for the loss of conversion premium on the upside.

4. As with conventional common stock hedges, higher ratios should be used with convertibles when calls are trading below their exercise prices.

chapter 9

Undervalued warrants

A warrant may generally be defined as a negotiable security issued by a company which represents a long-term option to purchase common stock directly from the company on specified terms. The terms are sometimes extensive and complex, thus offering unusual opportunities to the informed investor and disappointment to others.

Warrants are often referred to as high-risk or speculative investments. "Funny money" was a popular description prior to the prestigious AT&T issue in 1970. Like most Wall Street clichés, these terms are frequently inapplicable and have often discouraged conservative investors from considering warrants for their portfolios. Under certain circumstances, a warrant may actually be a more prudent investment than its underlying common stock and should be purchased by the conservative investor as a superior *alternative* to the common. It is the conservative, *undervalued* warrant that offers potential for spectacular stock market success when combined with other investment tools—tools that most investors are capable of using but that are frequently overlooked or

misused, even by the professionals. These techniques will be presented shortly, but first let us review the most important factors
influencing a warrant's value.

Exercise terms

The exercise price is the amount of money to be submitted
with each warrant upon surrendering it to the company for the
stated number of common stock shares. If the exercise terms for
XYZ Company warrants are one share of common for $10, then
$10 would be submitted with each warrant and one common
share would be received in return. If the exercise terms are two
shares for $10, then $10 would still be submitted with each
warrant but two common shares would be received. In both cases,
the exercise price is $10. As will be demonstrated later, when
other than one share of common stock is received in the exchange,
the exercise price must be *adjusted* before determining warrant
values.

Scheduled changes of exercise terms

Warrant terms occasionally contain provisions for periodic
changes in the exercise price. These changes are usually upward
and can therefore retard the warrant's appreciation potential.
They must be taken into consideration when computing values.
For example, the exercise price for Loews warrants, which expire
in 1980, was $35 until November 1972, at which time it was
automatically increased to $37.50. A further increase to $40 will
take place during November 1976. Warrant provisions may also
include periodic reductions in the number of common stock shares
to be received, which in effect is comparable to increasing the
exercise price.

Protection against stock splits and stock dividends

The amount of common stock to be received for each warrant may also be changed as a result of stock splits, but this type of revision should have little effect on the warrant's value. Braniff International warrants were originally exercisable into one share of common for $73. A 3 for 1 stock split in 1968 required that the exercise terms be revised to three shares for $73. The stock split had no effect on the warrant's inherent value or market price.

Through antidilution clauses in warrant agreements, most warrants are also protected against stock dividends (small stock splits) and against issuance of additional common stock or convertible securities by the company at prices below the warrant's exercise price. These factors may result in small adjustments to the exercise terms and will have little or no effect on the warrant's value or trading price. Braniff also issued a stock dividend in 1972 causing an additional revision in the warrant's exercise terms to 3.183 shares for $73.

Expiration date

In addition to the number of shares of common stock to be received and the price to be paid to exercise the privilege, the time period during which the option is valid is of major importance. This may be a few months, several years, or even perpetual. The majority of new warrants issued have a life of five to ten years.

A warrant with a remaining life of more than three years is generally considered to be long term and may be evaluated with other long-term warrants by using standardized techniques to be provided shortly. As the expiration date draws to within two years, the degree of risk may be substantially increased and short-term evaluation methods must be used, as shown for listed call options in chapter 4.

Where the exercise price is to be periodically increased, it may be necessary to evaluate the warrant as both short term and long term. Prior to November 1976, the Loews warrant should be considered short term at an exercise price of $37.50 and long term at $40. Except where otherwise indicated, all exercise terms used in our warrant computations will be those prevailing three years hence. A study of the Loews warrant would, therefore, be based on the higher exercise price of $40.

Note that when warrants expire, those holding them during the final days must exercise them to salvage any value that they may have at the time. Prior to the expiration date, warrants should seldom be purchased with the intention of exercising them. An exception to this rule would occur if one were interested in purchasing the common stock, and the warrants were available at or below their conversion value. Purchase and exercise of the warrants would then result in a saving to the investor.

Senior securities usable at par value

When warrants are issued with bonds, the bonds may often be used at full par value in lieu of cash in exercising the warrant, at the option of the warrant holder. If the bond is selling above par value, it would not be considered, since it would be more economical to use cash instead of the bond. If the bond is selling below par (usually the case, since the bond normally drops in price when the warrant is detached after issuance) the *effective* exercise price may be reduced quite drastically. For example, Loews 6.875s–93 bond, trading at 70, would reduce the $40 exercise price to an effective exercise price of $28 ($40 × 70/100 = $28). In other words, if one were planning to convert his Loews warrants into common, he would submit bonds purchased for $700 but valued at $1,000 for exercise purposes, instead of cash.

One must be cautious of deeply discounted bonds in applying the effective exercise price to warrant price projections. An improvement in the prospects of the company under study will normally result in a higher bond price. The appreciation potential of the warrant would then be reduced accordingly as the bond's price increased.

Be careful also to note the length of time that the bonds may be usable at par value because it may be less than the warrant's life. As when a warrant's exercise price is increased, if the usable bond life expires prior to the warrant, the warrant may have to be evaluated from both short-term and long-term standpoints.

Are there enough bonds for full warrant conversion?

Another important factor which must be considered is the size of the bond issue in relation to the number of bonds required for exercise of the entire warrant issue. Although most bond issues exceed the exercise quantity, some fall far short. Only about 30 percent of the General Host warrant issue could presently be exercised by the use of their 7s–94 bonds. This percentage could be reduced still further if the company were to make additional purchases of their own bonds on the open market, a practice frequently used by many companies to reduce interest payments and to improve net worth. This could cause a "squeeze" on the bonds if the common stock were to rise to the point where exercise of the warrant was anticipated. As the bonds are purchased for exercise purposes, their price would rise toward par, thus raising the effective exercise price of the warrant back up to the $40 range. A realistic analysis of the General Host warrant would therefore exclude the bonds from consideration.

Callable warrants

Warrants that are callable by the company may present the investor with annoying problems that are often encountered with convertible bonds selling above their call prices. Fortunately, only a few warrant terms include such provisions but, when they do, warrant purchases should be made with caution since any premium above conversion value would be immediately lost if the warrants were called.

NORMAL VALUE CURVES FOR
LONG-TERM WARRANTS

Several different normal value curves for warrants are presented in the literature. Each is similar in construction but contains significant differences depending on the formulas used or personal observations of historical warrant price patterns. I have found the following simple formula to be the most practical for use when studying *long-term* warrants on *speculative* common stocks.[1]

$$W = \sqrt{E^2 + S^2} - E$$

where:

W = Warrant price
E = Exercise price
S = Stock price

This formula may be used to plot a curve for each warrant under consideration, but fortunately it is not necessary to prepare individual curves for every warrant. Like the family of normal value curves for call options presented in chapter 4, a standardized curve may be prepared for all long-term warrants on speculative stocks. This is accomplished by dividing both the warrant and stock prices by the exercise price in the above formula. Representative factors are obtained as follows:

S/E	W/E
0.5	0.118
1.0	0.414
1.5	0.803
2.0	1.236
2.5	1.693

[1] S. T. Kassouf, *Evaluation of Convertible Securities* (New York: Analytical Publishers Co., 1966).

Adjusted warrant and exercise prices

When the exercise terms provide for other than one share of common stock for each warrant, or if there is a usable senior security selling below par value, the warrant price and exercise price must first be adjusted before computing S/E and W/E factors.

1. The warrant price is *adjusted* by dividing it by the number of shares of common stock to be received for each warrant.
2. The exercise price is first reduced, if there is a usable bond selling below par, to determine the *effective* exercise price. The effective exercise price is then *adjusted* by also dividing it by the number of shares of common stock to be received for each warrant.

The following example for the Braniff International (BNF) warrant will illustrate these procedures. In February 1976, the Braniff warrant was exercisable into 3.183 shares of common stock for $73. The Braniff 5.75s–86 were usable at par value and were selling at 68. At stock and warrant prices of $12.50 and $11.00, calculations were:

$$
\begin{aligned}
\text{Adjusted warrant price} &= \$11.00 \div 3.183 &&= \$\ 3.46 \\
\text{Effective exercise price} &= \$73.00 \times 68/100 &&= \$49.64 \\
\text{Adjusted exercise price} &= \$49.64 \div 3.183 &&= \$15.60 \\
S/E &= \$12.50 \div \$15.60 &&=\ \ \ 0.80 \\
W/E &= \$\ 3.46 \div \$15.60 &&=\ \ \ 0.22
\end{aligned}
$$

These S/E and W/E factors for Braniff are plotted on the normal value curve of Exhibit 9–1. It is noted that the warrant fell somewhat below the curve, indicating that it was undervalued in February 1976.

Factors affecting normal value

Like call options, warrants to purchase common stock are naturally worth most when there is the possibility of a substantial

EXHIBIT 9–1: Normal value curve for long-term warrants on speculative stocks

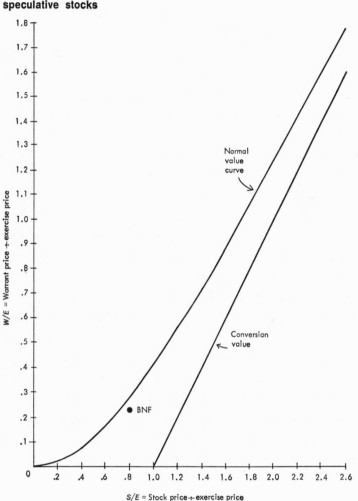

increase in the price of the common. Conversely, warrants to purchase stable, high-quality stocks would be expected to command lower premiums.

A major factor relating to a stock's quality and stability, and therefore having a pronounced influence on a warrant's normal value, is the dividend payout on the common stock. All other factors being equal, stocks with high yields will appreciate in value at a slower rate than stocks of companies that do not distribute part of their earnings to their shareholders. The return on investment to the common shareholders may be the same in both cases when dividends and price appreciation are added together. However, since a warrant does not benefit from dividends, it will be worth considerably more in the case where no dividend is paid on the common. A simple example will serve to illustrate this characteristic.

Assume that both A and B common stocks are selling at $50 and both have five-year warrants that are exercisable into one share of common for $50. A's common stock yields 5 percent while B's pays no dividend. If, after five years, A's common stock appreciates in value by 25 percent to $62.50, the stockholders would have received a total return on their investment of $25 or $50 percent ($12.50 price appreciation plus $12.50 in dividends). To equal this total return, the price of B's common must appreciate in price by the full 50 percent to $75. At the expiration date, B's warrants would have a conversion value twice that of A's—$25 versus $12.50. We would therefore expect that B's warrants would have sold at a greater premium than A's when both stocks were trading at the initial $50 price level.

Exhibit 9–2 illustrates empirically derived modifications to the normal value curves based on common stock yield. Experience indicates that these curves are representative of the majority of warrants you will encounter and will, therefore, contribute to the accuracy of your warrant evaluations. Five different value bands are shown based on a warrant's underlying common stock yield as follows:

Band 5 = 0–2 percent stock yield
    4 = 2–4 percent
    3 = 4–6 percent
    2 = 6–8 percent
    1 = above 8 percent
Note: Area 6 represents all warrants selling above band 5.

EXHIBIT 9–2:   Normal value curves for long-term warrants based on stock yield

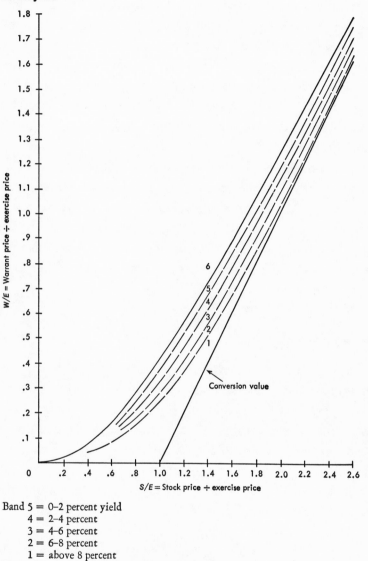

Band 5 = 0–2 percent yield
      4 = 2–4 percent
      3 = 4–6 percent
      2 = 6–8 percent
      1 = above 8 percent
Note: Area 6 represents all warrants above band 5.

For example, if a warrant's common stock yields 5 percent, the warrant would be considered properly priced if it were selling in band 3. Above band 3, it would be overpriced and below band 3 it would be undervalued. Note that a stock dividend will have the same negative effect as a cash dividend on a warrant's normal value if the warrant's terms are not adjusted to reflect these small stock splits. The assignment of a normal value band must therefore take into consideration both cash dividends and unprotected stock dividends.

If a common stock exhibits a higher than normal degree of price stability, its warrant should be assigned to a value band below that based on yield alone—similar to the procedures used in chapter 4 for call options. In the area of warrants, there is no substitute for good judgment. The normal value curves should be used only as a guide for initial screening of potential buy or sell candidates.

Warrant leverage

A warrant possesses leverage when it is expected to appreciate in value at a greater percentage rate than its underlying common stock on a price increase by the common. This leverage may be determined from the normal value curves by assuming that the common will advance to a given price and then estimating the corresponding price advance for the warrant. For example, if the warrant were expected to increase 200 percent upon a 100 percent rise by the common, it would have an upside leverage factor of 2.0.

Since warrants should be considered for purchase only when they offer significant leverage advantages over their common stocks, useful additions to the normal value curves are the leverage lines as illustrated in Exhibit 9–3. These leverage lines are based on the common stock advancing 100 percent in price while the

EXHIBIT 9–3:   Normal value curves for long-term warrants based on stock yield

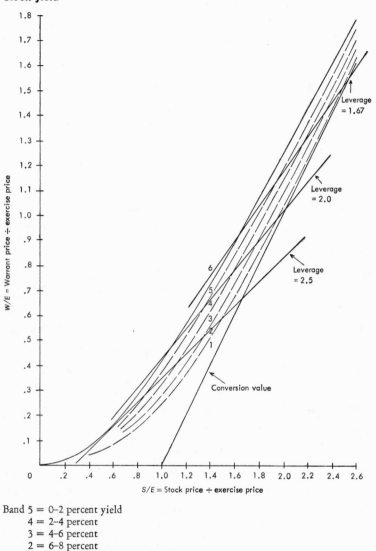

Band 5 = 0–2 percent yield
    4 = 2–4 percent
    3 = 4–6 percent
    2 = 6–8 percent
    1 = above 8 percent
Note: Area 6 represents all warrants above band 5.

warrant is still long term and also assuming that it remains on its normal value curve during the stock's advance. For example, the 2.0 leverage line intersects the top curve at $S/E = 1.0$ and the conversion value line at $S/E = 2.0$. A warrant trading on the top curve would be expected to advance 200 percent (from $W/E = 0.414$ up to $W/E = 1.236$) if the common stock doubles from $S/E = 1.0$ up to $S/E = 2.0$. A warrant trading on the conversion value line would also advance 200 percent (from $W/E = 1.0$ up to $W/E = 3.0$) as the common stock doubles ($S/E = 2.0$ up to $S/E = 4.0$).

As will be noted from a study of these curves, greater leverage is attained when the stock is selling below the exercise price. As the common stock rises above the exercise price, the warrant leverage diminishes. At some high price level for the common, the warrant will lose most of its leverage and will advance or decline at about the same percentage rate as the common.

These varying leverage characteristics are perfectly logical. When the common is selling below the warrant's exercise price, we would expect greater potential gain to compensate for the possibility that the warrant may have little or no value upon expiration. As the common stock moves above the exercise price, the risk is reduced because the warrant may still have substantial intrinsic value upon expiration.

A good rule of thumb is that warrants should be considered for purchase when they possess upside leverage of 2.0 or higher. They would then be selling in the area below the 2.0 leverage line shown in Exhibit 9–3. They should, of course, also be selling in, or below, their normal value band. The area between the leverage lines of 2.0 and 1.67 would be considered a "hold" area; above the 1.67 line is a "sell" area. In any event, a warrant should never be purchased unless its underlying common stock has been evaluated and you have made a favorable decision on the common. The warrant should only be considered as an alternate investment to the common stock.

UNDERVALUED WARRANTS

Our discussion so far has shown that a normally priced warrant would often advance at a percentage rate in excess of twice that of its common stock. To obtain this favorable leverage during an upside move, we must expect the warrant to also decline faster than its common in a down market. It might, therefore, be expected that the positive upside leverage would be offset by negative downside leverage. Although this is frequently the case for overpriced warrants, normally priced warrants, as evaluated by the previously discussed procedures, provide an overall mathematical advantage over purchase of their common stock.

Consider a long-term warrant whose common stock pays no dividend and has exhibited high price volatility—the warrant would be expected to sell on its normal value curve at the top of band 5. If the common stock were trading at the warrant's exercise price ($S/E = 1.0$), the W/E factor for the warrant would be 0.414. Assuming a 100 percent price advance by the common (to $S/E = 2.0$), the warrant would be expected to increase in value by approximately 200 percent (to $W/E = 1.236$). On the downside, if the common were to decline 50 percent (to $S/E = 0.5$), we would expect the warrant to decline about 71.5 percent to a W/E factor of 0.118. The warrant would have positive upside leverage and negative downside leverage, characteristics expected for all normally priced warrants. These price relationships may be expressed by the same formula used to evaluate convertibles in chapter 3 to determine if the warrant offers a mathematical advantage over its common stock.

$$MA = \frac{\text{Percent warrant advance}}{\text{100 percent stock advance}} \times \frac{\text{50 percent stock decline}}{\text{Percent warrant decline}}$$

$$= \frac{200}{100} \times \frac{50}{71.5} = 1.4$$

Although a ratio of 1.4 indicates a positive advantage for the warrant over its underlying common stock, sophisticated warrant buyers will normally search out situations that offer even greater advantages.

Undervalued warrants

Undervalued warrants offer unique opportunities for spectacular capital gains. An undervalued warrant may advance several times faster than its common stock during a bull market move while declining only modestly more than its common on the downside.

Consider a warrant that should be selling on the normal value curve at the top of band 5, as in the previous example, but is actually trading at a price 18 percent lower ($W/E = 0.414 \times 0.82 = 0.34$). Assuming that this undervalued condition is temporary, let us determine what performance can be expected if the warrant returns to its normal value after either an advance of 100 percent or a decline of 50 percent by its common, as in the previous example.

Upside gain   = 260 percent (from 0.34 up to W/E of 1.236)
Downside loss =   65 percent (from 0.34 down to W/E of 0.118)
$$\text{Mathematical advantage} = \frac{260}{100} \times \frac{50}{65} = 2.0$$

Given the above undervalued warrant opportunity, the aggressive investor would purchase the warrant instead of the common. A more conservative investor, one who recognizes the importance of preserving capital in declining markets for long-term investment success, might apportion his investment funds equally between warrants and cash as a prudent alternative to investing in the common stock. Potential results from a $10,000 investment in the common stock versus warrants and cash in equal amounts, assuming that the stock either advanced 100 percent or declined 50 percent in 12 months, are presented in the following table. Commissions are excluded to simplify the calculations.

	Stock price move	
	−50%	+100%
Stock position		
Upside capital gain = $10,000 × 100%............		$10,000
Downside capital loss = $10,000 × 50%............	($5,000)	
Dividends received................................	0	0
Net profit or (loss)...............................	($5,000)	$10,000
Return on investment............................	− 50%	+100%
Warrant/cash position		
Upside capital gain = $5,000 × 260%............		$13,000
Downside capital loss = $5,000 × 65%.............	($3,250)	
Interest received = $5,000 × 8%..............	400	400
Net profit or (loss)...............................	($2,850)	$13,400
Return on investment............................	−28.5%	+134%

EXHIBIT 9-4: General guides for buying warrants

1. Warrants should be evaluated only as an alternative investment to their common stock. Be sure you have studied and like the stock before buying the warrant.

2. Warrants should be long term (three years or more) to minimize the downward price pressure caused by an approaching expiration date.

3. The warrant should provide an advantage over purchase of the common—greater potential upside reward that more than compensates for the expected higher downside risk. Application of the normal value curves and leverage lines previously illustrated will help to assure that the warrant is fairly priced. A mathematical advantage, or risk/reward ratio, may be calculated as follows:

$$MA = \frac{\text{Percent warrant advance}}{100\,\text{percent stock advance}} \times \frac{50\,\text{percent stock decline}}{\text{Percent warrant decline}}$$

A ratio in excess of 1.0 would indicate a positive advantage but 1.5 would be considered a more desirable ratio to compensate for other disadvantages of warrant owner-ship (look for an even higher ratio if the stock pays a large dividend or is relatively stable).

4. Never purchase an overpriced warrant simply for its upside leverage—there are superior ways to obtain leverage if desired, i.e., buying the common stock on margin.

5. Unless you are a skilled trader, do not buy warrants on margin. Your equity could be totally eliminated in a bear market. In fact, it is recommended that a cash reserve be retained to permit bargain hunting after major market declines.

6. Be prepared to close out the position, even at a loss, when the warrant's life is only about two years—an approaching expiration date may seriously affect the warrant's price.

7. Sell the warrant if it becomes mathematically overpriced, even if the common stock has not changed appreciably. The funds should be switched into the common or used in another warrant having more favorable risk/reward characteristics.

8. All other factors being equal, select warrants that are listed on a major stock exchange and are also actively traded.

9. Since warrants are generally volatile securities, they should not be bought and then forgotten. The price action of both the warrant and its common stock should be watched weekly or even more frequently for maximum success.

10. The warrant certificates should be kept in street name at your brokerage firm to permit prompt action when the circumstances require it.

EXHIBIT 9-5: **Warrants having common stocks listed on the New York Stock Exchange (excluding real estate investment trusts)**

	Where traded	Exercise terms			Expiration date	Usable senior security	Notes
		Number of shares	Total dollars	Effective to			
APL Corp...................	OTC	1.000	14.00	12/31/88	12/31/88		
A-T-O Corp.................	PAC	1.000	35.00	10/15/78	10/15/78		
Alleghany Corp.............	ASE	1.000	3.75	perpetual	none		
Allied Products.............	OTC	1.000	58.00	7/01/83	7/01/83	7.0-84	
Amax Inc...................	ASE	1.000	47.50	10/01/77	10/01/77	see note	1
American Motors Corp.......	OTC	1.050	12.00	10/01/76	10/01/76		
Atlantic Richfield...........	ASE	1.000	127.50	12/31/76	12/31/76		
Atlas Corp..................	ASE	1.000	6.25	perpetual	none	$1.00 Pfd.	2
Avco Corp..................	NYS	1.000	56.00	11/30/78	11/30/78	7.5-93	
Bangor Punta...............	ASE	1.038	55.00	3/31/81	3/31/81		3
Braniff International Corp....	ASE	3.183	73.00	12/01/86	12/01/86	5.75-86	
Brown Co...................	ASE	1.000	16.50	5/15/80	5/15/80	9.0-95	
Budget Industries............	PAC	1.100	14.00	10/31/79	11/01/83	see note	4
			17.00	10/31/81			
			20.00	11/01/83			
CMI Investment.............	ASE	1.000	31.75	8/28/76	8/28/76		5
Carrier Corp................	ASE	1.000	27.33	7/15/76	7/15/76		
Chris-Craft.................	PAC	1.053	25.00	6/01/79	6/01/79	10.0-85	
Chrysler Corp...............	NYS	1.000	34.00	5/15/76	5/15/76		
Commonwealth Edison "A"..	NYS	1.000	30.00	4/30/81	none		6
Commonwealth Edison "B"..	NYS	1.000	30.00	4/30/81	none		6
Continental Telephone.......	ASE	1.040	22.41	11/05/76	11/05/76		
Delta Airlines...............	OTC	1.000	48.00	5/01/78	5/01/78		
Diversified Industries........	ASE	1.000	9.25	7/15/76	7/15/76		
Dreyfus Corp...............	OTC	1.000	45.00	8/25/79	8/25/79		
E-Systems..................	OTC	0.520	21.35	8/15/78	8/15/78		
Fibreboard Corp.............	ASE	1.000	22.50	12/01/78	12/01/78		
Fuqua Industries............	OTC	1.000	50.00	12/31/77	12/31/80		7
			55.00	12/31/80			
General Development........	NYS	1.020	28.25	7/15/78	7/15/78		
General Host...............	PAC	1.000	40.00	1/31/79	1/31/79	7.0-94	
Goodrich, B. F.............	ASE	1.000	30.00	8/15/79	8/15/79		
Gould Inc..................	ASE	1.000	36.67	6/30/76	6/30/76		
Greyhound.................	NYS	1.000	23.50	5/14/80	5/14/80		
Gulf & Western Industries....	NYS	1.136	27.50	1/31/78	1/31/78		
ITEL.......................	OTC	1.115	29.00	1/15/79	1/15/79	6.75-89	
Kane Miller.................	ASE	1.250	24.25	1/15/80	1/15/80		
LTV Corp..................	ASE	2.018	115.00	1/15/78	1/15/78		

EXHIBIT 9–5 *(continued)*

	Where traded	*Number of shares*	*Total dollars*	*Effective to*	*Expiration date*	*Usable senior security*	*Notes*

	Where traded	*Number of shares*	*Total dollars*	*Effective to*	*Expiration date*	*Usable senior security*	*Notes*
LTV Corp...............	OTC	1.109	40.00	1/15/78	1/15/78		
LTV Corp...............	OTC	0.666	37.50	4/01/79	4/01/79		8
Loews Corp............	ASE	1.000	37.50	11/29/76	11/29/80	6.875–93	
			40.00	11/29/80			
Louisiana Land & Exploration............	ASE	1.000	40.50	6/15/76	6/15/76		9
McCrory Corp..........	ASE	1.000	20.00	3/15/76	3/15/81		10
			22.50	3/15/81			
Molycorp..............	ASE	1.000	15.00	4/07/77	4/07/77		
NVF Co...............	PAC	8.600	21.95	1/31/79	1/31/79	5.0–94	
National Industries Inc......	ASE	1.000	21.40	10/31/78	10/31/78		
North Central Airlines.......	NYS	1.000	5.50	10/31/79	10/31/79		
Northwest Industries........	NYS	1.000	25.00	3/31/79	3/31/79	7.5–94	
Occidental Petroleum........	NYS	1.000	16.25	4/22/80	4/22/80		11
PSA Inc...............	ASE	1.000	23.40	10/01/77	10/01/77	6.0–87	
Penn Dixie Industries........	ASE	1.081	8.00	5/01/78	5/01/83		
			11.00	5/01/83			
Rapid-American Corp........	ASE	1.000	35.00	5/15/94	5/15/94	7.5–85	12
Reliance Group Inc..........	OTC	1.000	15.86	7/01/87	7/01/87	5.75–87	
Reliance Group Inc..........	ASE	1.000	32.07	6/04/78	6/04/78		
Standard Prudential..........	ASE	1.000	15.00	12/31/83	12/31/83		13
Telex Corp.............	ASE	1.000	11.00	11/01/76	11/01/76		
Tenneco Inc............	ASE	1.070	32.17	4/01/79	4/01/79	6.0–79	
Tesoro Petroleum Corp.......	ASE	1.000	13.80	8/24/76	8/24/76		
Textron Inc.............	ASE	1.000	10.00	5/01/79	5/01/84		
			11.25	5/01/84			
USM Corp.............	OTC	1.073	39.00	7/24/82	7/24/82	see note	14
UV Industries Inc..........	ASE	1.065	44.00	1/15/79	1/15/79		
United Brands Co..........	OTC	2.000	69.00	3/01/78	3/01/78	6.75–88	
United Brands Co..........	ASE	1.000	46.00	2/01/79	2/01/79		
United Telecommunications..	NYS	1.030	17.44	4/14/77	4/14/77		
Ward Foods............	ASE	1.050	60.00	1/02/79	1/02/79		
Warner Communications.....	ASE	1.000	37.00	1/08/80	1/08/80		15
Webb (Del E.) Corp.........	OTC	1.000	6.25	12/01/76	12/01/76		
Western Pacific Industries....	ASE	1.000	20.50	1/10/77	1/10/77		
Whittaker Corp...........	ASE	1.000	50.00	5/05/79	5/05/79		

Caution: The following notes pertain to normal factors that may affect the warrant's exercise terms. They do not include matters relating to a company's right (or intention) to extend the warrant's life or to reduce its exercise price. The extent of dilution protection against stock dividends, spin-offs, and other possible adjustments are also excluded.

EXHIBIT 9–5 *(concluded)*

Notes:

1. The use of the Amax price adjustment certificate (OTC) will reduce the exercise price by $5.00 to $42.50. In addition, the 8.0–86 bond is usable at 92.6 percent of par.

2. The $1.00 preferred stock (OTC) is usable at its $20 par value in lieu of cash for exercising the warrant.

3. The warrant is callable at $57.09. Company may also permit the use of certain debt securities at market in lieu of cash.

4. The 6.0–88 bond is usable at par in lieu of cash after 11/1/78.

5. The American Stock Exchange banned additional short sales of the warrant after 6/24/74.

6. The warrant is alternately convertible into 0.333 shares of common at any time without payment, even after the conventional warrant terms expire on 4/30/81.

7. The warrant is callable at $50.

8. The warrant trades as Jones & Laughlin Industries warrant.

9. The warrant trades as Amerada Hess-Louisiana Land.

10. Under a proposed merger into Rapid-American, each warrant would become an option to buy 0.5 shares of Rapid-American at the indicated exercise prices.

11. During the 90-day period ending 3/23/80, the company specifically reserves the right to extend the warrant life up to five years if common stock price does not exceed 110 percent of the exercise price; each unexercised warrant will be exchanged for 0.01 shares of common stock at expiration.

12. The warrant is callable at $20. Note that the usability of the bonds expires on 5/15/85 when the bonds mature.

13. The warrant is callable at $20.

14. Nine percent loan stock '82 is usable at par in lieu of cash.

15. Warrant is identified as $0.05 preferred C. The warrant is alternately convertible into one share of common for 15 warrants. The warrant is callable at $2.50 after 7/7/79.

EXHIBIT 9–6: Bonds usable in lieu of cash for exercising warrants

	Description	Where traded	Issue size (in millions)	Percent usable*	Notes
Allied Products...............	7.0 –84	NYS	$ 14	+76	
Amax Inc....................	8.0 –86	NYS	74	+53	1
Avco Corp...................	7.5 –93	NYS	77	−45	
Braniff International Corp.....	5.75 –86	NYS	49	+71	
Brown Co....................	9.0 –95	PAC	11	−62	2
Chris-Craft..................	10.0 –85	PAC	5	−18	
General Host.................	7.0 –94	NYS	77	−29	
ITEL........................	6.75 –89	OTC	14	+65	3
Loews.......................	6.875–93	NYS	394	+60	
NVF Co.....................	5.0 –94	ASE	83	+ 7	
Northwest Industries..........	7.5 –94	NYS	33	+40	
PSA Inc.....................	6.0 –87	NYS	21	+48	
Rapid-American Corp.........	7.5 –85	NYS	76	−53	
Reliance Group Inc............	5.75 –87	ASE	12	+94	4
Tenneco Inc..................	6.0 –79	NYS	100	+80	
United Brands Co.............	6.75 –88	NYS	29	+69	

* Is the usable bond issue large enough for exercise of the entire warrant issue? + means yes, − means no. The number following + gives the percentage of the bond issue required for full exercise of the warrant issue. The number following − gives the percentage of the warrant issue that can be exercised by using the full bond issue.

Notes:
1. Bonds are usable at 92.6 percent of par.
2. Bonds are traded flat since interest may be paid in common stock in lieu of cash.
3. Bonds are identified as ITEL Computer Leasing.
4. Bonds are identified as Leasco Capital Equipment.

chapter 10
Hedging undervalued warrants

As demonstrated in chapter 9, a conservative technique for taking advantage of an undervalued warrant is to apportion your investment funds equally between the warrant and cash. This tactic permits better performance during a rising market than owning the common stock, while significantly reducing downside risk. However, the combination investment of undervalued warrants and cash, while superior to the purchase of the common stock, does not make the most efficient use of one's capital. Only a portion of the investment funds are placed in the favorably leveraged security—the undervalued warrant. The balance is held in a passive cash position. The safest, and most profitable, long-term strategy is the warrant hedge.

THE WARRANT HEDGE

A warrant hedge simply involves the short sale of common stock against a warrant. Like the convertible hedger in chapter 3, the warrant hedger plans to take advantage of the undervalued warrant without exposing his investment capital to unnecessary risk. Also like the convertible hedger, the warrant hedger prefers that the underlying common stock pay no dividend and have a history of high price volatility. The warrant hedger, however, is not even concerned that the company may be a potential bankruptcy candidate as his hedge will protect him fully from such a catastrophe.

In a rising market, the profits secured from the favorably leveraged warrant are expected to exceed losses on the common stock sold short—by a significant amount. In a declining market, it would be expected that profits received from the short sale of common would partially or even completely offset losses on the warrants held long. This strategy permits the conservative investor to be fully invested in the warrant without having a portion of his capital tied up in an inactive cash position. Also, like in a convertible hedge, no funds or other collateral are required to be held in deposit on the short sale of stock against a warrant.

Let us examine a possible warrant hedge position for the same undervalued warrant discussed in chapter 9 having the following characteristics:

> Upside leverage................... 2.6
> Downside leverage.................0.65
> Mathematical advantage........... 2.0

Our entire $10,000 investment will be utilized to purchase warrants—no cash will be retained. Against this $10,000 investment on the long side, we will sell short $13,000 worth of common stock. Since no additional collateral is needed for the short sale, our net investment, unleveraged, is only $10,000. Excluding brokerage commissions, as in the previous example, the results in the accompanying table are anticipated.

Compare this hedge position with the alternate unhedged investments presented in chapter 9.

Presto—as if by magic—the warrant hedge position eliminated

	Stock price move	
	−50%	*+100%*
Warrant hedge position		
Downside		
Profit on stock sold short = \$13,000 × 50% = \$6,500		
Loss on warrants = \$10,000 × 65% = (6,500)		
Upside		
Profit on warrants = \$10,000 × 260% =		\$26,000
Loss on stock sold short = \$13,000 × 100% =		(13,000)
Net profit or (loss)............................ \$	0	\$13,000
Return on investment.........................	0%	+130%

	Stock price move	
	−50%	*+100%*
Common stock..............................	−50%	+100%
Undervalued warrant/50 percent cash..........	−28%	+134%
Undervalued warrant hedge position...........	− 0%	+130%

downside risk while actually outperforming ownership of the common stock on the upside.

Chapters could be written about the theoretical ramifications of hedging undervalued warrants. However, it is believed that an actual case history will best serve to illustrate the numerous techniques and factors involved. Fortunately for review purposes, this example also includes the majority of skills required for evaluating warrants as discussed in the previous chapter.

AN ACTUAL WARRANT HEDGE POSITION IN LTV

In January 1969, LTV's common stock was trading on the New York Stock Exchange at \$100 per share, having declined from its high of \$169. Numerous investment advisory services and brokerage firms were recommending purchase at that time. However, few of these "professionals" were aware of vastly superior alternatives to the conventional purchase of LTV common stock.

LTV warrants were concurrently trading on the American Stock Exchange at $42 each. These warrants were the option to purchase 1.113 shares of LTV stock for $115 until their January 1978 expiration date. The LTV 5s–88 bonds were usable at par value in lieu of cash for conversion purposes through January 15, 1973, and were selling at 60.

At prices of $100 and $42 for the common and warrant, the "speculative" warrant was a far superior purchase. Like all undervalued warrants, it offered unique investment opportunities compared to purchase of its underlying common stock. A step-by-step evaluation of possible *hedge* positions in LTV warrants would have proceeded in the following manner.

1. *Warrant life.* The warrant life was considered to be long term, even though the usable bonds were effective for a shorter time than the warrant expiration date—the bonds were usable at par value for conversion purposes for a period of four years.

2. *S/E and W/E calculations.* Following the procedures presented in chapter 9, calculations were:

$$\text{Adjusted warrant price} = \$42.00 \div 1.113 = \$37.74$$
$$\text{Effective exercise price} = \$115.00 \times 60/100 = \$69.00$$
$$\text{Adjusted exercise price} = \$69.00 \div 1.113 = \$62.00$$
$$S/E = \$100.00 \div \$62.00 = 1.61$$
$$W/E = \$37.74 \div \$62.00 = 0.61$$

The S/E and W/E factors are plotted on Exhibit 10–1 and we were elated to discover that the warrants were selling right on their conversion value line! Since the yield on LTV common was only 1.3 percent, these warrants were trading at a discount of approximately 30 percent from their normal value (band 5). In addition, the price volatility and speculative appeal of LTV enhanced the attraction of a warrant hedge. A very fortunate opportunity was presented to alert, sophisticated investors.

EXHIBIT 10-1:   Warrant in January 1969

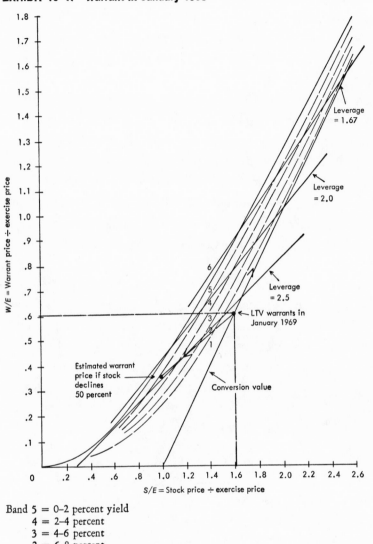

Band 5 = 0–2 percent yield
    4 = 2–4 percent
    3 = 4–6 percent
    2 = 6–8 percent
    1 = above 8 percent
Note: Area 6 represents all warrants above band 5.

3. *Consideration given to the 5s–88 bonds.*   The LTV bonds, trading at 60, were obviously speculative—well below investment grade caliber. Disregarding possible changes in money rates, we could expect them to fluctuate in price somewhat in harmony with the common stock. Stock price changes would certainly reflect the future prospects for LTV and accordingly its ability to meet bond interest payments. We would, therefore, have considered bond price changes in our future price projections and would have assigned bond prices of, say, 50 and 70 in the event the stock declined 50 percent or advanced 100 percent, respectively.

4. *Warrant price estimate if stock declined 50 percent.*   Due to the speculative nature of LTV common and the long warrant life, it would have been reasonable to expect that the warrant would have sold at its normal value rating if the stock dropped 50 percent to $50 per share. If LTV maintained the $1.33 dividend on its common stock, the normal value rating would have been band 4. If the dividend were passed, a reasonable possibility if the stock price were to drop in half, band 5 would have been the normal value rating for the LTV warrant. A conservative assumption would have been that the warrant would have sold at the top of band 4, in which case calculations to determine the warrant's probable price would have been:

Effective exercise price $= \$115.00 \times 50/100 = \$57.50$
Adjusted exercise price $= \$57.50 \div 1.113   = \$51.66$
$S/E = \$50.00 \div \$51.66 = 0.97$
W/E from Exhibit 10–1 $= 0.35$
Adjusted warrant price $= 0.35 \times \$51.66   = \$18.08$
Estimated warrant price $= \$18.08 \times 1.113   = \$20.00$

Note that the above steps are the reverse of the normal procedures for determining whether a warrant is fairly valued based on current price levels. In this case we are estimating the warrant's price after a major move by the common stock.

5. *Warrant price estimate if stock advanced 100 percent.* Assuming that the warrant would remain at its conversion value on a price rise by the common stock to $200 per share, calculations would have been:

Effective exercise price   = $115.00 × 70/100 = $80.50
Adjusted exercise price   = $80.50 ÷ 1.113   = $72.33
S/E = $200.00 ÷ $72.33 = 2.77
W/E at conversion value = 1.77
Adjusted warrant price   = 1.77 × $72.33   = $128.00
Estimated warrant price = $128.00 × 1.113   = $142.00

6. *Leverage projections.* Leverage calculations and a determination of the mathematical advantage of the LTV warrant confirmed the initial conclusion that the warrant was substantially undervalued.

Upside leverage = ($142.00 − $42.00) ÷ $42.00 = 2.38
Downside leverage = ($42.00 − $20.00) ÷ $42.00 = 0.52
$$\text{Mathematical advantage} = \frac{2.38}{1.00} \times \frac{0.50}{0.52} = 2.3$$

Upon completion of the above analysis of the LTV warrant, the investor would have had several choices as to how to best take advantage of the situation. Depending on the investor's objective and his opinion of future prospects for LTV, a variety of different hedge positions could have been evaluated. For example, consider the following two alternatives:

Bullish hedge—profits on the upside at little or no downside risk.

Bearish hedge—profits on the downside at little or no upside risk.

Assuming the purchase of $10,000 worth of warrants and excluding brokerage commissions and dividends on the stock sold short, anticipated performance results for these alternate hedge positions are shown in the table below.

	Stock price move	
	−50%	+100%
Bullish hedge: Stock sold short = $10,400		
Downside		
Profit on stock sold short = $10,400 × 50% = $ 5,200		
Loss on warrants = $10,000 × 52% = (5,200)		
Upside		
Profit on warrants = $10,000 × 238% =		$23,800
Loss on stock sold short = $10,400 × 100% =		(10,400)
Net profit or (loss)............................ $	0	$13,400
Return on investment.........................	0%	+134%
Bearish hedge: Stock sold short = $23,800		
Downside		
Profit on stock sold short = $23,800 × 50% = $11,900		
Loss on warrants = $10,000 × 52% = (5,200)		
Upside		
Profit on warrants = $10,000 × 238% =		$23,800
Loss on stock sold short = $23,800 × 100% =		(23,800)
Net profit or (loss)............................ $ 6,700		$ 0
Return on investment.........................	+67%	0%

As shown above, the bullish hedge offered a 134 percent potential gain at no estimated downside risk—heads you win but tails you don't lose! The bearish hedge offered a 67 percent downside potential at no estimated upside risk—tails you win but heads you don't lose!

Conclusion of the LTV story

As was painfully evident to buyers of LTV common stock in January 1969 at $100 per share, or to those who later purchased the stock at even lower prices, the stock quickly dropped like a one-way elevator to about $10 per share in December 1970. It was still trading in the area of $10 over five years later. Those who held LTV stock during this debacle suffered a 90 percent loss on their capital. Those speculators who had purchased LTV common on margin saw their equity completely evaporate long before the stock hit bottom. However, sophisticated investors who established hedge positions in the LTV warrants would have lost nothing or even enjoyed profits, depending on the specific hedge and how long it was held.

A BASIC SYSTEM FOR HEDGING
UNDERVALUED WARRANTS

My first book, *The Dow Jones-Irwin Guide to Convertible Securities,*[1] presented a mechanical system for hedging undervalued warrants and applied these procedures to a six-year investment period from 1967 through 1972. This basic system will be summarized here.

Procedures for evaluating, establishing, and maintaining hedge positions

1. Only listed warrants were considered since it was felt that historical price data available on over-the-counter warrants, many of which were not actively traded, were of questionable accuracy. Also, most OTC securities have small floating supplies; thus they cannot accept large amounts of capital without significantly affecting their price levels. It was believed, therefore, that the study, being limited to listed warrants only, would provide a more accurate documentation of historical performance as well as a better indication of future profit potential for warrant hedging.

2. All warrants must be long term to receive consideration— a life to expiration of three years or more. Exercise terms prevailing three years hence would be used for calculation purposes where the warrant terms were scheduled to be changed in the interim.

---

[1] Thomas C. Noddings, *The Dow Jones-Irwin Guide to Convertible Securities* (Homewood, Ill.: Dow Jones-Irwin, 1973).

3. Warrants would be purchased when they were computed to be undervalued in relation to their common stock, regardless of anyone's good or bad opinion on the prospects for the common.

4. Only warrants having normal value bands of 4 or 5 were considered so as to minimize the cost of dividends paid on the stock sold short. This limitation also improved the probability of the common stock having high price volatility —an important characteristic of a successful hedge program.

5. Undervalued warrants were defined as those trading in a rating band one or more levels below their normal value band. If there was a usable bond selling at an excessive discount, alternate calculations would be based on a more representative higher bond price, assuming improved prospects for the company.

6. Upside leverage for the warrant had to equal or exceed 2.0, as determined from leverage lines previously shown on the normal value curves.

7. The amount of common stock sold short was to be 130 percent of the market value of the warrants purchased. This 1.3 ratio was established to provide an approximate break-even position in declining markets. This bullish ratio offered the highest probability for profits over a market cycle, as was shown for bullish convertible hedges in chapter 3.

8. Positions would be closed out if the warrants became overpriced or if their upside leverage was reduced to below 1.67. Positions would also be closed if the remaining warrant life was reduced to less than two years.

9. Warrants were evaluated and specific buy, hold, and sell decisions were made only once every six months—January and July of each year. By limiting the study to six-month intervals, I believed it would contribute to more conserva-

tive results and also be of meaningful value to those investors unable to monitor their portfolios on a continual basis.

10. It was assumed that at the end of each six-month period portfolio adjustments would have been made so that all positions represented an equal portion of the portfolio and the short-to-long ratio would be 1.3 for each position. These adjustments were necessary to assure that performance for the subsequent six-month period would not be distorted by prior results.

11. To assure a realistic study, deductions were made in the profit and loss calculations for applicable investment expenses—commissions, margin interest, and dividends paid on stock sold short.

12. The six-year study evaluated performance results based both on the purchase of the warrants for cash and on margin as will be shown.

Specific buy, hold, and sell actions

1. *Establish* hedge positions when:
   a. Warrants are undervalued *and*
   b. Upside leverage is greater than 2.0 *and*
   c. Warrant life exceeds three years.
2. *Hold* hedge positions when:
   a. Warrants are normally valued *and*
   b. Upside leverage is greater that 1.67 *and*
   c. Warrant life exceeds two years.
3. *Close out* hedge positions when:
   a. Warrants become overpriced *or*
   b. Upside leverage is less than 1.67 *or*
   c. Warrant life is less than two years.

Anticipated performance in different types of markets

Prior to application of the above procedures to the six-year test period, it will be of interest to review the anticipated performance results for different stock market conditions which we can expect to encounter. Cash purchase of the warrants is assumed.

Declining markets. During broad declining markets, similar to the 1969–70 collapse, we would expect the equity in the account to remain relatively constant because profits on the short sales would offset warrant losses. However, since the short positions are marked to the market (paper profits are credited to the account), buying power is developed as the security prices fall. Additional investments would be established with this surplus buying power. Also, since the warrants are expected to decline at a faster rate than the common stock, short positions will be periodically reduced, or additional warrants purchased, to maintain the 1.3 short-to-long ratio.

To illustrate the above points, consider the following hedge position for a warrant having the previously discussed leverage characteristics of 2.6 on the upside and 0.65 on the downside.

Warrants purchased..................... $10,000
Common stock sold short................ $13,000
Equity (investment).................... $10,000

If the common stock and warrants were to decline 50 and 65 percent, respectively, profits on the short side would exactly equal losses on the warrants. Equity would have remained constant at our initial investment of $10,000. The status of our account after this decline, assuming that this was the only position, would be:

Value of warrants held long................ $ 3,500 ($6,500 loss)
Value of common stock sold short............ $ 6,500 ($6,500 profit)
Equity...................................... $10,000 (unchanged)
Credit balance.............................. $ 6,500

Short-to-long ratio = $6,500 ÷ $3,500 = 1.86

If, after this price decline, the warrants were still undervalued in relation to their underlying common stock, additional warrants would be purchased to reestablish the 1.3 ratio of stock sold short to warrants purchased. If the warrants were normally valued at this point, a portion of the short position would be covered instead of buying additional warrants. If the warrants were overpriced, the entire position would be closed out and the funds redeployed in another situation having better risk/reward characteristics.

Advancing markets.   During broad advancing markets, similar to the 1967–68 period, we would anticipate an increase in our account's equity because warrant profits would be expected to exceed losses on the common stock sold short. Since the popularity of various stock groups rotates during bull markets, our portfolio of hedged investments will naturally do best when the secondary and speculative stocks, which we prefer for warrant hedging, are in favor. As the short positions are marked to the market on the upside, our account would be debited with the paper losses. We would, therefore, plan to reduce our positions to offset the buildup of a debit balance. Also, since the warrants are expected to advance faster than the common stock, short positions will be periodically increased, or warrants sold, to maintain the 1.3 short-to-long ratio.

Consider again the previous hedge position based on the common stock and warrants advancing 100 percent and 260 percent, respectively. Our equity would have increased by $13,000 ($26,000 — $13,000) and the status of our account would be:

Value of warrants held long...................... $36,000 ($26,000 profit)
Value of common stock sold short................ $26,000 ($13,000 loss)
Equity = $10,000 + $13,000 profit................ $23,000
Debit balance.................................... $13,000

Short-to-long ratio = $26,000 ÷ $36,000 = 0.72

If, after this price advance, the warrants were still undervalued, additional common stock would be sold short to reestablish the 1.3 ratio. If the warrants were normally valued, a portion of the warrants would be sold instead of shorting more stock. If they became overpriced, the total position would be closed out.

Sideways markets. This is the most unpredictable and difficult type of market for the warrant hedger to encounter. By periodically adding to or reducing short sales as required to maintain the 1.3 ratio, some profits may be obtained if the price swings of individual positions are broad enough to permit these trades. From the negative aspect, it is possible to experience a slow decline in the account's equity resulting from dividends paid on stock sold short and a decline in warrant values as time passes, depending on the time remaining to their expiration date. Probably the most important variable is whether speculative securities are in favor or not during the period that the overall market is in the sideways movement. If they are in favor, there will most likely be sufficient market action to produce some profits. If they are not, as they were not during the 1971–72 period, it will probably be a very dull and disappointing market for the warrant hedger.

The following pages demonstrate how the mechanical hedging system would have performed during the six-year period between 1967 and 1972—a period in the stock market's history that includes each of the typical types of markets discussed above, and a period when most everyone had difficulty achieving satisfactory profits from their equity investments.

THE SIX-YEAR STUDY

The Dow Jones-Irwin Guide To Convertible Securities documented all warrants that were possible candidates for hedging beginning in January 1967. *S/E* and *W/E* calculations were made for each in accordance with previously established procedures.

Each warrant was assigned a normal value band based on its common stock yield. Its actual value band was then determined by plotting its S/E and W/E factors on the normal value curves and noting into which band those factors fell. Buy, hold, and sell decisions were made by applying the mechanical rules previously developed.

There were only seven warrants available for consideration in January 1967. During the ensuing years, increased warrant popularity swelled the selection list to 40 by mid-1970. At that time, numerous nonconglomerate-type companies began using imaginative financing arrangements in an effort to reduce the excessive cost of borrowing brought about by the historically high interest rates prevailing at the time. Other companies also found warrants to be a helpful aid in their new equity financing.

Summary of all positions taken during the six-year study

Exhibit 10–2 presents a summary of all positions established during the six-year study. A few pertinent conclusions may be drawn.

1. The chance that a warrant will become overpriced is greatest during a major market decline as most speculators apparently place excessive values on "cheap" warrants.

2. An undervalued warrant will generally remain undervalued as its common stock advances. A hedge position will not normally be closed out on the upside until its leverage is reduced to the point where little more can be gained by holding the position (the 1.67 leverage line).

3. Most warrants will decline at a greater percentage rate than their common stocks, thus confirming the need for excess short selling to preserve capital (the 1.3 short-to-long ratio).

EXHIBIT 10–2:   Positions taken in undervalued warrents (January 1967 through January 1973)

Warrant	Date purchased	Date closed	Months held	Stock gain or loss	Warrant gain or loss	Reason position was closed*
Hilton Hotels.....................	1/67	1/69	24	+319	+1115	A
Uris Buildings...................	1/67	1/68	12	+105	+ 271	A
Realty Equities..................	7/67	7/68	12	+104	+ 228	A
Braniff Airways..................	7/68	7/69	12	− 37	− 42	C
Gulf & Western Industries.........	1/69	7/69	6	− 49	− 54	C
Ling-Temco-Vought Corp.........	1/69	1/70	12	− 72	− 82	C
McCrory Corp....................	1/69	1/71	24	− 51	− 68	C
Wilson & Co.....................	1/69	7/70	18	− 76	− 76	C
General Host....................	7/69	1/70	6	− 40	− 38	C
National General................	7/69	1/70	6	− 35	− 26	C
Gould Inc.......................	1/70	7/70	6	− 36	− 44	C
Kaufman & Broad................	1/70	7/71	18	+ 29	+ 84	A
Kinney National Services†.........	1/70		36+			
Loew's Theatres.................	1/70	7/70	6	− 46	− 50	C
Continental Telephone............	1/71	1/73	24	+ 2	− 29	E
Loews..........................	1/71		24+			
Daylin Inc......................	7/71		18+			
Gould Inc.......................	7/71		18+			
General Development.............	1/72	1/73	12	− 47	− 56	C
Louisiana Land & Exploration.....	1/72		12+			
National General................	1/72		12+			
Carrier Corp....................	7/72		6+			

* A.   Warrant leverage was reduced to below 1.67 on an upside move.
  B.   Warrant became overpriced on an upside move.
  C.   Warrant became overpriced on a downside move.
  D.   Warrant became overpriced on a sideways move.
  E.   Warrant life remaining was less than two years.
† Present name is Warner Communications.

4.   The vast majority of hedge positions were held for a year or longer, indicating that patience is required for warrant hedging as in other long-term investment programs.

5.   Warrants closed out on the upside increased in percentage by more than twice as much as the increase of their common stocks as we had anticipated—even though they remained undervalued during the advance.

PERFORMANCE RESULTS FROM
THE BASIC SYSTEM

Exhibit 10–3 presents performance data for the warrants and their common stocks for each of the 12 six-month periods during the six-year study from January 1967 to January 1973. Gains or losses for each warrant and stock were determined, and average gains or losses were calculated on the basis that equal amounts of each position were held in the portfolio. The following points of interest may be drawn from an analysis of this data.

1. Of the 12 six-month periods, stock prices advanced six times, declined three, and were essentially neutral three times (a neutral or sideways market is arbitrarily defined as one where the common stocks advanced or declined by less than 10 percent during the six-month period). The price movements were in general harmony with stock market averages—especially those that reflect a broad spectrum of stocks, i.e., Value Line's 1,500-stock average.

2. During the nine periods of advancing or declining prices, the warrants advanced or declined on average at greater percentage rates than their common stocks, as expected.

3. During the six periods of rising prices, the common stocks advanced 40 percent on average, while the warrants advanced 80 percent. These relative price increases confirmed our anticipated results for undervalued warrants having upside leverage of 2.0 or higher.

4. During the three periods of falling prices, the common stocks declined 36 percent on average, versus 42 percent for the warrants. Here again the relative price performance was consistent with expected results since, as previously indicated, even undervalued warrants normally possess negative leverage on the downside.

EXHIBIT 10–3: The six-year study—Stock and warrant performance

	Stock prices			Warrant prices		
Position	Begin-ning	End-ing	Percent gain or loss	Begin-ning	End-ing	Percent gain or loss
January–June 1967						
Hilton Hotels................	32.00	59.12	+ 84.8	6.75	19.75	+192.6
Uris Buildings..............	16.25	21.25	+ 30.8	6.12	11.88	+ 93.9
Average gain or loss.......			+ 57.8			+143.2
July–December 1967						
Hilton Hotels..............	59.12	82.50	+ 39.5	19.75	32.12	+ 62.6
Realty Equities.............	12.38	10.00	− 19.2	6.25	6.12	− 2.0
Uris Buildings..............	21.25	33.25	+ 56.5	11.88	22.75	+ 91.6
Average gain or loss.......			+ 25.6			+ 50.7
January–June 1968						
Hilton Hotels................	82.50	104.62	+ 26.8	32.12	58.88	+ 83.3
Realty Equities.............	10.00	25.25	+152.5	6.12	20.50	+234.7
Average gain or loss.......			+ 89.6			+159.0
July–December 1968						
Braniff Airways.............	22.88	21.88	− 4.4	28.50	28.50	0
Hilton Hotels..............	104.62	134.00	+ 28.1	58.88	82.00	+ 39.3
Average gain or loss.......			+ 11.8			+ 19.6
January–June 1969						
Braniff Airways.............	21.88	14.50	− 33.7	28.50	16.50	− 42.1
Gulf & Western Industries....	51.25	26.25	− 48.8	18.12	8.25	− 54.5
Ling-Temco-Vought Corp....	98.00	40.00	− 59.2	41.25	13.12	− 68.2
McCrory Corp..............	36.00	24.25	− 32.6	16.25	8.88	− 46.1
Wilson & Co................	37.12	24.25	− 34.7	13.75	6.88	− 50.0
Average gain or loss.......			− 41.8			− 52.2
July–December 1969						
General Host................	24.00	14.50	− 39.6	5.62	3.50	− 37.8
Ling-Temco-Vought Corp....	40.00	27.00	− 32.5	13.12	7.62	− 41.9
McCrory Corp..............	24.25	23.75	− 2.1	8.88	7.62	− 14.1
National General...........	29.62	19.38	− 34.6	8.62	6.38	− 26.1
Wilson & Co................	24.25	19.75	− 18.6	6.88	5.25	− 23.6
Average gain or loss.......			− 25.5			− 28.7
January–June 1970						
Gould Inc..................	36.75	23.50	− 36.1	8.50	4.75	− 44.1
Kaufman & Broad...........	49.00	32.12	− 34.4	22.25	13.88	− 37.6
Kinney National Services....	30.25	21.88	− 29.3	8.75	5.50	− 37.1
Loew's Theatres............	37.38	20.00	− 46.3	16.00	8.00	− 50.0
McCrory Corp..............	23.75	15.38	− 35.3	7.62	3.50	− 54.1
Wilson & Co................	19.75	8.88	− 55.1	5.25	3.25	− 38.1
Average gain or loss.......			− 39.4			− 43.5
July–December 1970						
Kaufman & Broad...........	32.12	44.75	+ 39.3	13.88	23.75	+ 71.2
Kinney National Services....	21.38	29.00	+ 35.7	5.50	7.25	+ 31.8
McCrory Corp..............	15.38	17.75	+ 15.4	3.50	5.12	+ 46.4
Average gain or loss.......			+ 30.1			+ 49.8

EXHIBIT 10–3 (continued)

	Stock prices			Warrant prices		
Position	Begin-ning	End-ing	Percent gain or loss	Begin-ning	End-ing	Percent gain or loss
January–June 1971						
Continental Telephone	25.25	23.25	− 7.9	7.75	7.38	− 4.8
Kaufman & Broad	44.75	63.00	+ 40.8	23.75	41.00	+ 72.6
Kinney National Services	29.00	34.25	+ 18.1	7.25	12.25	+ 69.0
Loews	34.88	54.25	+ 55.6	14.00	27.88	+ 99.1
Average gain or loss			+ 26.6			+ 59.0
July–December 1971						
Continental Telephone	23.25	22.38	− 3.8	7.38	6.38	− 13.6
Daylin Inc	21.25	23.75	+ 11.8	7.38	8.25	+ 11.9
Gould Inc	36.25	44.25	+ 22.1	8.62	11.25	+ 30.4
Kinney National Services	34.25	31.25	− 8.8	12.25	9.75	− 20.4
Loews	54.25	46.38	− 14.5	27.88	22.00	− 21.1
Average gain or loss			+ 1.4			− 2.6
January–June 1972						
Continental Telephone	22.38	21.00	− 6.1	6.38	4.88	− 23.5
Daylin Inc	23.75	17.75	− 25.3	8.25	6.00	− 27.3
General Development	25.88	33.25	+ 28.5	9.00	11.88	+ 31.9
Gould Inc	44.25	32.75	− 26.0	11.25	10.75	− 4.4
Kinney National Services	31.25	48.38	+ 54.8	9.75	19.12	+ 96.2
Loews	46.38	53.50	+ 15.4	22.00	23.62	+ 7.4
Louisiana Land & Exploration	51.12	44.75	− 12.5	18.50	14.50	− 21.6
National General	25.00	23.75	− 5.0	6.38	5.88	− 7.8
Average gain or loss			+ 3.0			+ 6.4
July–December 1972						
Carrier Corp	29.50	28.38	− 3.9	9.83	8.25	− 16.1
Continental Telephone	21.00	25.75	+ 22.6	4.88	5.50	+ 12.8
Daylin Inc	17.75	16.25	− 8.5	6.00	4.75	− 20.8
General Development	33.25	13.75	− 58.6	11.88	4.00	− 66.3
Gould Inc	32.75	32.38	− 1.1	10.75	8.38	− 22.1
Loews	53.50	46.75	− 12.6	23.62	18.12	− 23.3
Louisiana Land & Exploration	44.75	43.25	− 3.4	14.50	12.00	− 17.2
National General	23.75	32.75	+ 37.9	5.88	6.50	+ 10.6
Warner Communications*	48.38	36.88	− 23.8	19.12	12.38	− 35.3
Average gain or loss			− 5.7			− 19.7

* Formerly Kinney National Services.

5. From the above performance data, an overall mathematical advantage for the warrants over their common stocks may be computed as follows:

$$MA = \frac{\text{Upside warrant gain}}{\text{Upside stock gain}} \times \frac{\text{downside stock loss}}{\text{downside warrant loss}}$$
$$= \frac{80}{40} \times \frac{36}{42} = 1.7$$

6. During the three periods when prices were neutral, the relative performance between the warrants and common stocks was about as expected except for the last six-month period. During this period, warrants in general were extremely out of favor—they lagged behind when their common stocks advanced and declined appreciably faster when their stocks declined.

As a general conclusion, the actual results were surprisingly consistent with overall market movements and expected relative warrant/stock performance. Also, the six-year period, which included a major bull market, a major bear market, and a market of drifting prices, is probably quite representative of market cycles to be expected in the future. It would seem, therefore, that future predictions based on this study may be made with a high degree of confidence.

COMMON STOCK PERFORMANCE

Exhibit 10–4 shows the gains or losses on investments made in just the common stocks for each of the 12 six-month periods. The cumulative profit or loss column assumes that total equity would have been equally proportioned among the indicated stocks in the portfolio at each six-month interval. As shown by the cumulative profit or loss figures, one would have increased his equity by 79 percent if he had maintained a portfolio of these stocks for the six-year period. This 79 percent appreciation appears to be reason-

EXHIBIT 10–4: The six-year study—Common stock performance

Six-month period	Net profit or loss* (percent)	Cumulative profit or loss (percent)
January–June 1967	+57.8	+ 57.8
July–December 1967	+25.6	+ 98
January–June 1968	+89.6	+276
July–December 1968	+11.8	+320
January–June 1969	−41.8	+145
July–December 1969	−25.5	+ 82
January–June 1970	−39.4	+ 10
July–December 1970	+30.1	+ 44
January–June 1971	+26.6	+ 82
July–December 1971	+ 1.4	+ 84
January–June 1972	+ 3.0	+ 90
July–December 1972	− 5.7	+ 79

* Net profit or loss figures shown were taken from Exhibit 10-3. No deductions were made for commissions paid on stock purchases or sales as it was assumed that they would have been offset by dividends received.

able for a portfolio of speculative and growth securities, selected at random, when considering overall market action during that period of time. It was very close to the average gain for growth-type mutual funds having generally high volatility. It may, therefore, be concluded that the common stocks in our study were fairly representative of the general stock market for speculative and growth-type securities.

WARRANT PERFORMANCE

If investments were made in the warrants only, Exhibit 10–5 shows that equity would have increased by an astounding 284 percent—almost four times that of the common stocks. This vastly superior performance dramatically illustrates the advantages offered by the undervalued warrant. Note, however, that in spite of this exceptional performance, the warrant investor still would have had many sleepless nights. He would have witnessed his equity decline by over 80 percent during the 1969–70 bear

EXHIBIT 10–5:   The six-year study—Warrant performance

Six-month period	Net profit or loss* (percent)	Cumulative profit or loss (percent)
January–June 1967.............	+142.2	+142.2
July–December 1967.............	+ 49.7	+ 263
January–June 1968.............	+158.0	+ 835
July–December 1968.............	+ 18.6	+1009
January–June 1969.............	− 53.2	+ 419
July–December 1969.............	− 29.7	+ 265
January–June 1970.............	− 44.5	+ 103
July–December 1970.............	+ 48.4	+ 201
January–June 1971.............	+ 58.0	+ 376
July–December 1971.............	− 3.6	+ 359
January–June 1972.............	+ 5.4	+ 384
July–December 1972.............	− 20.7	+ 284

* A deduction of 1 percent was made from the figures of Exhibit 10–3 to compensate for commissions that would have been paid for warrant purchases and sales.

market. And how would he have felt if he had started his warrant investment program in January 1969—at the beginning of the decline? He would have still been behind 65 percent four years later, and he would have received little comfort from the fact that his warrant investments had provided mathematical advantages over their common stocks.

WARRANT/CASH PERFORMANCE

It was indicated in chapter 9 that a conservative investor might consider a combined investment of 50 percent warrants and 50 percent cash as a prudent alternative to the common stocks. This approach has considerable merit if one utilizes a constant ratio formula plan. Under this plan, as prices decline, a portion of one's cash position would be transferred to warrants to maintain the 50:50 ratio. As prices rise, some profits would be taken on the warrants and the proceeds retained as cash. The constant ratio formula plan thus assures that profits are taken when prices are high and that additional investments are made when prices are low.

The six-year performance results for this technique are presented in Exhibit 10–6, and it is noted that a warrant/cash investment program would also have substantially outperformed the common stock portfolio—249 percent versus 79 percent for the six-year period.

EXHIBIT 10–6: The six-year study—50 percent warrants and 50 percent cash performance

Six-month period	Net profit or loss* (percent)	Cumulative profit or loss (percent)
January–June 1967	+72.6	+ 72.6
July–December 1967	+26.4	+118
January–June 1968	+80.5	+294
July–December 1968	+10.8	+336
January–June 1969	−25.1	+227
July–December 1969	−13.4	+183
January–June 1970	−20.8	+124
July–December 1970	+25.9	+182
January–June 1971	+30.5	+268
July–December 1971	− 0.3	+267
January–June 1972	+ 4.2	+282
July–December 1972	− 8.8	+249

* The net profit or loss was based on averaging the warrant profit or loss from Exhibit 10–5 with cash earning 6 percent interest.

Exhibit 10–7 compares the common stock and warrant/cash performance results with Value Line's 1,500-stock average for the six-year period. Note how the warrant/cash portfolio closely paralleled the performance of the common stocks during rising markets. Although only half of one's equity was invested in the warrants, their inherent leverage on the upside permitted comparable performance to a 100 percent investment in the common stocks. On the other hand, the 50 percent cash portion of the portfolio limited downside losses compared to the common stocks.

EXHIBIT 10-7: The six-year study—Relative performance

BUYING ON MARGIN

The use of margin—funds borrowed from the stock brokerage firm—is a key tool for improving performance results for a hedge program. Since investing with borrowed funds normally amplifies both profit and loss, could one have improved on the overall favorable results shown for both the common stocks and warrants if he had margined his purchases throughout the six-year test period?

The calculations presented in Exhibits 10–8 and 10–9 show surprising results. Contrary to popular thinking of market speculators, the use of borrowed money to leverage speculative investments is a self-defeating technique. As shown in Exhibit 10–8, the six-year stock performance would have been reduced from the favorable 79 percent appreciation to only 7 percent. Exhibit 10–9

EXHIBIT 10–8: The six-year study—Common stock performance on 70 percent margin

Six-month period	Net profit or loss* (percent)	70 percent margin† profit or loss (percent)	Cumulative profit or loss (percent)
January–June 1967............	+57.8	+ 80.4	+ 80.4
July–December 1967............	+25.6	+ 34.4	+142
January–June 1968............	+89.6	+125.9	+448
July–December 1968............	+11.8	+ 14.7	+528
January–June 1969............	−41.8	− 61.9	+139
July–December 1969............	−25.5	− 38.6	+ 47
January–June 1970............	−39.4	− 58.4	− 39
July–December 1970............	+30.1	+ 40.9	− 14
January–June 1971............	+26.6	+ 35.9	+ 17
July–December 1971............	+ 1.4	− 0.1	+ 17
January–June 1971............	+ 3.0	+ 2.1	+ 19
July–December 1972............	− 5.7	− 10.3	+ 7

* The net profit or loss figures were taken from Exhibit 10–4.

† A deduction of 1.5 percent was made from the net figures, to compensate for margin interest, before determining the profit or loss based on 70 percent margin.

shows that warrant appreciation would have been lowered from 284 percent down to only 53 percent.

These figures assume that at each six-month interval, the account would have been adjusted to the 70 percent margin level. If equity had increased during the previous six months, additional purchases would have been made. If equity had declined, securities would have been sold. Margin purchases, therefore, tend to work opposite to dollar cost averaging. Securities are bought at high price levels and must be sold at depressed prices.

One might argue that on a market decline he would not have sold any securities; thus they would all be working for him on the next upswing in the market. However, to comply with New York Stock Exchange regulations, brokerage firms require a minimum of 30 percent maintenance margin (or higher depending on the securities held). If the equity in the account were to drop to below

EXHIBIT 10-9: The six-year study—Warrant performance on 70 percent margin

Six-month period	Net profit or loss* (percent)	70 percent margin† profit or loss (percent)	Cumulative profit or loss (percent)
January–June 1967	+142.2	+200.3	+ 200.3
July–December 1967	+ 49.7	+ 68.1	+ 405
January–June 1968	+158.0	+222.9	+1530
July–December 1968	+ 18.6	+ 23.7	+1916
January–June 1969	− 53.2	− 78.9	+ 325
July–December 1969	− 29.7	− 45.3	+ 133
January–June 1970	− 44.5	− 66.4	− 22
July–December 1970	+ 48.4	+ 66.9	+ 30
January–June 1971	+ 58.0	+ 80.0	+ 135
July–December 1971	− 3.6	− 8.0	+ 116
January–June 1972	+ 5.4	+ 4.9	+ 127
July–December 1972	− 20.7	− 32.4	+ 53

* The net profit or loss figures were taken from Exhibit 10-5.

† A deduction of 2 percent was made from the net figures before determining the profit or loss based on 70 percent margin. This compensates for extra commission expenses plus margin interest.

30 percent of the market value of the securities, additional cash must be deposited or securities must be sold. During the 1969–70 bear market, the 30 percent equity level would have been quickly penetrated. If the ensuing margin call was handled by a deposit of additional cash instead of selling some securities, the original equity would have been completely wiped out.

When one uses borrowed money for investment purposes, he had better be right in predicting price trends! Or, he should be investing in hedge positions.

WARRANT HEDGE PERFORMANCE—THE BASIC SYSTEM

Calculations for determining the performance results for the warrant hedge investment program are presented in Exhibit 10–10, based on the stock and warrant gains and losses from Exhibit 10–3. The profit or loss for the common stocks during each six-month period was multiplied by a factor of 1.3 to reflect the short-to-long ratio as specified by the mechanical system. During periods of rising prices, the losses experienced on the common stock sold short were deducted from warrant profits. As prices fell, profits were secured from the short sales whereas the warrants produced losses. A 3 percent charge was deducted from the gross profit for each six-month period to compensate for the approximate commissions that would have been paid and for dividends paid on stock sold short. All calculations shown in Exhibit 10–10 assume the use of no leverage—this will be evaluated later. Following is a review of the warrant hedge program for each of the four distinctive market periods experienced during the six-year study.

January 1967–January 1969. The overall stock market produced a major bull market move during this two-year period, as demonstrated by Value Line's 1,500-stock average which advanced nearly 50 percent. As previously illustrated in Exhibit 10–4, a portfolio of the common stocks represented in our warrant hedge positions would have gained 320 percent during this same period —they were obviously much more speculative than the average stock. Along with this strong advance by the common stocks, our warrant hedge positions turned in a very respectable performance gain of 167 percent.

January 1969–July 1970. This was the worst period in the stock market's history since the depression. The blue-chip Dow Jones Industrial Average dropped 37 percent from the 1,000 area down to 630—Value Line's 1,500-stock average declined more

EXHIBIT 10–10:   The six-year study—Warrant hedge performance

Six-month period	Gross profit or loss (percent)	Net profit or loss* (percent)	Cumulative profit or loss (percent)
January–June 1967			
Profit on warrants $= +143.2$			
Loss on stock $= 1.3 \times 57.8 = -75.1$			
Net profit $= +68.1$	$+68.1$	$+65.1$	$+65.1$
July–December 1967			
Profit on warrants $= +50.7$			
Loss on stock $= 1.3 \times 25.6 = -33.3$			
Net profit $= +17.4$	$+17.4$	$+14.4$	$+89$
January–June 1968			
Profit on warrants $= +159.0$			
Loss on stock $= 1.3 \times 89.6 = -116.5$			
Net profit $= +42.5$	$+42.5$	$+39.5$	$+163$
July–December 1968			
Profit on warrants $= +19.6$			
Loss on stock $= 1.3 \times 11.8 = -15.3$			
Net profit $= +4.3$	$+4.3$	$+1.3$	$+167$
January–June 1969			
Profit on stock $= 1.3 \times 41.8 = +54.3$			
Loss on warrants $= -52.2$			
Net profit $= +2.1$	$+2.1$	-0.9	$+164$
July–December 1969			
Profit on stock $= 1.3 \times 25.5 = +33.2$			
Loss on warrants $= -28.7$			
Net profit $= +4.5$	$+4.5$	$+1.5$	$+168$
January–June 1970			
Profit on stock $\times 1.3 \times 39.4 = +51.2$			
Loss on warrants $= -43.5$			
Net profit $= +7.7$	$+7.7$	$+4.7$	$+181$
July–December 1970			
Profit on warrants $= +49.8$			
Loss on stock $= 1.3 \times 30.1 = -39.1$			
Net profit $= +10.7$	$+10.7$	$+7.7$	$+203$
January–June 1971			
Profit on warrants $= +59.0$			
Loss on stock $= 1.3 \times 26.6 = -34.6$			
Net profit $= +24.4$	$+24.4$	$+21.4$	$+267$
July–December 1971			
Loss on warrants $= -2.6$			
Loss on stock $= 1.3 \times 1.4 = -1.8$			
Net loss $= -4.4$	-4.4	-7.4	$+240$

EXHIBIT 10–10 *(continued)*

Six-month period				Gross profit or loss (percent)	Net profit or loss* (percent)	Cumulative profit or loss (percent)
January–June 1972						
Profit on warrants		= +	6.4			
Loss on stock = 1.3 ×	3.0	= −	3.9			
Net profit		=	+ 2.5	− 0.5	+239	
July–December 1972						
Profit on stock = 1.3 ×	5.7	= +	7.4			
Loss on warrants		= −	19.7			
Net loss		=	−12.3	−15.3	+187	

* Three percent was deducted from the gross profit or loss for each period to compensate for commissions paid on warrants and stocks and for dividends paid on stocks sold short.

than 50 percent. The more speculative stocks represented in our warrant hedging program "bombed" by almost 75 percent, giving back nearly all their gain of the previous two years. The warrant hedge program, however, turned in a stellar performance and actually provided a net gain of 5 percent during this 18-month bear market. Our overall performance from the hedge program increased to 181 percent from the 167 percent level at the end of 1968.

July 1970–July 1971. The market rebounded sharply from its depressed condition and was led by blue-chip and glamour stocks. Value Line's average turned in a modest 28 percent gain and our more volatile stocks advanced 65 percent. The warrant hedge program also provided a modest gain of about 30 percent. The hedge program performance stood at plus 267 percent whereas the overall stock market had still not reached its pinnacle of earlier years.

July 1971–January 1973. Except for a handful of blue-chip and glamour stocks, the overall stock market drifted sideways during this 18-month period—Value Line's 1,500-stock average remained essentially unchanged as did the stocks represented in our hedge program. The warrants acted more poorly than their stocks as was expected due to the passage of time plus the fact that speculative securities were definitely out of favor during this market cycle. Although it was a disappointing 18 months, our six-year performance was still up by 187 percent—an annualized return on our investment of nearly 20 percent from a system that involved no market judgment and was "managed" only twice a year!

WARRANT HEDGE PERFORMANCE ON MARGIN

Exhibit 10–11 presents the performance figures for the six-year warrant hedge program adjusted to reflect the leverage and extra expenses associated with investments made on 70 percent margin. Unlike the pronounced negative effect that borrowing imposed on straight purchases of either the common stock or warrants, the leveraged warrant hedge program provided improved overall per-

EXHIBIT 10–11:   The six-year study—Warrant hedge performance on 70 percent margin

Six-month period	Net profit or loss* (percent)	70 percent margin† profit or loss (percent)	Cumulative profit or loss (percent)
January–June 1967	+65.1	+89.4	+ 89.4
July–December 1967	+14.4	+17.0	+122
January–June 1968	+39.5	+52.9	+239
July–December 1968	+ 1.3	− 1.7	+233
January–June 1969	− 0.9	− 4.9	+217
July–December 1969	+ 1.5	− 1.4	+212
January–June 1970	+ 4.7	+ 3.1	+222
July–December 1970	+ 7.7	+ 7.4	+246
January–June 1971	+21.4	+27.0	+339
July–December 1971	− 7.4	−14.1	+277
January–June 1972	− 0.5	− 4.3	+261
July–December 1972	−15.3	−25.4	+169

* The net profit or loss figures were taken from Exhibit 10–10.

† A deduction of 2.5 percent was made from the net figures before determining the profit or loss based on 70 percent margin. This compensates for extra commission and dividend expenses plus margin interest.

formance right up until the final six months of the study. As expected, it magnified profits during advancing markets while having little adverse effect during periods of decline. During the last 18 months, when the market drifted sideways, the leveraged hedge program performed more poorly than the unleveraged investments, as would be expected. Exhibit 10–12 compares both the leveraged and unleveraged hedge program with Value Line's 1,500-stock average over the six-year period.

An important reason for employing leverage in a warrant hedg-

EXHIBIT 10–12:   The six-year study—Warrant hedge performance

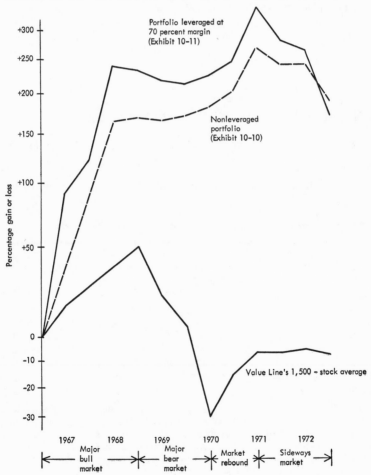

ing program is to secure tax advantages. Assuming no other investments, the hedge program would be expected to provide net long-term capital gains during the advancing markets where profits were achieved. If, on average, an annual net profit of 15 percent were achieved from warrant hedging, it would normally consist of about 20 percent in long-term capital gains less about 5 percent paid for margin interest and dividends paid on stock sold short—both are tax-deductible expense items. For an investor in the 50 percent tax bracket, the net tax would be computed approximately as follows:

$$
\begin{aligned}
\text{Tax on long-term capital gains} &= 20 \times 25\% &&= 5.0\% \\
\text{Less savings on deductible expenses} &= 5 \times 50\% &&= 2.5\% \\
\text{Net tax} & &&= 2.5\% \\
\text{Aftertax profit} & &&= 12.5\%
\end{aligned}
$$

AN ADDITIONAL 2½-YEAR "TRACK RECORD"

Exhibit 10–13 shows the warrant hedge recommendations I provided to the investment advisory service, as discussed in chapter 3. Each hedge was evaluated and constructed in accordance

EXHIBIT 10–13: Warrant hedges (June 1973 through December 1975)

Warrant hedge	Date recommended	Date closed	months	Profit or loss	Annualized return
LCA	6/26/73	8/10/73	1.5	+59%	+472%
Loews Corp.	6/26/73	8/10/73	1.5	+ 9	+ 72
Louisiana Land & Exploration	6/26/73	2/15/74	7.5	+55	+ 88
General Host	6/26/73	12/31/75	30.0	−14	− 6
United National	8/10/73	12/03/74	15.5	+ 3	+ 2
Brown Co.	8/10/73	12/31/75	28.5	−12	− 5
AMAX Inc.	11/16/73	6/16/75	19.0	+10	+ 6
Government Employees Insurance	2/16/74	11/15/74	9.0	+ 3	+ 4
Averages (eight positions)			14	+14%	+ 79%

Note: These hedges were recommended for an investment advisory service. Each hedge was designed for profits during bull markets and at modest risk in sideways or bear markets, without attempting to predict future price trends. If a hedge position was proposed more than once (or if a similar hedge position in the same company was suggested) while the initial recommendation was still rated a buy or hold, only the initial recommendation is shown. Profit or loss figures are based on nonleveraged positions and all commission expenses and dividends paid are included.

with the basic system's procedures for hedging undervalued warrants—expected upside profits at limited downside risk without attempting to forecast the future.

As shown by this additional 2½ year track record, warrant hedging not only protected one's capital during the worst bear market in 40 years but actually produced a very handsome profit.

ALTERNATIVES TO THE BASIC SYSTEM

To conservatively document the anticipated performance that would have been achieved from hedging undervalued warrants during the six-year study, rigid rules were established and followed without modification. This approach eliminated all judgment factors—either on overall market direction or on individual securities. It also obviated the need to closely monitor one's portfolio since action was considered only twice each year. However, if one has the interest and the time to aggressively manage a warrant hedge portfolio, he should be able to achieve results even superior to those obtained under the basic system—and he will probably have a great deal more fun at the same time.

Continuous review of all warrant opportunities

The easiest and probably the most profitable modification to the basic system is the continuous review of current positions and new hedging opportunities. As soon as a warrant becomes overvalued (or even normally valued, depending on other available situations), the position should be closed out and the funds employed in other hedge positions offering superior risk/reward prospects. Note that many new warrants, particularly those of large issues, begin trading at depressed price levels. This is probably the result of numerous investors receiving warrants as part of an issue of bonds or other securities. Since many investors probably purchase the package to obtain the senior security, they may quickly sell the unwanted warrants. This creates an unbalanced supply/demand condition that is frequently only temporary. The excess supply may last for a few days or even months, but it would be expected to eventually come into balance. Some specific examples from my actual investment experiences will illustrate these points.

Like in the mechanical system, the author established a hedge position in Kinney National Services in early 1970. Under the basic system, the position would still have been held as of January 1973 with but nominal paper profits. However, in actual practice, the warrants became temporarily overpriced in May 1971 and the hedge position was closed out at a sizable profit. The position was reestablished later at more favorable price relationships.

National General warrants were considered overpriced in both January 1971 and July 1971 and were, therefore, excluded from consideration under the basic system at those times. However, during this six-month period, price fluctuations permitted a position to be established and closed out at a significant short-term profit.

In November 1970, Tenneco issued new five-year warrants having exercise terms of one share of common stock for $24.25. Despite the high yield on the common stock, the warrants were attractive for purchase. On November 24, the warrants were bought at a price of $3.625 when the stock was trading at $19.50. At the end of the year, about one month later, Tenneco stock and warrants had risen to $24 and $5.75, at which point one reviewing the warrant field would probably not have established a hedge position in Tenneco. Most of the potential profit of the Tenneco hedge would have already been achieved—the short-term price advance of 23 percent by the common stock resulted in a 60 percent advance by the warrant. An investor who evaluates his portfolio more regularly than once every six months (per the mechanical system) will see some of the more lucrative trading opportunities illustrated by the above examples.

Over-the-counter warrants

Another area that can help to improve performance, as well as broaden the selection list for greater portfolio diversification, is the over-the-counter market. Even those warrants that become listed are usually first traded over-the-counter while their application for listing is being processed. The possibility that a warrant will trade at an underpriced level during this initial time period is quite high, as it normally takes some time for warrant services to react and for the general public to become sold on a new warrant's merits after it is issued. Remember that when hedging, you should not be as concerned about a company's fundamentals as you would if you were considering purchase of its common stock. When you discover an undervalued warrant, move quickly. The Tenneco warrant was actually bought in the over-the-counter market the day before it was listed on the New York Stock Exchange. On being listed, it quickly advanced to higher price levels as it attracted the attention of the investment public.

Fine tuning the hedge portfolio

If we can assume that professional investment analysts and advisors are earning their salaries and that stock market services are worth the expense, then it should be possible to outperform the basic system by following professional advice or even one's own personal judgment. The hedge portfolio would be fine tuned by adjusting the amount of common stock sold short for each individual position, depending on the expected future price trend for that security. To illustrate this point, my actual investment approach to the previously mentioned Tenneco warrant may be of interest.

I had an optimistic opinion of the future prospects for Tenneco, while watching with dismay its decline during the 1969–70 bear market from over $30 to the $19–$20 range in November 1970.

A price under $20 for this blue-chip security seemed absurd. It was earning $2 per share with improved prospects for the future. Its dividend was secure and provided a yield of almost 7 percent. The overall market was already recovering from its panic low in May of that year and was being led by blue-chip, high-yield stocks. Everything seemed to favor an improved price level for Tenneco's common stock—probably shortly after the offering of stock and warrants was consummated.

As mentioned earlier, the Tenneco warrants were purchased at the bargain price of $3.625. A hedge position could have been established at that time and would have been, if the basic system was being followed without modifications based on judgment. Since it was felt that the price of Tenneco common was unduly and temporarily depressed, it was decided that higher price levels would be sought before selling the common stock short. This judgment proved to be correct as Tenneco common advanced to above $25 per share within the following two months. At that point, short positions were established in the common stock on a scale-up basis. It was also interesting to note that, as the stock advanced, the warrant actually moved higher on the normal rating curves. At prices of $29 and $9.50 in March 1971, the warrants were fully valued and the hedge position was closed out at a net profit in excess of 100 percent. A 50 percent price advance by the common stock since the November 24, 1970 purchase date had resulted in a 160 percent warrant price increase—an upside leverage factor of 3.2.

Trading against warrants for profits during sideways markets

As was illustrated earlier, a major risk for warrant hedging is the probable deterioration of equity during a sideways market.

Continuous review of one's portfolio will help reduce this risk but will probably not eliminate it completely.

Another technique for fine tuning a hedge portfolio to reduce the risk of a sideways market is to trade the short side of a hedge position against the warrants. This simply involves adding to the short side of the portfolio during market rallies and then covering these additional short sales on market dips. This approach would be expected to produce some profits during an extended sideways movement at the expense of reduced gains if the market sustained a major upside advance.

Predicting major market swings

An approach that can substantially improve performance, but one that is probably less predictable than individual situations like Tenneco, is the correct forecasting of future market price trends. Let us suppose that one had been able to forecast the overall market movements during the six-year test period with reasonable accuracy—there are certain investment services that claim to have accomplished this feat. What would the typical investor have done under these circumstances? He probably would have been fully invested in common stocks during the 1967–68 bull market and then switched a portion of his equity into a cash position in early 1969, prior to the market crash. In mid-1970, he would have returned to a fully invested stock position. With luck, he might have doubled his equity during the six-year period—an admirable performance but significantly poorer than that achieved by the mechanical system for hedging warrants.

The warrant hedge investor has better alternatives at his disposal than having any of his funds tied up in a passive cash position. While remaining fully invested at all times, he can simply adjust the amount of common stock sold short against the war-

EXHIBIT 10–14: Warrant hedge performance based on accurate market judgment

Six-month period	Gross profit or loss (percent)	70 percent margin* profit or loss (percent)	Cumulative profit or loss (percent)
January–June 1967			
Profit on warrants X +143.2			
Loss on stock = 1.0 × 57.8 = − 57.8			
Net profit = +85.4	+114.9	+ 114.9	
July–December 1967			
Profit on warrants = + 50.7			
Loss on stock = 1.0 × 25.6 = − 25.6			
Net profit = +24.1	+ 28.7	+ 177	
January–June 1968			
Profit on warrants = +159.0			
Loss on stock = 1.0 × 89.6 = − 89.6			
Net profit = +69.4	+ 92.0	+ 431	
July–December 1968			
Profit on warrants = + 19.6			
Loss on stock = 1.0 × 11.8 = − 11.8			
Net profit = + 7.8	+ 4.0	+ 452	
January–June 1969			
Profit on stock = 2.0 × 41.8 = + 83.6			
Loss on warrants = − 52.2			
Net profit = +31.4	+ 34.9	+ 645	
July–December 1969			
Profit on stock = 2.0 × 25.5 = + 51.0			
Loss on warrants = − 28.7			
Net profit = +22.3	+ 21.9	+ 808	
January–June 1970			
Profit on stock = 2.0 × 39.4 = + 78.8			
Loss on warrants = − 43.5			
Net profit = +35.3	+ 40.4	+1,175	
July–December 1970			
Profit on warrants = + 49.8			
Loss on stock = 1.0 × 30.1 = − 30.1			
Net profit = +19.7	+ 21.0	+1,443	
January–June 1971			
Profit on warrants = + 59.0			
Loss on stock = 1.0 × 26.6 = − 26.6			
Net profit = +32.4	+ 39.1	+2,046	
July–December 1971			
Loss on warrants = − 2.6			
Loss on stock = 1.0 × 1.4 = − 1.4			
Net loss = − 4.0	− 12.9	+1,769	

EXHIBIT 10–14 *(continued)*

			Gross profit or loss (*percent*)	*70 percent margin* profit or loss* (*percent*)	*Cumulative profit or loss* (*percent*)
Six-month period					
January–June 1972					
Profit on warrants	= +	6.4			
Loss on stock = 1.0 × 3.0	= −	3.0			
Net profit	=	+ 3.4	− 2.3	+1,726
July–December 1972					
Profit on stock = 1.0 × 5.7	= +	5.7			
Loss on warrants	= −	19.7			
Net loss	=	−14.0	− 27.1	+1,231

* To compensate for commissions, dividends, and margin interest, 5 percent and 7 percent were deducted from gross profit figures for periods of short sale ratios of 1.0 and 2.0, respectively, before determining the profit or loss based on 70 percent margin.

rants. Let us suppose the warrant hedger was equally skilled at forecasting overall market price movements. Let us also assume he had made adjustments to his short-to-long ratio in anticipation of the market trends. Instead of the mechanical 1.3 ratio, we will assume that he had employed the following:

	Short-to-long ratio
January 1967–December 1968...............	1.0
January 1969–June 1970....................	2.0
July 1970–January 1973....................	1.0

By cutting back on the short side to a 1.0 ratio during advancing markets, the hedger would have increased his upside capital appreciation over the mechanical system at a somewhat higher downside risk if his judgment proved to be incorrect—a risk that was substantially less than a conventional portfolio of common stocks. The 2.0 short-to-long ratio employed during the market crash promised downside profits at little or no risk if the market continued its upward movement.

By exercising accurate market judgment, but again only evaluating his portfolio twice each year, the warrant hedge investor would have increased his equity by 1,200 percent during the six-year period! For the skeptical reader, Exhibit 10–14 provides the detailed calculations in support of this conclusion.

GENERAL GUIDES FOR HEDGING WARRANTS

1. Warrants should be substantially undervalued—a mathematical advantage of 1.5 or higher, providing an upside leverage of 2.0 or higher.

2. Warrants should be long term (three years or more) to minimize the downward price pressure caused by an approaching expiration date.

3. Select warrants on common stocks that pay little or no dividends—the short seller must pay these dividends.

4. Since a properly designed hedge would be expected to protect one against major loss, even in the event of bankruptcy, the best hedge positions are in stocks having high price volatility.

5. Make sure that the stock is available for short selling and that there is a reasonable probability that it can be held short as long as desired.

6. Both warrants and common stock should be actively traded to permit establishing and closing out positions at favorable price relationships.

7. The dollar amount of common stock sold short versus warrants purchased should be designed to meet one's specific objectives for that situation. This ratio will generally fall within a range of 1.0 to 2.0.

8. Warrants are held in the brokerage account, even if purchased for cash, to permit the short sale of common stock without having to deposit margin on the short side.

9. A major price move is usually required before closing out a position for profit—do not consider warrant hedging for short-term trading.

Possible risks in warrant hedging

Risk	Recommended action to minimize risk
1. A major market decline will substantially reduce warrant prices.	Amount of stock sold short should be carefully selected to minimize downside risk (bullish hedge) or to achieve profits on the downside if desired (neutral or bearish hedge).
2. Warrant price will go to its conversion value upon expiration.	Hedge positions should normally be closed out within about two years of the expiration date—even if a loss must be taken.
3. A sideways market will cause warrant prices to drift downward in relation to their stocks as time passes.	Only long-term warrants should be selected to minimize downward price pressure. Common stocks should have high price volatility to improve the chances for major price moves within a sideways market.
4. Short sales cannot be protected as a result of a tender offer or other circumstances that could cause a forced close-out of the position at unfavorable price relationships (i.e., the common rises in response to a tender offer while warrants lag behind).	Avoid obvious problem stocks where possible. Diversification will limit overall port-folio risk.
5. Warrant values are reduced as a result of a merger whereby the common stock is exchanged for less volatile securities.	Avoid obvious problem stocks where possible. Diversification will limit overall portfolio risk.
6. Dividends paid on stocks sold short will cause an equity deterioration unless offset by profit opportunities.	Select common stocks that pay little or no dividends.
7. Margin interest paid will also cause an equity deterioration unless offset by profit opportunities.	If leverage is employed for hedging warrants, it is recommended that income-type situations also be included in the overall portfolio to offset the margin interest.
8. Warrants, in general, become out of favour during a sideways market movement as they did during the latter half of 1972.	There is no direct action that can be taken to avoid this risk. Trading the short side against the warrants will reduce it somewhat at the expense of lower profits if the market were to sustain a major price advance.

10. Close out the position if warrants become overvalued—the funds should be used in another situation having more favorable risk/reward characteristics.

11. Be prepared to close out the position, even at a loss, when the warrant's life is only about two years.

12. Avoid situations where the common stock will likely be tendered or merged with another company.

chapter 11

Selling calls against warrants

The sale of overpriced call options against undervalued warrants is one of the most dynamic and potentially profitable hedging strategies available to the sophisticated investor. To illustrate the possible risks and rewards, let us evaluate an actual warrant/call option hedge opportunity which existed in the spring of 1975.

Gulf & Western common stock and warrants closed out 1974 at $25 and $4 per share, respectively. The three-year warrant, having an exercise price above $50, was considered to be about normally valued at that time and was of no particular interest to hedgers. However, warrant hedgers did not have long to wait for an opportunity to develop. The stock market rally in the early months of 1975 carried Gulf & Western's common stock to a new recovery high of $35 in April 1975—a very respectable four-month advance of 40 percent. The Gulf & Western warrant, however, seriously lagged behind its common and advanced only 25 percent to $5 per share—a most disappointing performance for a highly leveraged security, but not uncommon in a stock market dominated by large institutional investors who would never even consider the purchase of a warrant for their portfolios.

At stock and warrant prices of $35 and $5 in April 1975, the warrant was definitely undervalued. It was trading at the price of a call option having only 18 months to run instead of its 27 months to expiration on January 31, 1978. A warrant/stock hedge, similar to the tactics presented in chapter 10, could have been considered, but there was an even better strategy available. Six-month call options on Gulf & Western stock, having a $35 exercise price, were trading on the CBOE at 4½—an above-normal premium of about 13 percent. The alert hedgers took advantage of these favorable warrant and call option prices by establishing warrant/call option hedges similar to the position shown below.

Possible Hedge Position

Buy 2,000 warrants at $5	$10,000
Sell 10 Oct-35 calls at $450	−4,500
Commissions	+ 400
Net debit to the account	$ 5,900

NET INVESTMENT

The collateral required to establish the hedge was 50 percent of the warrant cost plus the amount required to sell 10 naked call options—or about $11,300 total. Since most investors usually have extra collateral available, the actual investment was generally considered to be $5,900—the net debit to the account from the two transactions.

RISK/REWARD ESTIMATES

The following risk/reward estimates were made assuming that the warrant would remain undervalued relative to its underlying common stock during the next six months up to the call's expiration date in October. Round-trip commissions for both the warrants and calls were included in the estimates; however, if the warrants were still undervalued in October, as assumed, they could be held for selling additional calls. Despite these conservative assumptions, the potential return from the hedge position far exceeded conventional types of hedges. The calculations are shown below.

	Assumed stock price at call's expiration date				
	25	30	35	40	50
Estimated warrant price..........	3	4	5	7	12
Estimated call price..............	0	0	0	5	15
Profit and (loss) estimates (pretax)					
Warrants.....................	(4,000)	(2,000)	0	4,000	14,000
Call options..................	4,500	4,500	4,500	(500)	(10,500)
Commissions.................	(620)	(650)	(670)	(850)	(1,060)
Net profit or (loss).............	(120)	1,850	3,830	2,650	2,440
Return on investment...........	−2%	+31%	+ 65%	+45%	+41%
Annualized return on investment	−4%	+62%	+130%	+90%	+82%

Note: If the warrants returned to their normal value, instead of remaining undervalued as assumed, the rate of return would be much higher.

POSSIBLE RISKS

The obvious risk, as illustrated by the above analysis, is that Gulf & Western common stock might return to $25 per share, or even lower. In this event, the downside risk would be compounded by the adverse tax consequences of income received on calls sold versus capital loss on warrants purchased. But these risks are more than offset by the favorable potential from either a sideways or advancing market—both pretax and aftertax.

The less obvious risk is that the warrant might continue to lag behind its stock on a further advance. For example, if the stock advanced to $40, while the warrant remained at $5, the indicated profit of $2,650 would turn into a loss of $1,350. Although this was a real possibility, at that point the warrant would be so grossly undervalued that future calls sold against it would provide an even more attractive risk/reward opportunity. Of course, the possibility that the warrant would continue to lag behind is probably more than offset by the greater probability that it would begin to catch up and return to its normal value.

After considering all factors relative to the risks and rewards for this warrant/call option hedge in Gulf & Western, it seemed that the potential for unusually large gains far exceeded the potential for loss.

CONCLUSION OF THE GULF & WESTERN STORY

The actual experience with the Gulf & Western warrant/call option hedge was indeed a pleasant one. The stock advanced to $44 in July, while the warrant kept pace as predicted by rising to $10. The hedge offered short-term profit-taking opportunities to those investors unconcerned with long-term capital gains. Others held out until the call's expiration date for the advantage of a long-term capital gain on the warrants. At closing prices of 39½, 8¼, and 4½ for the stock, warrants, and calls, respectively, the net profit of $5,650 provided an annualized return of about 190 percent.

For your convenience, Exhibit 11–1 provides a listing of warrants that have common stocks with listed call options.

EXHIBIT 11–1:   Warrants having listed call options

	Number of shares	Total dollars	Effective to	Expiration date	Usable senior security	Notes
Warrant						
				Exercise terms		

Warrant	Number of shares	Total dollars	Effective to	Expiration date	Usable senior security	Notes
Atlantic Richfield................	1.000	127.50	12/31/76	12/31/76		
Braniff International Corp.........	3.183	73.00	12/ 1/86	12/ 1/86	5.75 –86	
Commonwealth Edison...........	1.000	30.00	4/30/81	none		1
Delta Airlines..................	1.000	48.00	5/01/78	5/01/78		
Greyhound.....................	1.000	23.50	5/14/80	5/14/80		
Gulf & Western Industries........	1.033	27.50	1/31/78	1/31/78		
Loews Corp....................	1.000	37.50	11/29/76	11/29/80	6.875–93	
		40.00	11/29/80			
Louisiana Land & Exploration....	1.000	40.50	6/15/76	6/15/76		2
Occidental Petroleum............	1.000	16.25	4/22/80	4/22/80		3
Tenneco Inc....................	1.070	32.17	4/01/79	4/01/79	6.00 –79	
Tesoro Petroleum Corp...........	1.000	13.80	8/24/76	8/24/76		

Notes:

1.   Warrants ("A" and "B") are exercisable into one common share upon payment of $30 through 4/30/81 and are alternately convertible into 0.333 common at any time without payment.

2.   Issued by Amerada Hess. Trades as Amerada Hess–Louisiana Land warrant.

3.   During the 90-day period ending 3/23/80, company specifically reserves the right to extend the warrant up to five years if common price does not exceed 110% of exercise price; each unexercised warrant will be exchanged for 0.01 shares at expiration.

chapter **12**

Reverse warrant
hedging

A *reverse* warrant hedge is the strategy opposite to the regular
warrant hedge presented in chapter 10. Unlike the purchase of
long-term, undervalued warrants, it involves the short sale of
overpriced warrants nearing their expiration date. The short sale
is hedged by the purchase of the underlying common stock or
other securities that are convertible into the common. In many
respects, the reverse warrant hedge is similar to the sale of listed
call options against stocks or convertibles. The major advantage
offered by the warrant hedge, compared to the call option hedge, is
that market inefficiencies occasionally permit warrants to become
grossly overpriced. You should hedge only the grossly overpriced
warrant, since basic differences between the two strategies will
generally favor the sale of listed call options. The major factors to consider when evaluating a reverse warrant hedge candidate, and problems relating to the short selling of warrants
are:

1. The warrant should be definitely overpriced. The normal
value curves of chapter 9 may be used to roughly determine
value, bearing in mind that these curves apply to warrants having

a life to expiration of three years or more. Or, you may use the normal value curves for listed call options if the warrant life is only a year or two.

2.   The warrant should generally have a life to expiration of less than three years to make a reverse warrant hedge position attractive on an *annualized* basis. Offsetting the desirability of a short time period to expiration, for maximum annualized return on your investment, is the need to establish the position early enough to assure the warrant's availability for short selling. It is important to get into a reverse warrant hedge position before the crowd.

3.   The warrant should be listed on a major stock exchange and be actively traded to facilitate borrowing for short selling. Since many of the listed warrants that you might evaluate for hedge candidates will not be widely held in margin accounts, availability for short selling may be a major problem. Even after taking a position, there is no guarantee that your broker will be able to protect the short position indefinitely. The problem becomes especially acute since the warrants decline in price as they approach their expiration date. This price reduction causes a natural movement of warrants from margin accounts to cash accounts where they become unavailable for borrowing.

4.   Another problem in the area of warrant hedging is the possibility that the company may extend the warrant's life or take some other adverse action that will suddenly increase the inherent value of the warrants you have sold short. This has become a factor in recent years because of a tax court ruling that requires the company to report the proceeds from the original warrant sale as income if the warrants expire worthless. Challenges to this ruling and other attempts to avoid the tax consequences will probably keep this matter in a state of uncertainty and confusion for some time.

5.   Both sides of the reverse warrant hedge position must be margined. The funds deposited for margining the short side will reduce the debit balance in your account, but you cannot use the proceeds from the short sale as you can from the sale of call options.

6.   Warrants must be purchased prior to their expiration date for covering the short sale. Even though they may be worthless upon expiration, the lender is still entitled to the return of his warrant certificates. In actual practice, the reverse warrant hedge will usually be closed out some time prior to the expiration date and the funds redeployed in better situations.

7.   Like the sale of listed call options, the reverse warrant hedge does not normally provide full downside protection. The quality of the company must therefore be considered when selecting a reverse hedge position. The best situations will usually be found in quality stocks having low price volatility.

8.   Undervalued convertible bonds or convertible preferred stocks should always be considered as an alternative to the common stock for the long side of the hedge. The convertible may increase the downside safety while providing greater yield.

9.   When the position is within a year of the warrant's expiration date, consider purchasing call options on the common stock in lieu of holding the stock (or convertible). This technique may substantially improve overall portfolio performance by releasing funds for other investments.

10.   Like other short sales, profit or loss on warrants sold short is treated as short-term capital gain or loss regardless of the time period they are held. This tax consequence will frequently offer advantages to the warrant hedger compared to the present tax treatment on the sale of call options. In bear markets, the short-term profit from the shorted warrants can normally be offset by long-term capital losses from long positions held in the hedge

portfolio. In bull markets, short-term capital loss from the warrants can give the hedger additional flexibility by allowing him to take short-term profits in other situations during the year.

Despite the fact that the negatives seem to outweigh the positives, reverse warrant hedging has been a source of extraordinarily high profits for hedgers over the years—especially for those who exercised good judgment by carefully selecting certain positions while avoiding others where potential problems were indicated. Like the straight warrant hedge in LTV, let us evaluate an actual case history of a *reverse* warrant hedge to illustrate the strategies and tactics that apply.

AN ACTUAL REVERSE WARRANT HEDGE POSITION—AMERICAN TELEPHONE & TELEGRAPH

In May 1972, AT&T common stock and warrants were both actively trading on the New York Stock Exchange. Prices were in the area of $42 and $7, respectively. Since the warrants were to expire in three years (May 15, 1975) and were the right to purchase common stock at $52 per share, well above the stock price at the time, the warrants were excellent candidates for reverse hedging. With about 31 million warrants outstanding and a short interest of less than 1 million shares, there was no problem obtaining the warrants for short sales.

A review of the warrant terms indicated that AT&T did not have the right to reduce the warrant's exercise price or extend its life. This was confirmed by a call to the company's legal department who also advised that, in their opinion, such action would require approval by the common stockholders, who would most likely reject it.

Assuming the purchase of 100 shares of common stock, alternate reverse hedge positions were evaluated on standard work sheets as illustrated by the following:

Exhibit 12–1—100 warrants sold short—*bullish* hedge.

Exhibit 12–2—200 warrants sold short—*neutral* hedge.

Exhibit 12–3—300 warrants sold short—*bearish* hedge.

Referring to the calculations in Exhibit 12–1, a step-by-step approach for estimating potential profit or loss proceeded as follows:

a. One hundred shares of common stock were purchased at $42 per share.

b. One hundred warrants were sold short at $7 per share.

c. The total position, including commissions, was the sum of these two transactions, or $4,940.

d. The net investment, at the 55 percent margin rate prevailing at the time, was $2,720.

e. The initial debit balance created was the difference between the $4,260 cost for the purchase of the common stock and the $2,720 required investment, or $1,540.

f. Since the major variable (and risk) is the price of AT&Ts common stock on the warrant's expiration date, four different prices were assumed for calculation purposes. These ranged from $30, which was considered to be the maximum downside possibility, to $70, which was believed to be the potential upside objective. The other prices selected were the stock's current price of $42 and the warrant's exercise price of $52. Note that the exercise price will always represent the maximum profit potential for any reverse hedge situation.

g. Warrant prices shown are conversion values at the various assumed stock prices. In actual practice, you will normally buy back expiring warrants at a price slightly higher than their actual conversion value but the net effect on profit and loss calculations will be small.

h. Profit and loss calculations are based on the indicated stock and warrant prices at expiration.

i. Round-trip commissions are included for meaningful estimates.

EXHIBIT 12–1

WORK SHEET

REVERSE WARRANT HEDGE EVALUATION

COMPANY _____ AT+T _____ DATE _May 1972_

A. DESCRIPTION OF SECURITIES

Security	Description	Traded	Price	Yield %
Common stock		NYS	42	6.7
Convertible bond				
Convertible preferred				
Warrant		NYS	7	

Warrant expiration date _5-15-75_ (_3.0_ years)

B. POSSIBLE HEDGE POSITION: Bullish _✓_ , Neutral _____ , or Bearish _____

(a) _Common_ purchased: _100_ shs. at $ _42.00_ each = $ _4,200_ + _60_ comm. = $ _4,260_
(b) Warrants sold short: _100_ shs. at $ _7.00_ each = $ _700_ – _20_ comm. = $ _680_
(c) Total $ _4,940_

(d) Investment = $ _4,940_ x _55_ % margin = $ _2,720_
(e) Initial debit balance = $ _4,260_ – $ _2,720_ = $ _1,540_

C. PROFIT OR LOSS ESTIMATES AT EXPIRATION DATE

(f) Stock price (assumed)	30	42	52	70
Estimated convertible price				
(g) Estimated warrant price (conversion value)	0	0	0	18
(h) Profit or (loss) – warrants	700	700	700	(1,100)
– common	(1,200)	0	1,000	2,800
– convertible				
(i) Commissions	135	(145)	150	185
(j) Estimated capital gain or (loss)	635	555	1,550	1,515
(k) Estimated return on investment	–23.3 %	+20.4 %	+57 %	+56 %
(l) Estimated annualized ROI	–7.8 %	+6.8 %	+19 %	+18.6 %

D. ESTIMATED ANNUAL CASH FLOW

(m) Estimated stock dividends or bond interest   = $ _280_
(n) Less estimated margin interest* = $ _1,540_ x _6.0_ % = (_92_)
(o) Estimated cash flow   = $ _188_ = _6.9_ %

*Based on the initial debit balance; however, this will fluctuate as the short account is marked to the market. The indicated interest rate is also subject to change.

j. The estimated net capital gain or loss was determined next.
k. The estimated return on investment was the net capital gain or loss divided by the $2,720 investment.
l. Annualized return on investment was determined by dividing the total return by the warrant's three-year life to expiration.

EXHIBIT 12–2

WORK SHEET

REVERSE WARRANT HEDGE EVALUATION

COMPANY ___*AT+T*___   DATE *May 1972*

A. DESCRIPTION OF SECURITIES

Security	Description	Traded	Price	Yield %
Common stock		*NYS*	*42*	*6.7*
Convertible bond				
Convertible preferred				
Warrant		*NYS*	*7*	

Warrant expiration date *5-15-75* (*3.0* years)

B. POSSIBLE HEDGE POSITION: Bullish_____, Neutral ___✓___, or Bearish_____

Common purchased: *100* shs. at $ *42.00* each = $ *4,200* + *60* comm. = $ *4,260*
Warrants sold short: *200* shs. at $ *7.00* each = $ *1,400* - *40* comm. = $ *1,360*
Total $ *5,620*

Investment = $ *5,620* x *55* % margin = $ *3,090*
Initial debit balance = $ *4,260* - $ *3,090* = $ *1,170*

C. PROFIT OR LOSS ESTIMATES AT EXPIRATION DATE

Stock price (assumed)	*30*	*42*	*52*	*70*
Estimated convertible price				
Estimated warrant price (conversion value)	*0*	*0*	*0*	*18*
Profit or (loss) – warrants	*1,400*	*1,400*	*1,400*	*(2,200)*
– common	*(1,200)*	*0*	*1,000*	*2,800*
– convertible				
Commissions	*(155)*	*(165)*	*(170)*	*(235)*
Estimated capital gain or (loss)	*45*	*1,235*	*2,230*	*365*
Estimated return on investment	*+1.5%*	*+40.0%*	*+72.2%*	*+11.8%*
Estimated annualized ROI	*+0.5%*	*+13.3%*	*+24.0%*	*+3.9%*

D. ESTIMATED ANNUAL CASH FLOW

Estimated stock dividends or bond interest   = $ *280*
Less estimated margin interest* = $ *1,170* x *6.0* %   = (*70*)
Estimated cash flow   = $ *210* = *6.8* %

*Based on the initial debit balance; however, this will fluctuate as the short account is marked to the market. The indicated interest rate is also subject to change.

m. Annual dividends to be received were estimated at $2.80 per share during the three-year period.

n. Estimated annual margin interest was based on the initial debit balance of $1,540 and a 6 percent interest rate. Both these factors are subject to change as the market value of the

EXHIBIT 12-3

WORK SHEET

REVERSE WARRANT HEDGE EVALUATION

COMPANY ___*AT+T*___   DATE *May 1972*

A. DESCRIPTION OF SECURITIES

Security	Description	Traded	Price	Yield %
Common stock		*NYS*	*42*	*6.7*
Convertible bond				
Convertible preferred				
Warrant		*NYS*	*7*	

Warrant expiration date *5-15-75* (*3.0* years)

B. POSSIBLE HEDGE POSITION: Bullish_____, Neutral_____, or Bearish __*✓*__

Common purchased: __*100*__ shs. at $ *42.00* each = $ *4,200* + *60* comm. = $ *4,260*
Warrants sold short: __*300*__ shs. at $ *7.00* each = $ *2,100* - *60* comm. = $ *2,040*
Total $ *6,300*

Investment = $ *6,300* × __*55*__ % margin = $ *3,465*
Initial debit balance = $ *4,260* - $ *3,465* = $ *795*

C. PROFIT OR LOSS ESTIMATES AT EXPIRATION DATE

Stock price (assumed)	*30*	*42*	*52*	*70*
Estimated convertible price				
Estimated warrant price (conversion value)	*0*	*0*	*0*	*18*
Profit or (loss) – warrants	*2,100*	*2,100*	*2,100*	(*3,300*)
– common	(*1,200*)	*0*	*1,000*	*2,800*
– convertible	(			
Commissions	*175*)	(*185*)	(*190*)	(*280*)
Estimated capital gain or (loss)	*725*	*1,915*	*2,910*	(*780*)
Estimated return on investment	*+20.9%*	*+55.3%*	*+84.0%*	*-22.5%*
Estimated annualized ROI	*+7.0%*	*+18.4%*	*+28.0%*	*-7.5%*

D. ESTIMATED ANNUAL CASH FLOW

Estimated stock dividends or bond interest   = $ *280*
Less estimated margin interest* = $ __*795*__ × __*6.0*__ % = (*48*)
Estimated cash flow   = $ __*232*__ = __*6.7*__ %

*Based on the initial debit balance; however, this will fluctuate as the short account is marked to the market. The indicated interest rate is also subject to change.

shorted warrants fluctuates and as interest rates change. The net results, however, would not be expected to be materially different.

o. The estimated annual cash flow was determined by deducting margin interest paid from dividends received. Note that this was actually higher than the common stock yield.

Exhibit 12–4 graphically presents the anticipated annual return on investment (including net cash flow) for each of the alternate reverse hedge positions. Also shown is the purchase of AT&T common stock for comparison purposes (dividends included).

Looking first at the bullish 1 for 1 ratio (100 warrants sold short), note that the reverse warrant hedge position was expected to outperform ownership of the common stock at all prices up to $67. If one were to construct a probability table for the price of AT&T common stock three years hence, it would probably show a very low possibility that AT&T would advance to that price level. Exhibit 12–4 conclusively demonstrated that the warrants, at a price of $7, were substantially overpriced in May 1972 and that a reverse warrant hedge was a superior alternative to the common stock.

The 1 for 1 ratio was recommended for the investor who was bullish on AT&T common. Others would have considered a

EXHIBIT 12–4: Alternate reverse warrant hedge positions in American Telephone & Telegraph

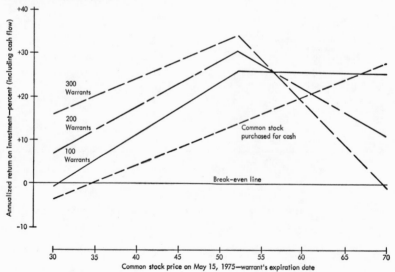

2 for 1 or 3 for 1 to increase their profit potential in the event that AT&T would end up selling somewhere below $56 (the crossover point for the three alternate hedge positions). Also, if one had sizable holdings of other common stocks or regular warrant hedges, a high ratio would have been considered for protection of his portfolio against a bear market or to optimize the total portfolio's performance in a sideways market.

Ratios even higher than 3 for 1 could also have been considered. However, a quick rise in the price of AT&T common to the high $40s or low $50s could have resulted in a near-term loss position plus fears of substantial loss if the stock were to continue moving higher. It was believed that a 3 for 1 ratio could be closed out, if desired, at about break-even if this were to occur.

A neutral 2 for 1 ratio was believed to be best for most investors. This offered a potential return of 20 percent annually if AT&T common were to end up selling at $42 or $61.50 on May 15, 1975, with a possible return of 30 percent if the ideal price of $52 was attained. No loss would be expected on the downside unless AT&T sold below $24 or on the upside above $80, both extremely unlikely events.

CONCLUSION OF THE AT&T STORY

The actual experience with the AT&T reverse warrant hedge position was most surprising. AT&T common stock became the darling of the institutional money managers during the latter half of 1972. In mid-November, only six months after establishing the hedge positions, the common had risen to $52—a healthy ten-point advance. On the other hand, the warrants lagged far behind the common and advanced only one point from $7 up to $8. This price relationship permitted a close-out of the hedge position at substantial profits—the annualized return on investment for the 2 for 1 hedge was greater than 50 percent. Also, note that the capital gains on the common stock were long term and that the losses on the warrants sold short were short term for tax purposes —a desirable combination for most investors.

Those investors who chose to hold their hedge positions, or those who took profits in November 1972 and reestablished hedges later, were even more surprised. When the warrants expired in May 1975, the common stock was trading right at the $52 exercise price. At the time, it seemed like the stock wanted to go higher but was prevented from moving through the $52 barrier due to the 31 million warrants outstanding. All hedgers received the maximum possible profits on their positions. The favored 2 for 1 hedge, for example, produced a return of over 90 percent for the three-year period.

MY EARLIER REVERSE WARRANT
HEDGE POSITIONS

My initial introduction to the field of convertible securities was the reverse warrant hedge in 1964. The first three positions taken are shown below and each involved different techniques. They are presented for informational purposes and to provide an indication of the potential profit available from this type of hedging strategy.

Sperry Rand.   Reverse warrant hedge positions of long common stock versus short warrants were established beginning in early 1965—almost three years prior to the warrant's expiration date in September 1967. Additional positions were taken through July 1965 and all were held until July 1966, when the common stock advanced above the warrant's exercise price. The total position was closed out at that time because there were other situations available that had more favorable risk/reward characteristics. A net profit of 27 percent was realized on the investment which was held, on average, for 14 months.

Universal American.   Reverse warrant hedge positions were established in this situation between September 1965 and July 1966—the warrants expired in March 1967. The initial hedge position included common stock purchased in the $7–$8 range— well below the warrant's $13.75 exercise price. As the common advanced to the $14 area in April 1966, the stock was sold and the funds switched into Universal American's convertible preferred stock, which was trading at its conversion value and paying a generous dividend versus no yield on the common. The total position was held until the March 1967 expiration date and then closed out at a net profit in excess of 30 percent on the funds invested. The average time period the position was held was about ten months.

Pacific Petroleums.   Like the two reverse warrant hedges above, the position in Pacific Petroleums, taken in early 1966, involved long common stock versus short warrants. As additional funds became available, the position was increased through July 1966 (the warrants expired in March 1968). In September 1967, six months prior to the warrant's expiration date, all common stock shares were sold. A small portion of the proceeds received was placed in six-month call options on the common stock which were selling at only half the trading price of the warrant even though the common stock was at the warrant's exercise price— additional evidence that short-term warrants are frequently overpriced. The balance of the funds received from the sale of the common stock was placed in other convertible situations. The new hedge position of long calls versus short warrants was held right up to the warrant's expiration date. A net profit of approximately 80 percent was obtained from the total hedge position which was held, on average, for about 21 months.

Note that in each of the above three reverse warrant hedges, the common stock was selling well below the warrant's exercise price at the time the positions were established. This price relationship is best for any reverse hedge as it offers potential profits on both the long and short sides of the position if the common advances to the area of the warrant's exercise price. In each case, the positions were closed out upon a price advance by the common stock.

AN ADDITIONAL 2½-YEAR "TRACK RECORD"

The 1973–74 bear market produced abundant opportunities for reverse warrant hedging as warrant prices lagged behind the wholesale liquidation of their underlying common stocks by institutional money managers. Never in the history of warrants, and probably never again, were so many outstanding reverse warrant hedges available. Between June 1973 and June 1975, I made 18 hedge recommendations for the previously mentioned investment advisory service. Exhibit 12–5 provides a complete record of these 18 recommendations and shows an annualized return of greater than 15 percent despite poor overall market performance during this period. At no time during the worst bear market in 40 years was this portfolio of reverse warrant hedges losing money even though optimum performance was expected from a sideways to up market.

EXHIBIT 12–5: Reverse warrant hedges (June 1973 through December 1975)

Reverse warrant hedge	Date recommended	Date closed	Months held	Profit or loss	Annualized return
Trans-World Airlines...............	6/26/73	9/28/73	3.0	+14%	+56%
Chrysler Corp......................	6/26/73	12/31/75	30.0	+ 7	+ 3
Tesoro Petroleum Corp.............	8/10/73	11/16/73	3.0	+11	+44
Tenneco Inc.......................	8/10/73	1/02/74	16.5	+17	+12
Gould Inc.........................	9/28/73	4/22/75	19.0	+17	+11
American Telephone & Telegraph......................	11/16/73	2/12/75	15.0	+13	+10
Telex Corp........................	11/16/73	12/31/75	25.5	+13	+ 6
Gulf & Western Industries..........	2/16/74	6/30/75	16.5	+ 8	+ 6
Mobil Oil Corp....................	5/15/74	2/12/75	9.0	+13	+17
Carrier Corp.......................	5/15/74	3/31/75	10.5	+26	+30
Tiger International................	5/15/74	3/31/75	10.5	+13	+15
Alza..............................	5/15/74	12/31/75	19.5	+25	+15
CMI Investment...................	5/15/74	12/31/75	19.5	+42	+26
Warner Communications...........	6/28/74	3/31/75	9.0	+26	+35
Louisiana Land & Exploration......	6/28/74	12/31/75	18.0	+28	+19
Tesoro Petroleum Corp.............	6/28/74	12/31/75	18.0	+28	+19
Northwest Industries...............	8/12/74	11/11/74	3.0	+ 7	+28
PSA Inc..........................	8/12/74	4/22/75	8.5	+14	+20
Averages (18 positions).........			14	+18%	+21%

Note: These hedges were recommended for an investment advisory service. Each hedge was designed for profits during sideways or modestly higher markets at limited risk, without attempting to predict future price trends. If a hedge position was proposed more than once (or if a similar hedge position in the same company was suggested) while the initial recommendation was still rated a buy or hold, only the initial recommendation is shown. Profit or loss figures are based on nonleveraged positions and all commission expenses, dividends, and bond interest are included.

chapter 13
Spreading call options

A call option spread is the simultaneous purchase and sale of different calls on the same underlying stock. The difference may be either the exercise dates of the options (calendar spread) or the exercise prices (price spread)—or a combination of both. Under certain circumstances, option spreads may be a better alternative than holding common stock unhedged or a useful tool for complementing your total investment portfolio. Nevertheless, most investors and brokers do not fully understand the risk/reward characteristics or take into consideration the aftertax results that may ensue from this sophisticated hedging strategy.

For a complete discussion of spreading terms, basic strategies, margin requirements, and tax consequences, let me refer you to the booklets available from the option exchanges. I could easily write this chapter by paraphrasing these booklets, but instead I will assume you already have knowledge of the tactics involved in spreading, and perhaps some actual experience. My primary purpose here is to help you avoid the *bad* spreads that are always available and to search out the occasional good spread that offers real risk/reward advantages relative to your total investment ob-

jective. We will start by evaluating the common calendar spread
—normally a poor spreading strategy for most investors.

CALENDAR SPREADS

Consider, for example, the sale of three-month calls on XYZ
Company against the purchase of six-month calls—a typical calendar spread. We will assume that both calls have a $50 exercise
price and that XYZ common is also trading at $50. We will
further assume that the six-month call is trading at a 15 percent
premium ($7.50) and that the three-month call is at a 10 percent
premium ($5.00)—a normal price relationship considering the
time remaining to expiration for both options. The position will
be held for three months and then closed out as the shorter-term
call expires. At this point we would expect the longer-term call to
be trading on the 10 percent premium curve of Exhibit 4–8, since
it will have three months remaining life.

Assuming the purchase and sale of ten calls each to avoid the
high brokerage commissions charged on small quantities, the net
investment is calculated as follows:

Cost of calls purchased = 10 × $750   = $7,500
Less proceeds from calls sold = 10 × $500 = −5,000
Plus commissions (approximate)   = + 300
Net investment   = $2,800

A risk/reward analysis for this spread position might be *misrepresented* as shown in the table.

	Stock price in three months		
	45	*50*	*55*
Estimated call prices			
Three-month call......................	0	0	5.00
Six-month call........................	3.00	5.00	8.00
Profit or (loss) estimates			
Three-month calls.....................	$5,000	$5,000	$ 0
Six-month calls........................	(4,500)	(2,500)	500
Profit or (loss) excluding commissions.....	$ 500	$2,500	$500
Return on investment...................	+18%	+89%	+18%

Not bad for a three-month investment—or is it? Common sense should make the experienced investor pause and ask: "How can profits be expected by spreading when both calls were initially trading at normal premiums?" The answer should be obvious, they can't be expected! The example intentionally misrepresented the risk/reward prospects by not considering possible price movements by XYZ stock beyond the indicated plus or minus 10 percent, and by excluding commission expenses from the profit and loss computations. A realistic risk/reward analysis is shown in the accompanying table. As illustrated, the typical calendar spread will produce profits only if the stock trades in a narrow price range. However, considering the possibility of broad price movements, this trading technique is not recommended for either the serious investor or speculator. It is best left to the floor traders who can take advantage of minor pricing inefficiencies between two options and who pay only nominal commissions.

An additional risk of calendar spreading is that the overall level of option premiums might decline during the three-month period that the spread position is held. The longer-term call would then be trading below the anticipated 10 percent premium curve, resulting in lower profit, or greater loss, than estimated. Note also that profit or loss on calls purchased will be short-term capital gain or loss while profit or loss on calls sold will be ordinary income or expense; there is no opportunity to obtain long-term gains versus ordinary expense as offered by some call option strategies.

| | \multicolumn{5}{c}{*Stock price in three months*} | | | |
	30	40	50	60	70
Estimated call prices					
Three-month call.........	0	0	0	10.00	20.00
Six-month call...........	0.50	1.75	5.00	11.75	20.50
Profit or (loss) estimates					
Three-month calls........	$5,000	$5,000	$5,000	($5,000)	($15,000)
Six-month calls...........	(7,000)	(5,750)	(2,500)	4,250	13,000
Commissions.............	(350)	(500)	(350)	(700)	(900)
Pretax profit or (loss)......	($2,350)	($1,250)	$2,150	($1,450)	($ 2,900)
Return on investment......	−84%	−45%	+80%	−52%	−104%

WHY SPREAD OPTIONS?

Under certain circumstances, there are real advantages to both the speculator and the conservative investor alike in considering option spreading as an alternative to the purchase of common stock or other conventional investment strategies. Most of these advantages will be offered by *price* spreads and may include:

1. High profit potential at predetermined risk compared to holding common stock or other securities unhedged.
2. Optimal return during a sideways market movement at controlled risk. This strategy could be a useful complement to a portfolio of unhedged securities.
3. Risk/reward advantages over the conventional covered or variable call option hedges against common stock.
4. Much less capital than the cost of purchasing stocks unhedged or selling calls against the stocks.
5. Tax advantages, if carefully designed and managed, for optimum aftertax return.

To illustrate the above points, let us examine a few different price spreads for six-month calls on XYZ stock, trading at $50, as shown below.

Available calls

Exercise price	Market price
$40	$12.00
50	7.50
60	4.50

We will assume that the calls have six months or more to run so that purchases may be held for long-term capital gains, if desired. For aftertax calculations, we will assume that the investor is in the 50 percent bracket—ordinary income or expense from calls sold will be calculated at 50 percent while capital gain or loss from calls purchased will be calculated at 25 percent. All positions will be based on ten calls purchased to avoid excessive commission costs, but commissions will be excluded from the calculations for ease of illustrating the strategies. Assuming that all positions are held until the calls' expiration date, call prices at their intrinsic values would be as shown in the accompanying table.

			Stock price at expiration date			
Estimated call prices	30	40	50	60	70
$40 call....................	0	0	10	20	30
$50 call....................	0	0	0	10	20
$60 call....................	0	0	0	0	10

A BULLISH PRICE SPREAD

Buy ten $40 calls at $12.00.......... $12,000
Sell ten $50 calls at $7.50........... −7,500
Net debit (investment)............. $ 4,500

	Stock price at expiration date				
	30	40	50	60	70
Capital gain or (loss) from $40 calls................	(12,000)	(12,000)	(2,000)	8,000	18,000
Ordinary income or (expense) from $50 calls............	7,500	7,500	7,500	(2,500)	(12,500)
Pretax profit or (loss)........	(4,500)	(4,500)	5,500*	5,500	5,500
Tax adjustments—capital....	3,000	3,000	500	(2,000)	(4,500)
Tax adjustments—income....	(3,750)	(3,750)	(3,750)	1,250	6,250
Aftertax return..........	(5,250)	(5,250)	2,250*	4,750	7,250

* Refer to chapter 7 for exercise strategies to convert the pretax profit of $5,500 into capital gains for aftertax advantages.

The price spread would compare favorably with the unhedged purchase of 600 shares of common stock, providing profit or loss as shown below.

	Stock price at expiration date				
	30	40	50	60	70
Capital gain or (loss)..........	(12,000)	(6,000)	0	6,000	12,000
Tax adjustment...............	3,000	1,500	0	(1,500)	3,000
Aftertax return..........	(9,000)	(4,500)	0	4,500	9,000

The spread offers about the same upside potential at less downside risk than unhedged common stock plus a much higher return in a sideways market movement. The spread position can also be taken for less than $5,000, compared to $30,000 for the stock. Investment of the $25,000 difference in money market instruments could provide substantial extras, especially if the stock is a low-dividend payer. There is no doubt that this spread is a superior alternative to the stock position—both pretax and after-tax.

Although commissions were omitted from both estimates for simplification, it should be noted that the actual commission expense to establish the spread position is usually less than that for the purchase of 600 shares of common.

EVEN-MONEY PRICE SPREADS

By definition, in an even-money price spread you receive as much for the calls you sell as you pay for those you purchase—no net debit. Two examples are illustrated below.

Example A:

Buy ten $40 calls at $12.00............ $12,000
Sell sixteen $50 calls at $7.50.......... −12,000
Net debit........................ $ 0

	Stock price at expiration date				
	30	40	50	60	70
Capital gain or (loss).......	(12,000)	(12,000)	(2,000)	8,000	18,000
Income or (expense)........	12,000	12,000	12,000	(4,000)	(20,000)
Pretax profit or (loss).......	0	0	10,000	4,000	(2,000)
Tax adjustments—capital...	3,000	3,000	500	(2,000)	(4,500)
Tax adjustments—income...	(6,000)	(6,000)	(6,000)	2,000	10,000
Aftertax return........	(3,000)	(3,000)	4,500	4,000	3,500

Example B:

Buy ten $40 calls at $12.00.......... $12,000
Sell ten $50 calls at $7.50........... −7,500
Sell ten $60 calls at $4.50........... −4,500
Net debit........................ $ 0

	Stock price at expiration date				
	30	40	50	60	70
Capital gain or (loss)......	(12,000)	(12,000)	(2,000)	8,000	18,000
Income or (expense)					
$50 calls...............	7,500	7,500	7,500	(2,500)	(12,500)
$60 calls...............	4,500	4,500	4,500	4,500	(5,500)
Pretax profit or (loss)......	0	0	10,000	10,000	0
Tax adjustments—capital..	3,000	3,000	500	(2,000)	(4,500)
Tax adjustments—income..	(6,000)	(6,000)	(6,000)	(1,000)	9,000
Aftertax return........	(3,000)	(3,000)	4,500	7,000	4,500

Either of these even-money price spreads compares favorably with unhedged stock purchases or the sale of call options against common stock. For example, let us compare them with this variable hedge position.

Buy 800 shares of stock at $50...... $40,000
Sell twelve $50 calls at $7.50........ −9,000
Net debit........................ $31,000

	Stock price at expiration date				
	30	40	50	60	70
Capital gain or (loss).........	(16,000)	(8,000)	0	8,000	16,000
Income or (expense)..........	9,000	9,000	9,000	(3,000)	(15,000)
Pretax profit or (loss)........	(7,000)	1,000	9,000	5,000	1,000
Tax adjustments—capital.....	4,000	2,000	0	(2,000)	(4,000)
Tax adjustments—income.....	(4,500)	(4,500)	(4,500)	1,500	7,500
Aftertax return..........	(7,500)	(1,500)	4,500	4,500	4,500

In addition to the reduced downside risk, another major advantage provided by the even-money price spreads compared to the conventional variable hedge strategy is the additional $31,000 that may be invested in money market instruments—or other income-producing situations like some of the convertible hedging strategies introduced earlier.

It should be stressed again that the spread examples shown in this chapter are representative but by no means a complete overview of the available market. Other publications should be studied before beginning an option-spreading program.

SUMMARY

The following guidelines should be used for selecting and managing price spreads.

1. The long call should normally be in the money and trading close to its intrinsic value. By itself, the call option combined with cash should be a good alternative to unhedged common stock, as illustrated in chapter 5.

2. The call (or calls) sold should have an exercise price above that of the call purchased and by itself should be a reasonable candidate for hedging against common stock per the strategies of chapter 6.

3. The number of calls sold versus calls purchased should be established based on the *aftertax* potential profit relative to risk. Note that profit and loss potentials based on the modest capital invested in the spread are both amplified compared to conventional strategies. Do not assume risks greater than you can afford to take.

4. Select spreads having more than six months to run if long-term capital gains are advantageous to you.

5. Monitor all spread positions continually to avoid an early assignment of call options sold. An assignment might result in a capital loss on the call instead of the more favorable ordinary loss if it were bought back.

6. If the stock price approaches your aftertax upside or downside break-even points, you may wish to use defensive strategies by revising the spread mix or switching to different exercise prices.

7. If the stock ends up at, or modestly above, the exercise price of the calls sold, consider letting them be exercised rather than buying them back. The exercise of your long calls (or the purchase of stock) in response to the assignment could convert ordinary income into capital gains (short term). See chapter 7 for a discussion of this tactic.

8. Other collateral should be maintained in the account whenever naked calls are sold, as in even-money spreads, to provide for increased margin requirements during a rising market.

chapter 14

Strategies with listed put options

This chapter is being written prior to the introduction of listed puts on the option exchanges. For this reason, I will not go into as great an amount of detail as in earlier chapters on call options. But I do want to alert you to the potential advantages (and pitfalls) that listed puts will offer, and I have prepared three exhibits for your future reference. Again, I assume that you have knowledge of the basic investment strategies and risk/reward characteristics for put options.

The three exhibits, to be discussed shortly, are built around six basic investment strategies. Listed in descending order from the most bullish to the most bearish, they are:

1. Buy 100 shares of stock.
2. Buy one call option.
3. Sell one put option (uncovered).
4. Sell one call option (uncovered).
5. Buy one put option.
6. Sell short 100 shares of stock.

All tactics relating to puts and calls involve one or more of these six basic strategies. If you understand the risk/reward characteristics of each, you should have no trouble evaluating any other suggested strategy—whether it be a strip, a strap, or whatever other complex tactics the investment community might dream up to complicate your life and to enrich its bank accounts.

Exhibit 14–1 illustrates the risk/reward characteristics for the six basic strategies, assuming that:

1. The common stock is trading at $50.
2. Six-month puts and calls, having $50 exercise prices, are both trading at $5 (10 percent premiums).
3. Commissions and dividends are excluded to simplify the illustrations.

As shown in the exhibit, it is assumed that the stock ends up in a price range of $30 to $70 upon expiration of the options. This assumption permits us to conveniently illustrate the potential risk and reward for each strategy. For example, the conventional strategy of purchasing common stock (strategy 1) offers a possible loss of $2,000 versus a potential gain of $2,000. The purchase of a call option (strategy 2), an alternative to buying common stock, limits the downside risk to the $500 premium paid while offering as full upside potential as the stock, minus the premium ($2,000 − $500 = $1,500). Of course, if the stock remained unchanged, the call option buyer would also lose the entire $500 premium while the stock buyer would suffer no loss. Note that the profit and loss figures shown are pretax; aftertax results may be substantially different and will be evaluated later.

The major purpose of Exhibit 14–1 is to demonstrate that for every basic strategy there is a mirror image alternative—you should never use one without first considering the other. Let us briefly review each of the six basic strategies and their alternatives. Guidelines will be developed for helping you determine which alternative offers the most favorable risk/reward prospects.

EXHIBIT 14–1:   Alternate strategies with listed puts and calls (pretax results)
Assumptions: 1. Stock is trading at $50.
2. Six-month puts and calls, having $50 exercise prices, are both trading at $5 (10 percent premiums).
3. Commissions and dividends are excluded.

	Prices at expiration date				
	30	40	50	60	70
Stock...	30	40	50	60	70
Call..	0	0	0	10	20
Put..	20	10	0	0	0

Bullish Strategies

1.	Buy 100 shares of stock............	(2,000)	(1,000)	0	1,000	2,000
1a.	Buy one call and sell one put.......	(2,000)	(1,000)	0	1,000	2,000
2.	Buy one call.....................	(500)	(500)	(500)	500	1,500
2a.	Buy 100 shares and buy one put.....	(500)	(500)	(500)	500	1,500
3.	Sell one put.....................	(1,500)	(500)	500	500	500
3a.	Buy 100 shares and sell one call.....	(1,500)	(500)	500	500	500

Bearish strategies

4.	Sell one call.....................	500	500	500	(500)	(1,500)
4a.	Short 100 shares and sell one put....	500	500	500	(500)	(1,500)
5.	Buy one put.....................	1,500	500	(500)	500)	(500)
5a.	Short 100 shares and buy one call...	1,500	500	(500)	(500)	(500)
6.	Short 100 shares of stock...........	2,000	1,000	0	(1,000)	(2,000)
6a.	Buy one put and sell one call.......	2,000	1,000	0	(1,000)	(2,000)

Neutral strategies

a.	Buy 100 shares and sell two calls...	(1,000)	0	1,000	0	(1,000)
b.	Short 100 shares and sell two puts....	(1,000)	0	1,000	0	(1,000)
c.	Sell one straddle..................	(1,000)	0	1,000	0	(1,000)

BULLISH STRATEGIES

1 versus 1a.   The risk/reward characteristics of buying common stock (1) are obvious to everyone, but the alternate strategy of buying a call and selling a put (1a) may offer substantial advantages. First, on the assumption that the premium received for selling the put is the same as the premium paid for buying the call, there would be no net debit charged to your account—compared to a debit of $5,000 for the purchase of stock. The collateral required for margining the naked put might earn a greater yield than that paid on the common. Second, if the put premium were higher than the call premium, you would actually receive a net credit to your account plus your potential profit is increased and your risk decreased by the difference in the premiums. Third, commission expenses for the put and call alternative might be lower than for the purchase of common stock. Note that the above advantages would apply regardless of whether overall option premiums are high or low as long as the relationship between the put and call premiums is as indicated.

2 versus 2a.   The alternative to the simple purchase of a call option (2) is the purchase of 100 shares of stock plus one put option (2a). The call option strategy will normally be the best unless the common stock is a high-dividend payer and/or the put premium is substantially lower than the call premium.

3 versus 3a.   The sale of an uncovered put option (3) is an excellent alternative to the conventional sale of a covered call against the underlying stock (3a)—possibly greater yield on the collateral used for selling the naked put versus the dividend paid on the stock, plus lower commission expenses.

BEARISH STRATEGIES

4 versus 4a.   The sale of a put against 100 shares of stock sold short (4a) represents the covered put-writing strategy and will probably be aggressively promoted by the brokerage industry as a way to earn premium income during bear markets. But, this strategy will seldom offer superior advantages to the simple sale of an uncovered call option (4) since dividends (if any) must be paid on the stock sold short, as well as higher commission expenses.

5 versus 5a.   The simple purchase of a put option (5) will normally offer advantages for bear market profits over the complex strategy of shorting 100 shares of stock against a call option (5a)—no dividends paid on stock sold short plus lower commissions.

6 versus 6a.   The more sophisticated strategy of buying a put and selling a call option (*6a*) will normally be more advantageous than the short sale of common stock (6), especially if the put premium is lower than the call premium and if the stock pays a dividend.

As noted in the above discussion for bullish and bearish strategies, the dividend paid on the common stock and premium differences between the put and call are important factors to consider

EXHIBIT 14–2:   Comparison of alternate strategies with listed puts and calls (Pretax results)

Put premium versus call premium ⟶	Stock pays no dividend			Stock dividend equals money market rate		
	Lower	Same	Higher	Lower	Same	Higher
Bullish Strategies						
1 or 1*a*	*	1*a*	1*a*	1	either	1*a*
2 or 2*a*	*	2	2	2*a*	either	2
3 or 3*a*	*	3	3	3*a*	either	3
Bearish strategies						
4 or 4*a*	4	either	4*a*	4	4	*
5 or 5*a*	5	either	5*a*	5	5	*
6 or 6*a*	6*a*	either	6	6*a*	6*a*	*
Neutral strategies						
a, b, or *c*	*a* or *c**	*b* or *c*	*b*	*a*	*a* or *c*	*b* or *c**

* The best strategy will depend on the precise difference between put and call premiums relative to interest earned on the collateral used to carry the positions.

when evaluating the available alternatives. Exhibit 14–2 summarizes these considerations and indicates the favored strategy depending on the circumstances. Commission expense differences are less important and are excluded, but they could tip the scales if all other factors were equal.

NEUTRAL STRATEGIES

Exhibits 14–1 and 14–2 also include neutral strategies for optimizing return on investment during a sideways market movement—the most common being the sale of two calls against 100 shares of stock (the variable hedge). Depending on the stock's yield versus money market rates and the difference between put and call premiums, the other alternatives may be better.

AFTERTAX RESULTS

As if life weren't complicated enough, the unique tax treatment presently applicable to put and call premiums may substantially modify the relative risk/reward characteristics of the alternate strategies. Aftertax results are shown in Exhibit 14–3; assuming

EXHIBIT 14–3:   Alternate strategies with listed puts and calls (Aftertax results)
Additional assumption: The investor is in the 50 percent tax bracket and all capital gains
—short term or long term— are at 25 percent (short-term gains are offset by other short-
term losses, or are converted into long term by other strategies; and losses are offset by
other gains).

			Prices at expiration			
		30	40	50	60	70
Stock		30	40	50	60	70
Call		0	0	0	10	20
Put		20	10	0	0	0
Bullish strategies						
1.	Buy 100 shares of stock	(1,500)	(750)	0	750	1,500
1a.	Buy one call and sell one put	(1,125)	(625)	(125)	625	1,375
2.	Buy one call	(375)	(375)	(375)	375	1,125
2a.	Buy 100 shares and buy one put	(375)	(375)	(375)	375	1,125
3.	Sell one put	(750)	(250)	250	250	250
3a.	Buy 100 shares and sell one call	(1,250)	(500)	250	500	750
Bearish strategies						
4.	Sell one call	250	250	250	(250)	(750)
4a.	Short 100 shares and sell one put	750	500	250	(500)	(1,250)
5.	Buy one put	1,125	375	(375)	(375)	(375)
5a.	Short 100 shares and buy one call	1,125	375	(375)	(375)	(375)
6.	Short 100 shares of stock	1,500	750	0	(750)	(1,500)
6a.	Buy one put and sell one call	1,375	625	(125)	(625)	(1,125)
Neutral strategies						
a.	Buy 100 shares and sell two calls	(1,000)	(250)	500	250	0
b.	Short 100 shares and sell two puts	0	250	500	(250)	(1,000)
c.	Sell one straddle	(500)	0	500	0	(500)

that the investor is in the 50 percent bracket, that in-the-money puts and calls sold are repurchased instead of allowed to be exercised, and that all capital gains or losses ultimately receive long-term tax treatment.[1]

One of the most interesting aspects of Exhibit 14–3 is the aftertax results of the three neutral strategies. The only truly neutral strategy is the sale of a straddle; the other two strategies have a strong aftertax upward or downward bias.

HOW SHOULD THE SOPHISTICATED INVESTOR EMPLOY PUT OPTIONS?

Since all of the basic strategies and their alternatives were related to the underlying common stock, and since earlier chapters showed that there are superior alternatives to stocks, how should we plan to employ put options in our overall investment program? As I presently see it, there will be two major uses of puts by the sophisticated investor.

1. *Downside protection.* Probably the most important use of puts will be to purchase them for downside protection of a portfolio of undervalued convertible bonds or preferreds— especially when put premiums are low. Or, a typical convertible hedger may want to sell calls when the overall level of premiums is high and buy puts when premiums are low— or use both strategies if call premiums are high and put premiums are low.

2. *Price spreads.* The best spreading opportunities for call options, as shown in chapter 13, were price spreads. However, they had an upward market bias—especially when considering aftertax results. Conversely then, put option price spreads may be employed for bear market profits or combined with call option price spreads for optimum return during a sideways market.

---

[1] Note: If the tax ruling concerning profit or loss on options sold is changed, as previously discussed, this exhibit may no longer be of value.

chapter 15

The most undervalued securities in today's market

Dual-purpose funds can be used by both conservative and aggressive investors to gain substantial advantages over conventional forms of investing. More income can be obtained than from corporate bonds, or greater capital appreciation can be sought at less risk than from the typical common stock portfolio. Dual-purpose funds are ideal tools for the individual investor. It is a shame that most do not understand them, but if everyone did, the advantages offered by these unique investments would no longer exist. What are the advantages? How are they measured? These questions will be answered, but first let us understand the subject at hand.

The dual-purpose funds are closed-end investment companies with portfolios similar to other professionally managed funds. However, as their name implies, fund ownership is divided equally into *two classes* of securities—income shares and capital shares. The *income* shares receive all the dividends and interest earned on the underlying portfolio while the *capital* shares get all the capital gains—or losses. Therefore, an investor can have $2 working toward his particular goal for each $1 that he invests. "Leveraged fund" is a term commonly used to describe this feature.

Dual-purpose funds also differ from other closed-end funds in another most important, but overlooked, area. Each dual-purpose fund has a specified *terminal date* when there will be a final accounting to both the income and the capital shareholders. The funds will either liquidate or become open-end investment companies (mutual funds)—as desired by the shareholders. The income shares will be redeemed at fixed redemption prices and the remaining assets will go to the capital shareholders. Payment will be in cash or in equivalent value of shares of the ongoing mutual fund (which may be redeemed at net asset value).

Before the terminal date, neither class of shares can be redeemed; but all are traded in the marketplace. Like other closed-end funds, their market prices may reflect either a discount or a premium relative to their net assets; they have generally sold at discounts since their inception in 1967. This discount is the most important advantage offered by the dual-purpose funds and is the reason they are, for the present, such a unique and clearly superior investment. This advantage is especially attractive because you know that unlike other funds, the terminal dates *provide fixed points in time when they must sell at their net asset values!* In other words, the discount *must disappear.*

At the present time, the seven dual-purpose funds shown below offer superior alternatives to conventional investments for income or capital appreciation or a combination of both objectives.

The purchase of an equal number of income and capital shares

Fund	*Investment adviser*	*Total assets* (*in million $*)
American DualVest Fund.......	Weiss, Peck & Greer	$33
Gemini Fund................	Wellington Management	44
Hemisphere Fund..............	CNA Management Corp.	17
Income and Capital Shares......	Phoenix Investment Counsel of Boston	26
Leverage Fund of Boston.......	Vance, Sanders & Co.	50
Putnam Duofund..............	The Putnam Management	24
Scudder Duo-Vest.............	Scudder, Stevens & Clark	93

of any of these dual-purpose funds would be comparable to investing in typical closed-end or mutual funds, or each income and capital share may be evaluated separately to determine its individual merits. Procedures for studying these securities will be provided but first we will trace the history of one of the funds to develop a better understanding of the advantages and related risks for these unusual securities.

GEMINI FUND

Gemini Fund began operations in March 1967 and, except for modest cash reserves from time to time, its portfolio has been fully invested in a broadly diversified list of common stocks. Approximately 1.7 million shares of both income and capital securities were issued. Each had a starting net asset value of $11 per share (the shares were actually sold to the public above their net asset values since a sales charge was added).

The total assets of the fund appreciated steadily through 1972, at which time they reached $55 million, compared to the starting value of about $37 million. The 1973–74 bear market reduced net assets to about $30 million and they then rebounded to $44 million at the end of 1975. Overall, Gemini performed very satisfactorily during this difficult nine-year market period when most stock market portfolios declined in value. In fact, Gemini Fund was the standout performer of the dual-purpose fund group.

The purchasers of *income* shares in 1967 were promised a minimum annual dividend of $0.56 per share plus the possibility of future increases if the dividends received from the fund's portfolio increased. They were also guaranteed an $11 redemption value on December 31, 1984, unless the total assets of the fund were to shrink below $18.5 million by that date (1.7 million shares × $11 per share). The income shareholders have not been disappointed. In fact, the annual dividends paid on their shares have grown to $1.38—or a yield of 12.5 percent on the original $11 investment. The shares have traded as high as 15½ and were recently well above their $11 redemption value despite the high interest rate levels prevailing in the medium- to long-term money markets.

Contrary to the investment objectives of the income shareholders, the buyers of *capital* shares in 1967 were seeking an aggressive way to participate in an advancing stock market. Had stocks continued to rise as they did during previous years, the capital shares would have advanced about twice as fast because of their inherent leverage. For example, if the total net assets of Gemini Fund had doubled to $74 million, the capital shares net asset value would have tripled to $33 per share—an appreciation of 200 percent. The capital shareholders would have also benefited from the lower tax rate applicable to capital gains. On the downside, however, the net asset value of the capital shares would have declined twice as fast as the total assets of the fund. Trading at $11 per share in 1967, the capital shares were simply a leveraged investment on the market—twice the upside potential but also twice the downside risk. The purchase of the capital shares provided an investment posture similar to buying conventional common stocks on 50 percent margin.

Despite the relatively good performance record of Gemini during the nine-year period, the capital shareholders actually fared worse than would have been expected. Like most closed-end funds, the shares quickly went to a discount from their net asset value and this discount widened as the public withdrew from the market. At the end of 1975, while their net asset value had advanced to over $15 per share, the capital shares were trading at only $9.75.

The large discount for Gemini's capital shares, as 1976 began, created a *once in a lifetime* investment opportunity. On December 31, 1984, the capital shares *must* trade at their net asset value whether the public is an active participant in the stock market or not. At about $10 per share, the capital shares promised to advance more than three times as fast as the net assets of the fund during the next nine years. On the downside, their risk was cushioned by the large discount from net asset value.

Anyone interested in taking a long-term investment posture in the stock market should have seriously considered Gemini's securities—or those of the other dual-purpose funds—instead of building his own stock portfolio. The advantages are overwhelming! They include, as an alternative to a common stock portfolio:

1. Built-in diversification.
2. Professional money management.
3. One-decision investing.

As a unique investment vehicle, the funds also offer:

1. *Discount* investing.
2. Leverage on your dollar (better than 2 for 1), offering the potential for outperforming an up market by a wide margin.

Let us now examine each of the income and capital shares of the seven funds as they existed on December 31, 1975, to determine which offered the best future risk/reward prospects.

THE DUAL-PURPOSE FUND INCOME SHARES

The income shares of the dual-purpose funds may be considered as alternate investments to corporate bonds or other income securities, or they may be combined with capital shares for an alternative to ordinary mutual funds or conventional common stock portfolios. Like bonds, their current yield and yield to maturity may be calculated. Exhibit 15–1 provides relevant information at 1975 year-end prices. As shown in Exhibit 15–1, the shares offered higher returns than most corporate bonds having similar maturity dates.

EXHIBIT 15–1:   The income shares (December 31, 1975 values)

	Market prices	Redemption		Estimated dividend*	Current yield*	Yield to maturity*
		Price	Date			
American DualVest Fund.....	$12.50	$15.00	6/29/79	$1.00	8.0%	12.5%
Gemini Fund...............	13.25	11.00	12/31/84	1.37	10.3	9.2
Hemisphere Fund...........	6.50	11.44	6/30/85	0.65	10.0	13.0
Income and Capital Shares....	9.25	10.00	3/31/82	0.78	8.4	9.5
Leverage Fund of Boston.....	12.625	13.72	1/03/82	1.03	8.2	9.3
Putnam Duofund............	16.50	19.75	1/03/83	1.34†	8.1	10.1
Scudder Duo-Vest...........	8.125	9.15	3/31/82	0.75	9.2	10.8

  * Current yield and yield to maturity were based on estimated dividends for 1976 as reported in the *Value Line Investment Survey*. No adjustments were made for possible dividend increases or decreases in future years.

  † $1.38 is the minimum annual dividend effective 12/31/76. Thereafter, the minimum dividend will be increased by approximately 10 cents per share at the end of each successive two-year period until such dividend is $1.58 beginning on 1/1/81.

Like the purchase of bonds, an investor considering these income shares should evaluate the quality of the underlying assets in the fund's portfolio and the amount of total assets relative to the redemption price (asset coverage). Exhibits 15–2 and 15–3 summarize the essential information at 1975 year-end prices, but the fund's most recent quarterly report should be consulted also for complete and current data. As shown in Exhibit 15–2, most of the income shares were well protected by excess assets, and Exhibit 15–3 indicates that the equity-type securities held were generally in quality companies. The obvious exception was Hemisphere Fund since its asset coverage was only nominal. However, much of Hemisphere's assets were invested in short-term money market instruments or bonds and the balance in high-quality common stocks. Of course, portfolio shifts by the funds to more aggressive investments would expose their income shares to greater risk than indicated—or a shift to cash or bonds would increase safety.

During the 1973–74 bear market, the total assets of some of the funds declined to levels where the full redemption value of their income shares was threatened. This caused their portfolio

EXHIBIT 15–2:   The income shares (December 31, 1975 portfolio analysis)

	Redemption price	Current total assets*	Asset coverage	Portfolio makeup	
				Cash and bonds†	Stocks‡
American DualVest Fund.......	$15.00	$20.70§	138%	30%	70%
Gemini Fund..................	11.00	26.32	239	0	100
Hemisphere Fund..............	11.44	11.89	104	45	55
Income and Capital Shares......	10.00	17.34§	173	20	80
Leverage Fund of Boston........	13.72	24.68	180	12	88
Putnam Duofund‖	19.75	31.72§	161	0	100
Scudder Duo-Vest..............	9.15	16.95	185	18	82

* Total assets equal income share redemption price plus capital share net asset value except as indicated (§).

† Includes short-term money market instruments plus corporate or government bonds.

‡ Includes common stocks and convertible securities.

§ Current asset value for income shares is less than redemption price—difference will be made up by terminal date by transfer of funds from capital shares to income shares:

> American DualVest $14.65
> Income and Capital Shares..................... 9.64
> Putnam Duofund.............................. 19.00

‖ Two capital shares for each income share.

managers to adopt defensive investment postures by switching some of their common stocks into cash or conservative income situations—Hemisphere Fund was 98 percent in cash and bonds at the end of 1974. Assuming the same defensive money management strategy in the future, it seems reasonable to expect that the full redemption values will be received at terminal dates even if the stock market were to decline in interim years.

At 1975 year-end price levels, the income share group offered exceptional alternatives to corporate bonds or other conservative income-type investments. Maturity dates from as short as 3½ years (American DualVest) to as long as 9½ years (Hemisphere Fund) provided additional flexibility for investment planning.

THE DUAL-PURPOSE FUND CAPITAL SHARES

My investment career has been devoted to the search for undervalued or overpriced securities in the areas of convertibles, war-

EXHIBIT 15–3: **Ten largest common stock and equity-related holdings for each fund (as of year-end 1975)**

American DualVest Fund
American Telephone & Telegraph
Union Carbide
International Business Machines
Alcoa
Studebaker-Worthington
UAL Inc.
El Paso Co.
Crum & Forster
Tropicana Products
Diamond Shamrock

Gemini Fund
American Telephone & Telegraph
Philadelphia Suburban Corp.
Interco Inc.
Martin-Marietta
Koppers
Studebaker-Worthington
Harsco Corp.
Ethyl Corp.
International Minerals & Chemicals
Philadelphia National

Hemisphere Fund
International Telephone & Telegraph
Ford Motor Co.
Dow Chemical
International Business Machines
National Starch
Caterpillar Tractor
Pittson Co.
Monsanto
International Paper
Exxon Corp.

Income and Capital Shares
American Telephone & Telegraph
ACF Industries
DuPont
Pioneer Corp.
Exxon Corp.
United Technologies
Phillips Petroleum
Federated Department Stores
Caterpillar Tractor
Amerada Hess

Leverage Fund of Boston
Exxon Corp.
Raytheon Co.
Boeing
Standard Oil of Indiana
Pay'n Save
Farmers Group
Atlantic Richfield
Northrop Corp.
R. J. Reynolds Industries
Monsanto

Putnam Duofund
Allied Stores
Owens-Illinois Inc.
R. J. Reynolds Industries
Monsanto
Pizza Hut Inc.
Celanese Corp.
International Paper
Colt Industries
Union Camp
Kaiser Aluminum & Chemicals

Scudder Duo-Vest
Exxon Corp.
Philip Morris
Nortrust
Stauffer Chemical
Time Inc.
Bethlehem Steel
Monsanto
Atlantic Richfield
Tektronix Inc.
International Business Machines

rants, options, and other special situations. This research has exposed many outstanding investment opportunities but none compares with the dual-purpose fund capital shares as they existed in January 1976. They were *grossly undervalued* relative to the underlying assets in their portfolios. This unusual situation was caused by the lack of interest by the investment public. The institutions aggressively purchased the stocks held by the dual-purpose funds but there was little public activity to keep the shares of the funds in line with their inherent values. And, for *strange* reasons, institutions do not buy the securities of other professionally managed funds—even at huge discounts. Since these securities will probably remain undervalued for some time in the future in today's institutionally dominated market, you should learn how to evaluate the risk/reward characteristics of these capital shares. The following material should be carefully studied—*then re-studied!*

The capital shares of the dual-purpose funds are essentially long-term call options (or warrants) on the underlying securities held by the funds. At their terminal dates, they will be worth the total value of the funds' portfolios less the fixed redemption prices paid to the income shareholders. Their potential upside appreciation and downside risk are directly related to their current discounts below net asset values, their inherent leverage, future stock market trends, and the investment skills of the funds' managers.

The net asset value of a capital share is equal to the total assets of the fund less the book value of its related income shares. This information is reported weekly in *The Wall Street Journal* and other financial publications as shown in Exhibit 15–4. As useful as this published information may seem, it does not provide the essential tools for measuring the true worth of these securities. It provides no information on their inherent leverage relative to the underlying equity-type investments in the fund—information needed for estimating future risk/reward opportunities.

EXHIBIT 15-4:   The capital shares (December 31, 1975 values as reported weekly in financial publications)

	Market price	Net asset value	Premium or discount
American DualVest Fund..................	$4.375	$ 6.05	− 28%
Gemini Fund...........................	9.75	15.32	− 36
Hemisphere Fund........................	1.75	0.45	+289
Income & Capital Shares.................	4.625	7.70	− 40
Leverage Fund of Boston.................	6.75	10.96	− 38
Putnam Duofund........................	3.875	6.36	− 39
Scudder Duo-Vest.......................	4.625	7.80	− 41

Exhibits 15–5 and 15–6 bridge this information gap. As shown in Exhibit 15–5, we will assume the equity securities held in each of the funds' portfolios will simply advance or decline by the same amount as the overall stock market in future years. The net asset value at terminal date for each of the capital shares may then be estimated as shown. The dollar figures are converted to percentage advances or declines as shown in Exhibit 15–6.

Finally, risk/reward ratios may be computed for measuring the current attractiveness of each capital share, relative to the overall stock market. I have selected a stock market advance of 50 percent versus a decline of 25 percent to calculate the risk/

EXHIBIT 15-5:   The capital shares (estimated values at terminal dates)

	Market price	Estimated capital share value at terminal date,* assuming that equity portion of portfolio changes by:				
		−50%	−25%	0%	+50%	+100%
American DualVest Fund	$4.375	$ 0	$2.08	$ 5.70	$12.94	$20.19
Gemini Fund.................	$9.75	2.16	8.74	15.32	28.48	41.64
Hemisphere Fund.............	1.75	0	0	0.45	3.72	6.99
Income and Capital Shares......	4.625	0.40	3.87	7.34	14.28	21.21
Leverage Fund of Boston.......	6.75	0.10	5.53	10.96	21.82	32.68
Putnam Duofund†.............	3.875	0	2.02	5.98	13.92	21.84
Scudder Duo-Vest.............	4.625	0.85	4.32	7.80	14.75	21.70

   * Estimated capital share value = current total assets (*CTA*), from Exhibit 15–2, plus or minus *CTA* × percent market change × percent of portfolio in equity investments, minus income share redemption value.
   † Two capital shares for each income share.

EXHIBIT 15-6: The capital shares (risk/reward analysis)

	Change in capital share value at terminal date, assuming that equity portion of portfolio changes by:					Risk/ Reward ratio*
	−50%	*−25%*	*−0%*	*+50%*	*+100%*	
American DualVest Fund......	−100%	− 53%	+30%	+196%	+361%	1.8
Gemini Fund.................	− 78	− 10	+57	+192	+327	9.6
Hemisphere Fund.............	−100	−100	−74	+113	+299	0.6
Income and Capital Shares......	− 91	− 16	+59	+209	+359	6.4
Leverage Fund of Boston.......	− 98	− 18	+62	+232	+384	6.9
Putnam Duofund..............	−100	− 48	+54	+259	+464	2.7
Scudder Duo-Vest.............	− 82	− 6	+69	+219	+369	18.2

$$* \text{Risk/Reward ratio} = \frac{25 \text{ percent market decline}}{\text{percent capital share decline}} \times \frac{\text{percent capital share advance}}{50 \text{ percent market advance}}$$

reward ratios but other numbers may also be used if you desire. Since, by definition, the risk/reward ratio for the "market" is 1.0, most of the dual-purpose fund capital shares offered substantial advantages.

CONCLUSIONS

Both the income shares and the capital shares of the dual-purpose funds have been overlooked by the investment public in the institutionally dominated stock market we have witnessed in recent times. They presently offer outstanding values and can be used by the sophisticated investor in a variety of ways to improve his investment performance. Here are a few strategies for your consideration.

1. Selected income shares offer greater current yield or yield to maturity than conventional income-type investments of comparable quality. Aggressive income-oriented investors may consider the purchase of these securities on margin.

2. Selected capital shares provide an aggressive investment approach for achieving exceptional long-term capital apprecia-

tion—assuming a rising stock market in future years. Speculators may consider the purchase of the capital shares on margin.

3. A combination of selected income shares and capital shares, in different funds, provides a superior alternative to most conventional portfolios of common stocks—an equal dollar amount invested in each offers greater upside potential at less downside risk. Investors in high tax brackets should consider combining capital shares with tax-exempt bonds as a superior aftertax alternative to the stock market.

chapter 16
The SUPERHEDGE!

The traditional hedging strategies illustrated throughout this book were designed to take advantage of securities that were significantly undervalued or overpriced relative to their underlying common stocks. The construction of a hedge, using these undervalued or overpriced securities, enabled us to optimize risk/reward ratios for maximum investment success.

The following table shows the basic hedging strategies that were evaluated.

Long security	Short security
Undervalued convertibles	Common stock call options
Undervalued warrants	Common stock call options
Common stock convertibles	*Overpriced warrants*
Common stock convertibles	*Overpriced call options*

As attractive as these various hedges are, I am pleased to announce the development of a new and exciting hedging strategy that promises even greater potential for profit and offers:

1. The use of *grossly undervalued* securities for the long side of the hedge—with *absolute assurance* that they will return to their normal market value in time.

2. The potential for maintaining the short side of the hedge in *overpriced* securities—or in securities that you believe will *underperform* the market over the near term.

3. Broad market diversification.

A SUPER HEDGING STRATEGY

Chapter 15 showed how drastically undervalued some of the dual-purpose fund capital shares have been in recent times and provided simple analytical tools for measuring their risk/reward characteristics, relative to the overall stock market, on a continuing basis. Although I have used these unique funds to complement conventional hedge portfolios for years, I was always intrigued by the possibility of employing them directly in some form of hedge against the overall market. Several concepts were evaluated but rejected. The opportunity finally surfaced as the listed call option market developed and expanded to over 100 different securities. Why not simply purchase the best dual-purpose capital shares and sell overpriced call options, on a diversified list of common stocks, against them?

What are the risks? What are the potential rewards? Can profit or loss projections be made for different stock market movements with reasonable accuracy? Let us evaluate a possible dual-purpose fund *superhedge* portfolio to see if these questions have predictable answers.

Using Gemini Fund capital share data from chapter 15, a $100,000 *superhedge* portfolio could be constructed as follows:

1. A total of $120,000 worth of Gemini capital shares are purchased—about 12,000 shares at $10.00 per share (including commissions).

2. Since each capital share represents $26.32 worth of under-
lying common stocks ($26.32 total assets × 100 percent in-
vested in stocks), the $120,000 market value of the capital
shares controls about $300,000 worth of stocks (12,000
shares × $26.32).

3. Call options are then sold against a diversified portfolio of
common stocks having a total market value of about
$300,000—20 different positions at about $15,000 each are
recommended for diversification.

4. Since all call options sold will be treated as being uncovered,
we will select out-of-the-money calls because of the favorable
margin requirements that apply. Assuming that the calls are
10 percent out of the money, the total value of the calls'
exercise prices would be about $330,000 ($300,000 ÷ 90
percent).

5. Assuming 6 to 7 percent premiums for typical six-month
calls, trading 10 percent out of the money, the account is
credited with about $20,000 in call premiums ($330,000 ×
$6\frac{1}{2}$ percent, minus commissions).

6. The net cash investment required to establish the *superhedge* is $100,000—the $120,000 cost of the Gemini capital
shares less the $20,000 received for call premiums.

7. The collateral value of the capital shares should be sufficient
for initially margining the uncovered calls. This is confirmed
by the following margin calculations.

Initial margin requirements
Capital shares: $120,000 × 50%	= $ 60,000
Call options: $300,000 × 30%	= 90,000
Minus amount out of the money	= −30,000
Minus premiums received	= −20,000
Total investment required	= $100,000

Note that the account would have a *maintenance* margin surplus
of $24,000 since 70 percent of the capital share's market value

would apply for maintenance ($120,000 × 70% = $84,000). This surplus is important to avoid nuisance maintenance margin calls if the underlying common stocks were to advance toward their calls' exercise prices, but it would probably be insufficient in the event of a major stock market rally.

ANTICIPATED PERFORMANCE IN DIFFERENT TYPES OF MARKETS

To evaluate the potential risks and rewards for the *superhedge* under different stock market conditions, we will first make these assumptions:

1. The stocks held by Gemini Fund in its portfolio will perform like the market.
2. The stocks underlying the call options sold will also perform like the market.
3. The capital shares of the fund will remain relatively under-valued over the near term, although they must ultimately trade at their net asset value.

We will also compare the risk/reward characteristics of the *superhedge* with conventional call option hedge portfolios where calls are sold against underlying shares of common stocks at their exercise prices (not out of the money as in the *superhedge*).

Declining markets. During a broadly declining market, we would expect a modest decline in our *superhedge* account's equity —losses on the capital shares minus the call premiums received. On the downside, the capital share's discount from net asset value should diminish as the shares build up inherent leverage, and as the public selling of these securities lags behind during an institutional-type bear market. Assuming a 20 percent stock market decline over a six-month period and a 25 percent discount for the capital shares (versus a 36 percent discount prior to the decline), our estimated position would be calculated as shown in the table below.

Total asset value of Gemini Fund = $26.32 − (20% × $26.32) =	$ 21.06
Minus income share redemption price	= − 11.00
Capital share net asset value	= $ 10.06
Estimated capital share price = $10.06 × 75%	= $ 7.55
Capital share loss = 12,000 shares × ($10.00 − 7.55)	= ($29,400)
Minus premiums received assuming that all call options expire worthless	= −20,000
Estimated net loss	= ($ 9,400)
	− 9.4%

Note that a conventional portfolio of covered call options would also be expected to be down about 10 percent for a 20 per-cent market decline. Of course, a market decline over 20 percent during the six-month period would result in greater losses for both the *superhedge* and the conventional hedge portfolio.

Sideways markets. A sideways market is a desirable en-vironment for any seller of call options and the *superhedge* strat-egy is no exception. In theory, the entire $20,000 received in premiums is the six-month profit potential; however, some of the underlying stocks might rise above their exercise prices, giving some calls intrinsic value at their expiration dates. If we assume that 75 percent of the potential profit is received, the annualized return is about 30 percent ($15,000 profit, or 15 percent for six months). In any event, the *superhedge* should outperform a con-ventional option hedge portfolio by a substantial amount during a sideways market movement—about twice the premium amount available for potential profits plus greater probability of capturing the premiums since the calls sold were out of the money.

Advancing markets. An advancing market is the ideal en-vironment for a covered call-selling program—a 1:1 ratio of calls sold versus stock held, as in the *superhedge.* In fact, the *superhedge* should perform even better than a conventional hedge portfolio since the stocks start out by 10 percent out of the money. If we assume that Gemini's capital shares will remain at a

36 percent discount during a near-term rising market, the profit potential may be estimated as shown in the following table.

	Capital share net asset value	Capital share price	Profit potential		
			Capital shares	Calls	Net
10 percent market advance........	$17.95	$11.49	$18,000	$20,000	$38,000
20 percent market advance........	20.58	13.17	38,000	(10,000)	28,000
30 percent market advance........	23.22	14.86	58,000	(40,000)	18,000
40 percent market advance........	25.85	16.54	78,000	(70,000)	8,000

The above estimates of potential profit are *maximums* assuming that all of the calls' underlying common stocks advance with the market. Since some will certainly rise faster while others lag behind or actually decline, the profit realized might be somewhat lower than shown, especially for only a modest market advance. This condition would be even more applicable for a conventional hedge portfolio where the stocks start out at the calls' exercise prices. All factors considered, the *superhedge* offers an annualized return of about 50 percent for most advancing markets versus about 20 percent for a conventional hedge portfolio.

Note that since we assumed that the discount would remain at 36 percent, an advancing market will increase the spread between net asset value and market price. At a 40 percent market advance, this represents an additional $48,000 that must show up by December 31, 1984.

The above studies for different stock market conditions indicate that the *superhedge* offers *far* greater profit potential than the conventional hedge portfolio of call options sold against common stocks. It also offers more potential than most traditional convertible hedging strategies. But there are negatives, and potential problems, in managing a *superhedge* portfolio. These include:

1. The need to margin the uncovered calls limits the strategy to a bullish posture, as shown, unless other collateral is available for margining additional call options. This problem

would be amplified if margin requirements were raised above the current rate of 50 percent.

2. An advancing market might require additional collateral for the very high margin requirements when uncovered calls move into the money, even though the total position was profitable.

3. Option losses must be funded in a bull market to avoid having to sell some of the underlying capital shares.

4. The long and short side of the portfolio may diverge, causing losses, or lower profits, than anticipated.

5. The market for capital shares is relatively thin—this precludes the commitment of large amounts of capital to the strategy.

6. Managing a *superhedge* portfolio involves *a lot of work* in selecting and monitoring the securities, and in designing the portfolio for tax consequences as previously presented in the book. The *superhedge* is not for everyone.

AN EIGHT-MONTH "TRACK RECORD"

Beginning in July 1975, an actual *superhedge* portfolio was started by a client of mine. With minor differences, it was designed like the *superhedge* portfolio presented in this chapter. The eight-month period through February 1976 included six months of a sideways to modestly lower market during the last half of 1975 and the exceptionally strong two-month advance in early 1976. Although specific information on this account is confidential, I can state that performance to date has actually exceeded our expectations—better than 50 percent annualized return![1]

---

[1] A word from the author: This account has contributed unique and specific techniques for managing a *superhedge* portfolio based on both theoretical and actual experience. This information will be considered for future publication after additional experience is obtained, but it is presently proprietary.

Index

American DualVest Fund, 232–43
American Telephone & Telegraph
  reverse warrant hedges, 205–12

Braniff International warrant, 136,
  140–41

Call options; *see* Listed call options
Chase Manhattan
  convertible bond, 11–14
  selling call options against convertible bond, 127–32
Citicorp convertible bond, 14–15
Consolidated Edison convertible preferred, 10
Convertible bonds and preferred stocks
  antidilution provisions, 21
  bonds versus preferreds, 17–18
  break-even time, 9
  call provisions, 21
  changes in terms, 20
  conversion premium, 8
  conversion value, 6–8
  delayed convertible, 19
  estimated price curve, 12
  expiration of conversion privileges, 21
  fabricated convertible, 19
  general guides for buying convertibles, 23

Convertible bonds and preferred stocks—*Cont.*
  hedging with
    call options, 117–33
    common stock, 24–39
    put options, 231
    warrants, 203
  investment value, 8–9
  margining purchases, 13–14, 23
  mergers and tender offers for common stock, 21
  model portfolios, 21–23
  normal value curve, 10
  normally valued convertibles, 6–11
  placing orders, 16–17
  plus cash convertible, 19
  preferreds in arrears, 20
  premium over investment value, 9
  risk/reward analysis, 10–11, 13
  short-term convertible bonds, 20
  special convertibles, 18–20
  tender offers for discounted bonds, 20
  undervalued convertibles, 5–6, 11–13
    for aggressive investors, 14–16
  unit convertible, 19
  unusual pluses and minuses, 20–21
  yield advantage, 9

251